FOR ORGANS, PIANOS & ELECTRONIC KEYBOARDS

143

THE SON… Paul McCa…
2ND EDITION

T0058984

ISBN 978-0-7935-2649-9

A Publication of

MPL COMMUNICATIONS, INC.

http://www.mplcommunications.com

Exclusively Distributed By

7777 W. Bluemound Rd. P.O. Box 13819 Milwaukee, WI 53213

For all works contained herein:
Unauthorized copying, arranging, adapting, recording, Internet posting, public performance, or other distribution of the printed music in this publication is an infringement of copyright. Infringers are liable under the law.

E-Z Play ® TODAY Music Notation © 1975 HAL LEONARD CORPORATION
E-Z PLAY and EASY ELECTRONIC KEYBOARD MUSIC are registered trademarks of HAL LEONARD CORPORATION.

Visit Hal Leonard Online at

Another Day

Registration 4
Rhythm: 8-Beat or Rock

Words and Music by Paul McCartney
and Linda McCartney

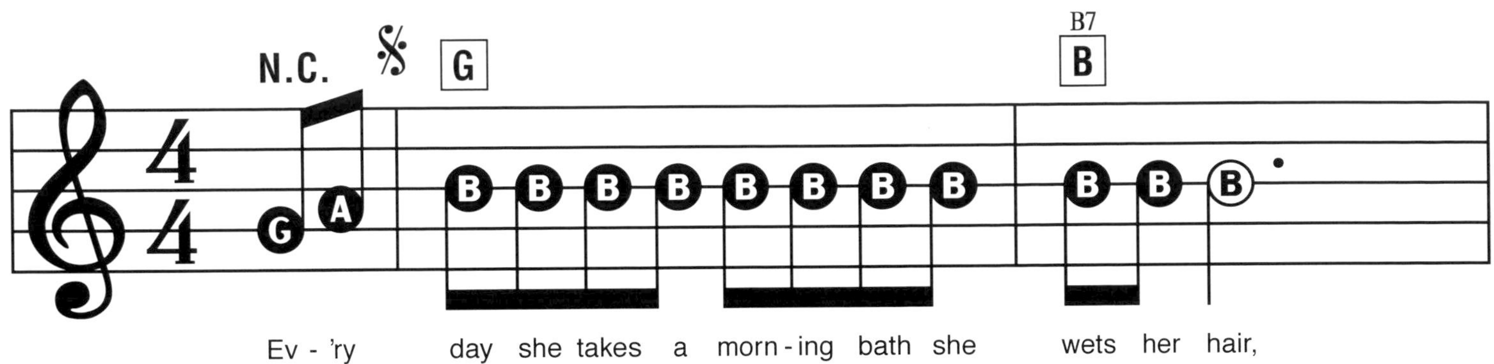

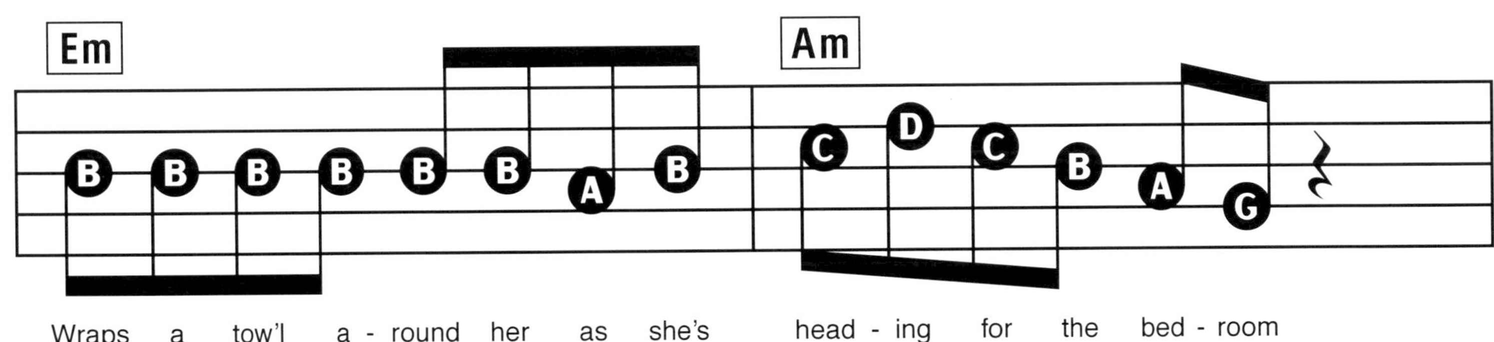

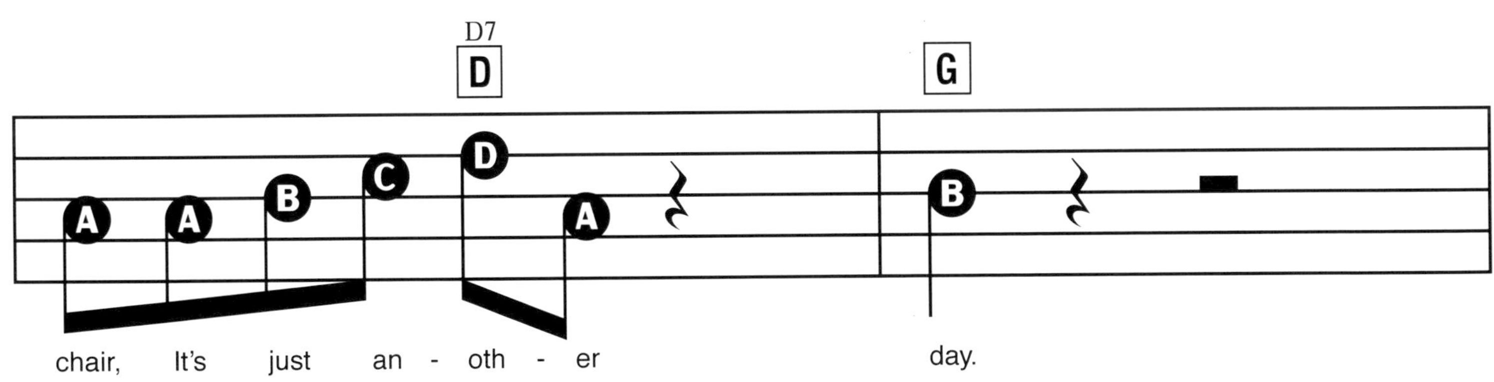

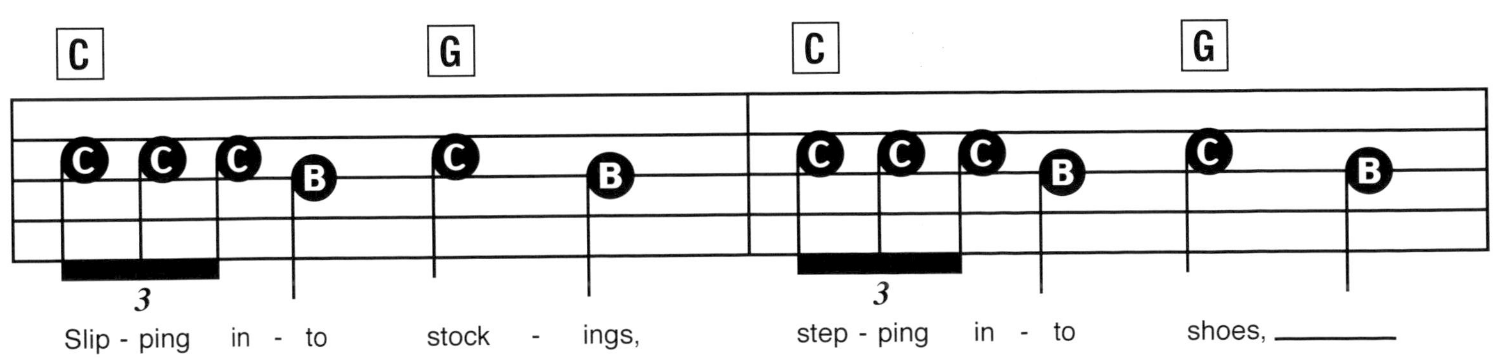

© 1971 (Renewed) PAUL and LINDA McCARTNEY
Administered by MPL COMMUNICATIONS, INC.
All Rights Reserved

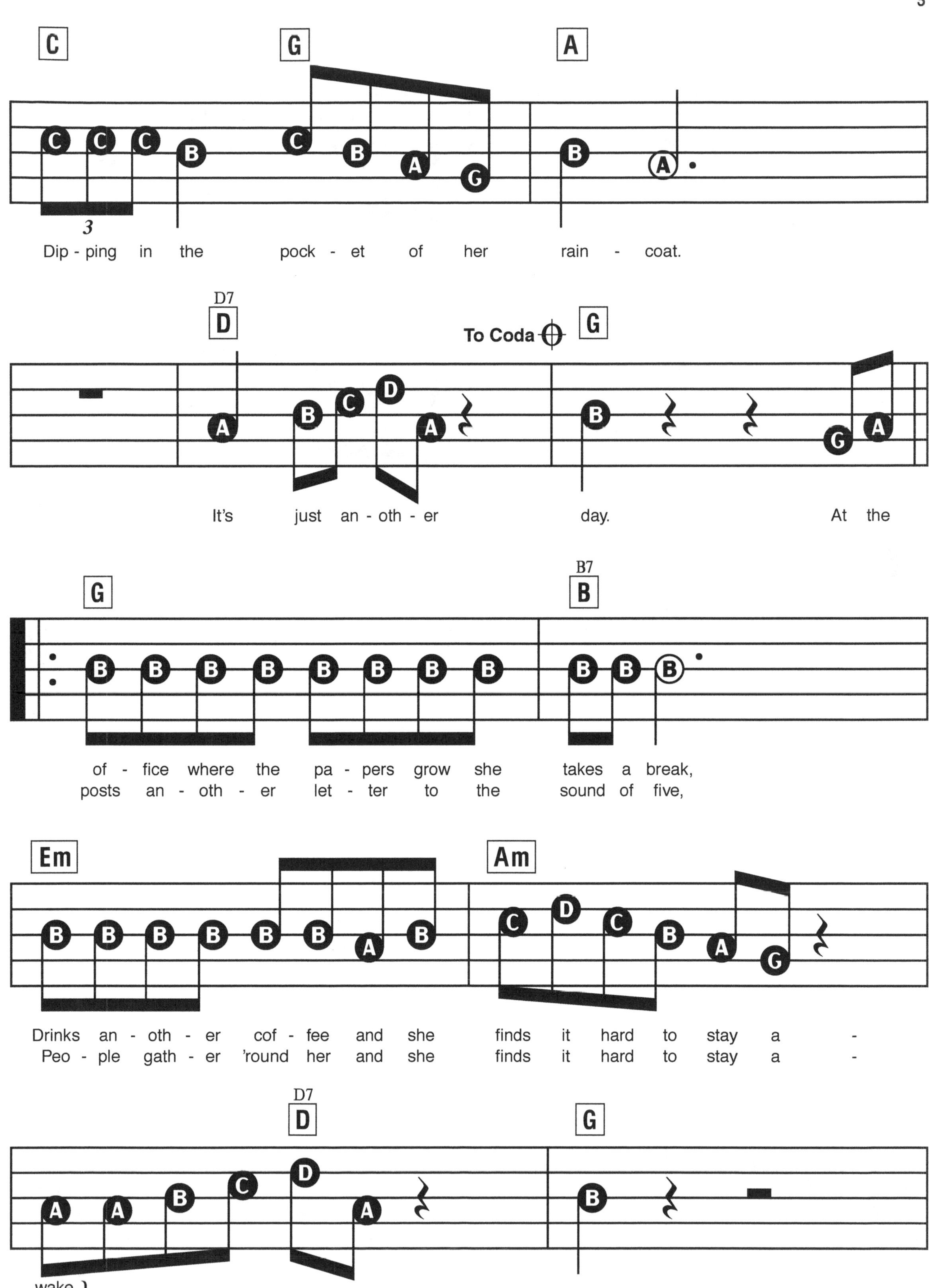
C G A
Dip - ping in the pock - et of her rain - coat.
D7 D
To Coda G
It's just an - oth - er day. At the
G B7 B
of - fice where the pa - pers grow she takes a break,
posts an - oth - er let - ter to the sound of five,
Em Am
Drinks an - oth - er cof - fee and she finds it hard to stay a -
Peo - ple gath - er 'round her and she finds it hard to stay a -
D7 D G
wake,
live,
It's just an - oth - er day.

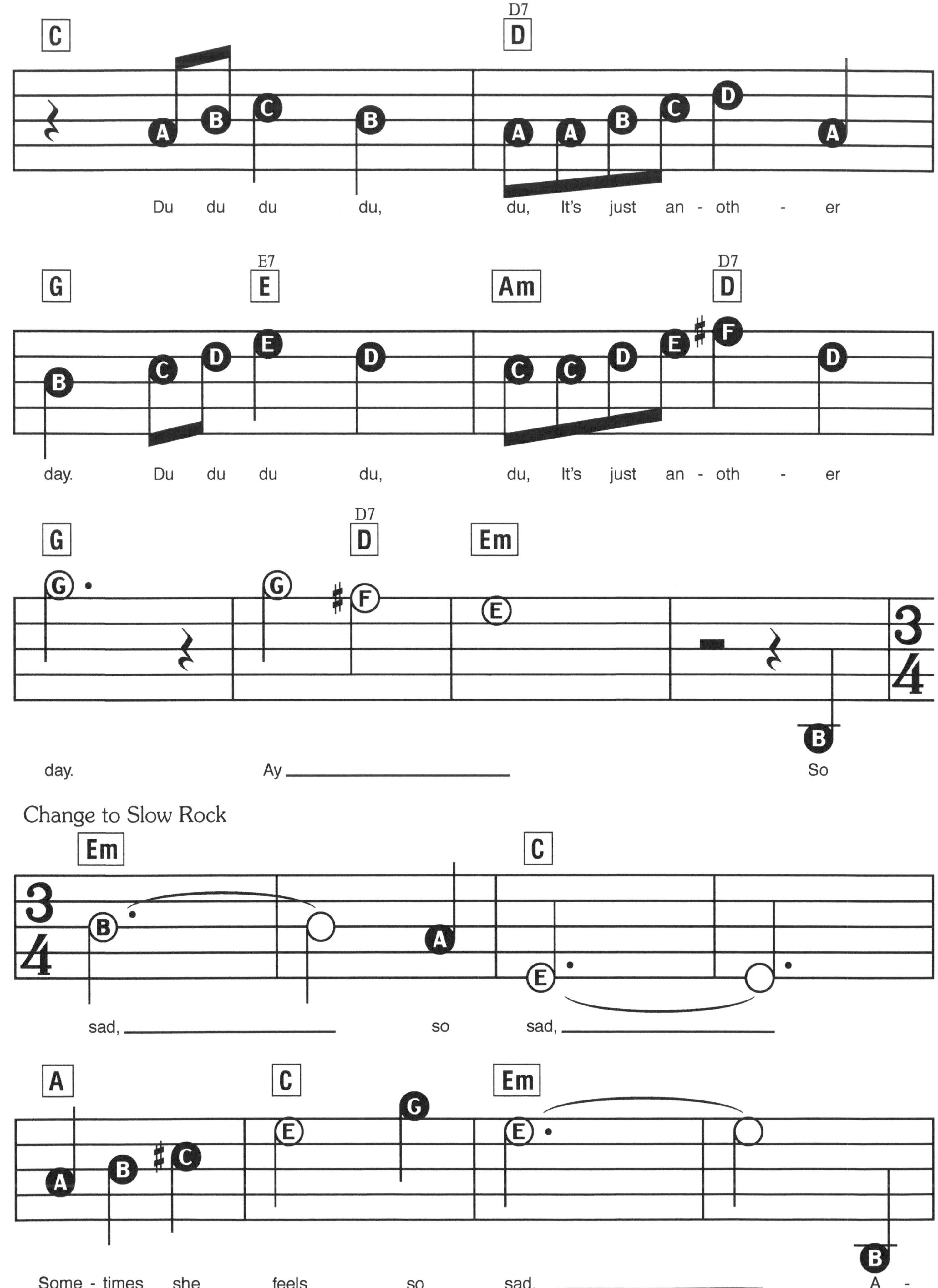
C
D7
D
Du du du du,
du, It's just an - oth - er
G
E7
E
Am
D7
D
day. Du du du du,
du, It's just an - oth - er
G
D7
D
Em
3
4
day.
Ay
So
Change to Slow Rock
Em
C
3
4
sad,
so
sad,
A
C
Em
Some - times she feels so sad.
A -

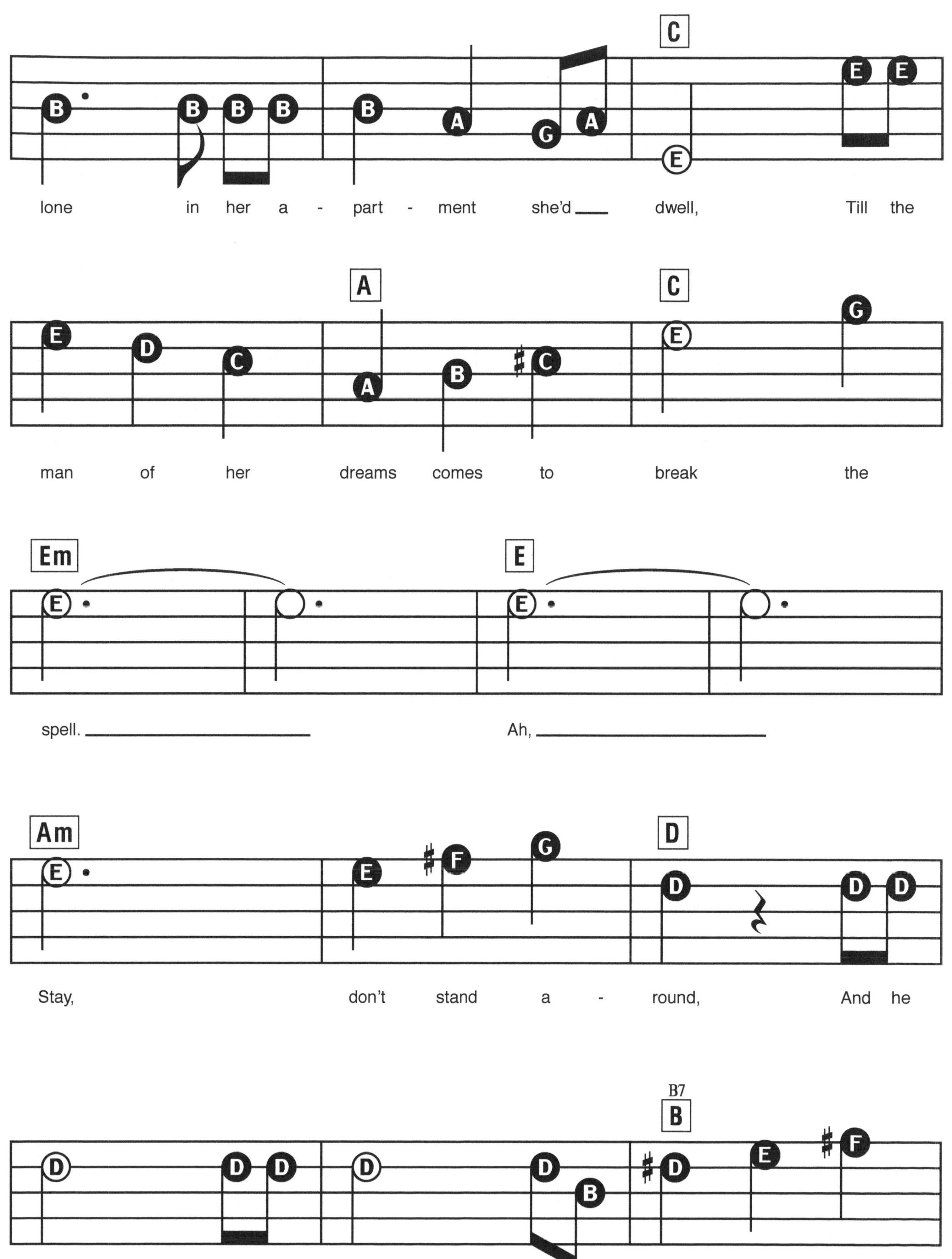
C
lone in her a - part - ment she'd dwell, Till the
A C
man of her dreams comes to break the
Em E
spell. Ah,
Am D
Stay, don't stand a - round, And he
B7
B
comes and he stays but he leaves the next

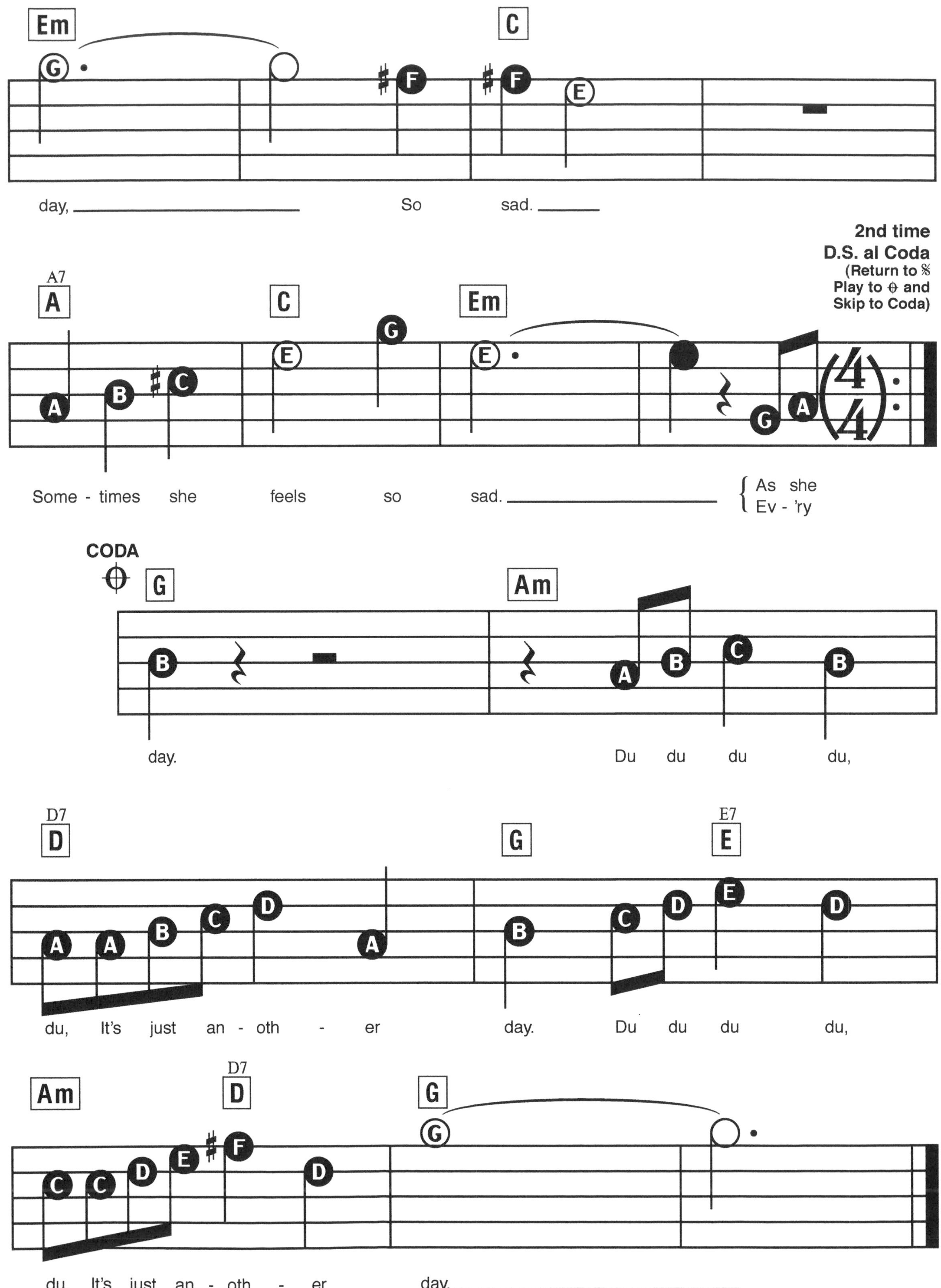
Em
C
day,
So sad.
2nd time
D.S. al Coda
(Return to 𝄋
Play to ⊕ and
Skip to Coda)
A7
A
C
Em
Some - times she feels so sad.
As she
Ev - 'ry
CODA
G
Am
day.
Du du du du,
D7
D
G
E7
E
du, It's just an - oth - er day.
Du du du du,
Am
D7
D
G
du, It's just an - oth - er day.

Arrow Through Me

Registration 4
Rhythm: 8-Beat or Rock

Words and Music by
Paul McCartney

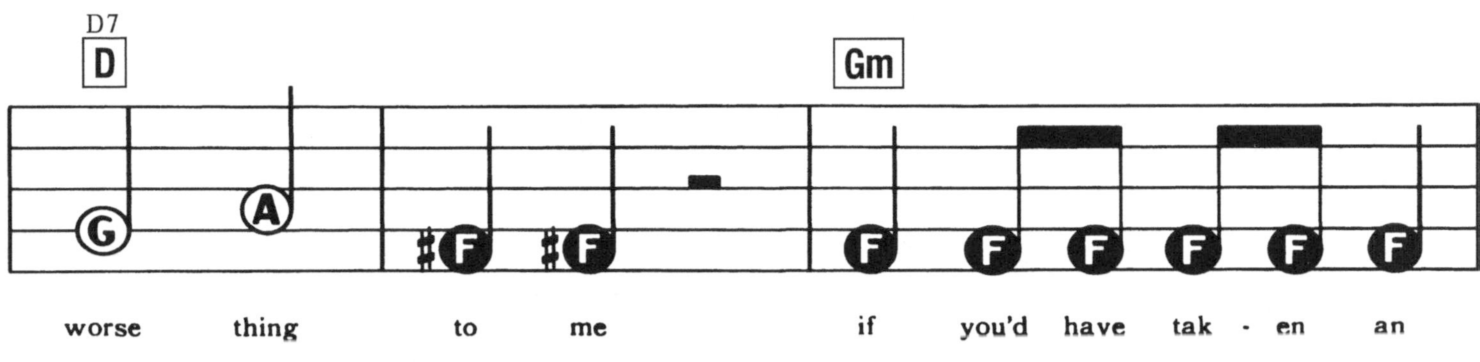

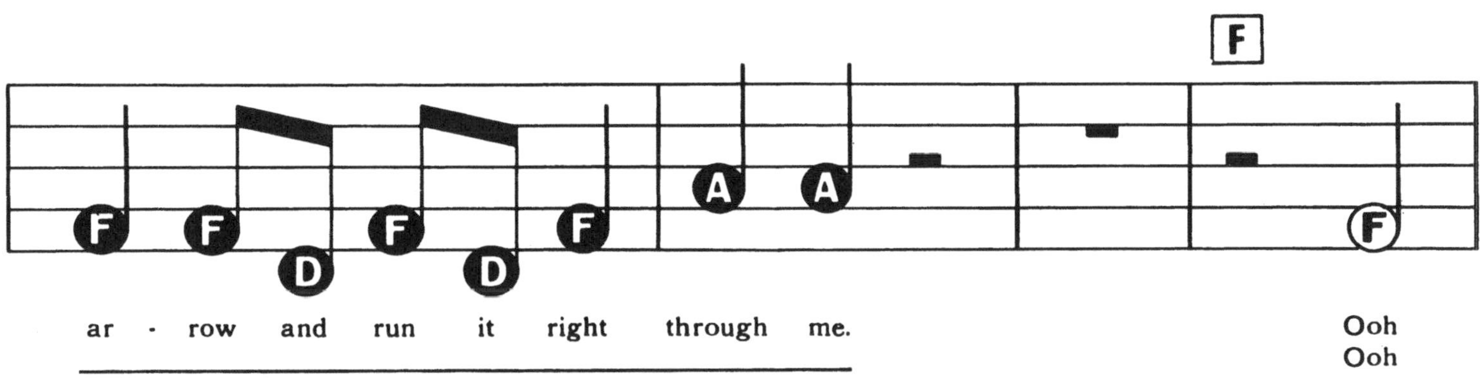

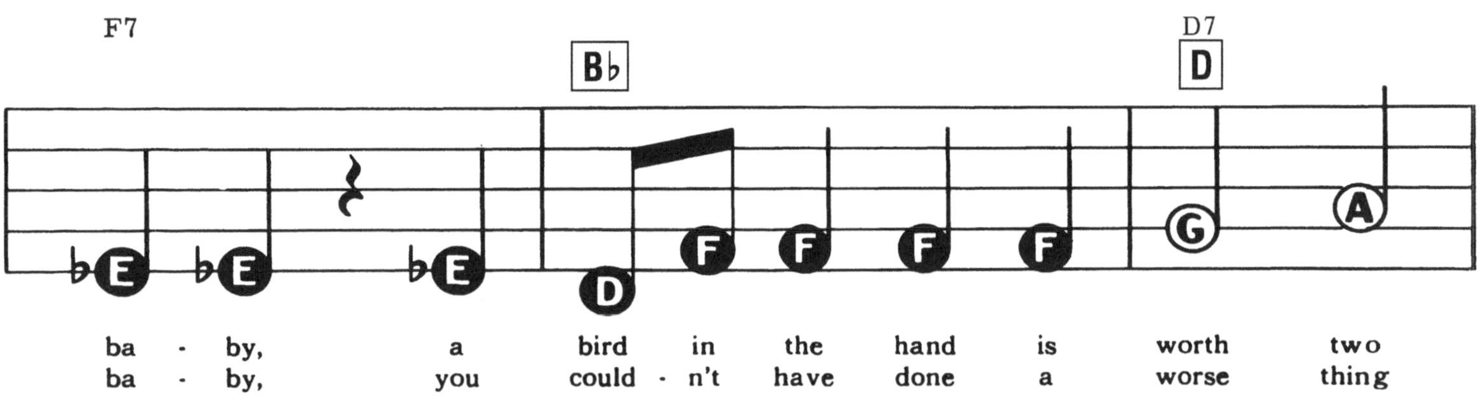

© 1979 MPL COMMUNICATIONS LTD.
Administered by MPL COMMUNICATIONS, INC.
All Rights Reserved

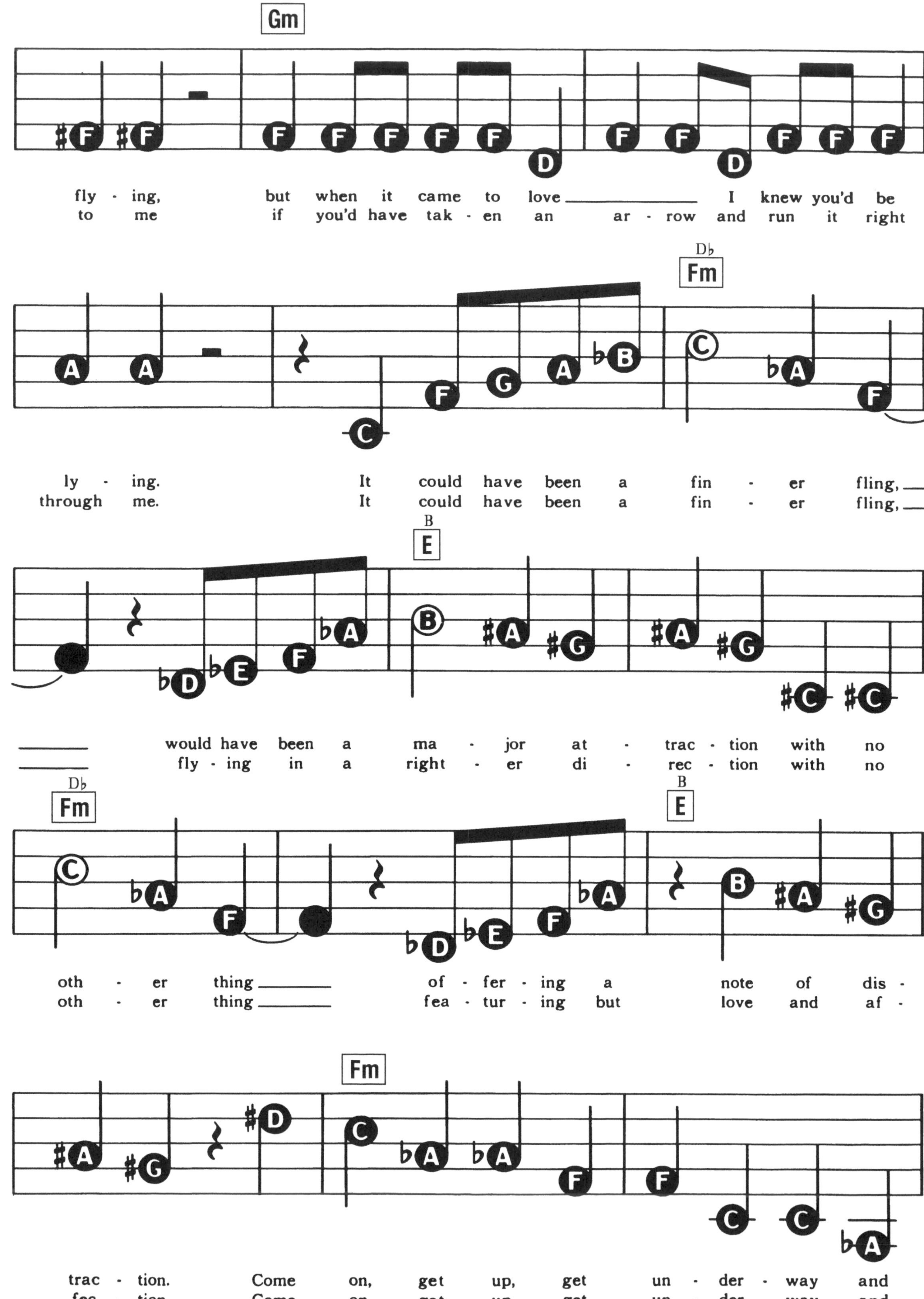
Gm
fly - ing, but when it came to love I knew you'd be
to me if you'd have tak - en an ar - row and run it right
Db
Fm
ly - ing. It could have been a fin - er fling,
through me. It could have been a fin - er fling,
B
E
would have been a ma - jor at - trac - tion with no
fly - ing in a right - er di - rec - tion with no
Db
Fm
B
E
oth - er thing of - fer - ing a note of dis -
oth - er thing fea - tur - ing but love and af -
Fm
trac - tion. Come on, get up, get un - der - way and
fec - tion. Come on, get up, get un - der - way and

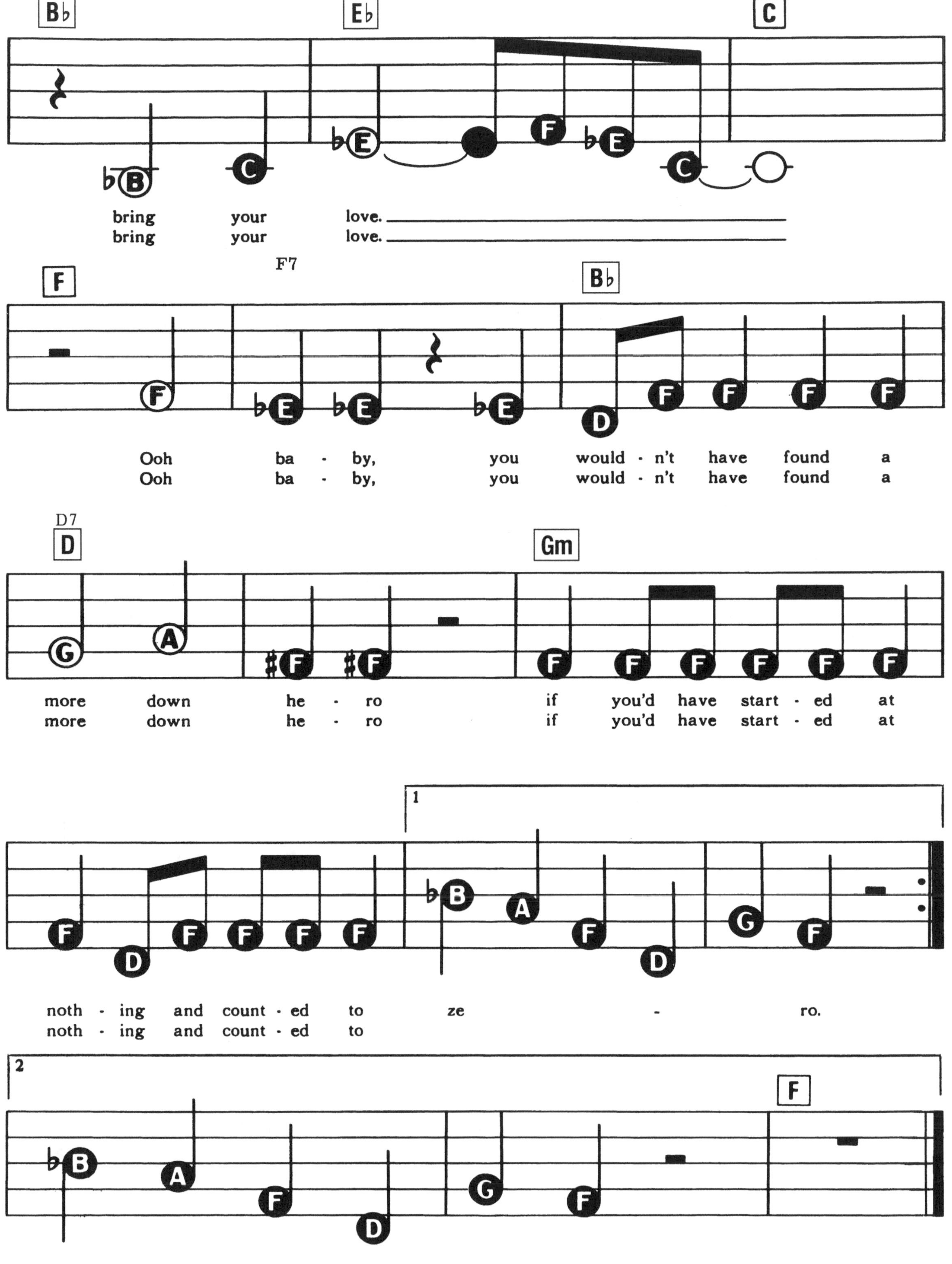
B♭
E♭
C
bring your love.
bring your love.
F
F7
B♭
Ooh ba - by, you would - n't have found a
Ooh ba - by, you would - n't have found a
D7
D
Gm
more down he - ro if you'd have start - ed at
more down he - ro if you'd have start - ed at
1
noth - ing and count - ed to ze - ro.
noth - ing and count - ed to
2
F
ze - ro.

Band on the Run

Registration 4
Rhythm: Rock

Words and Music by Paul McCartney
and Linda McCartney

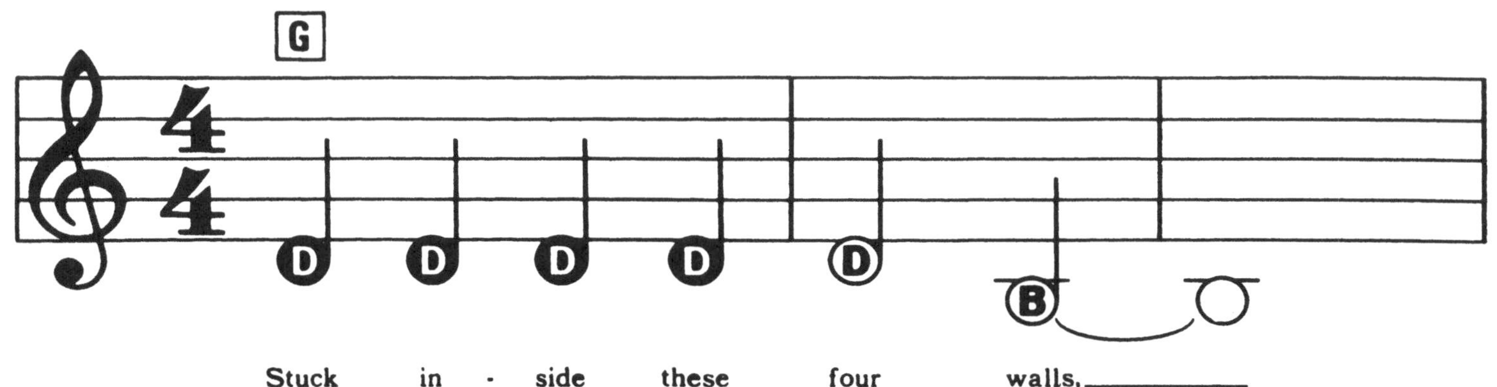

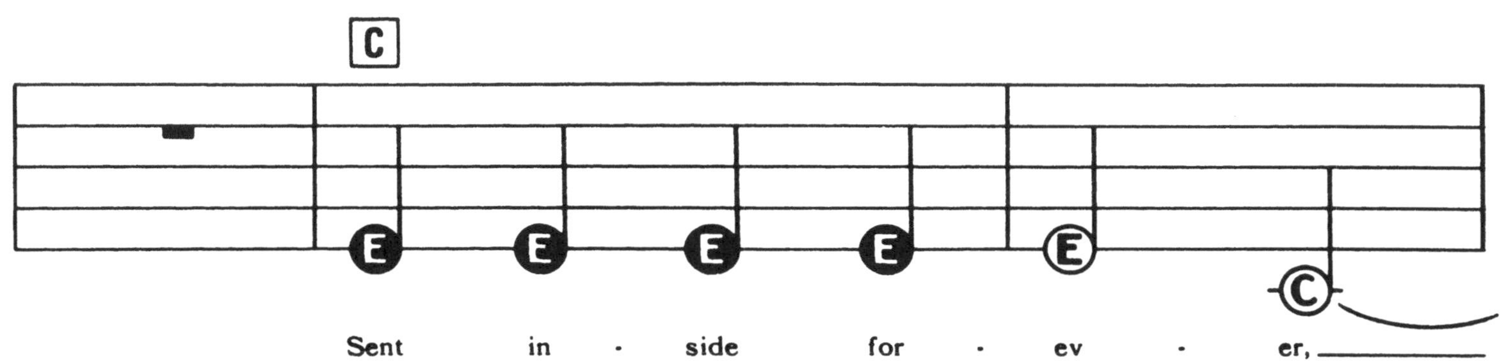

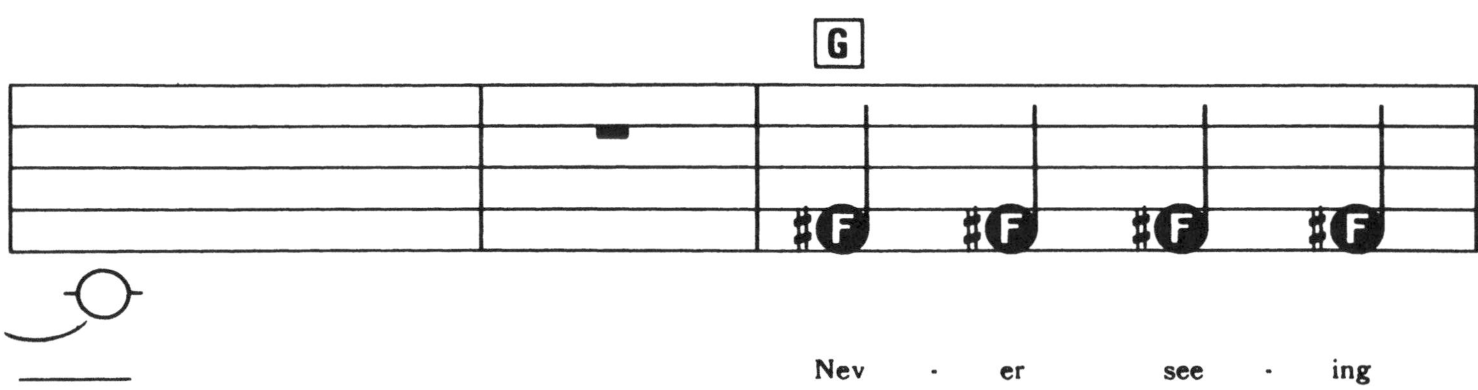

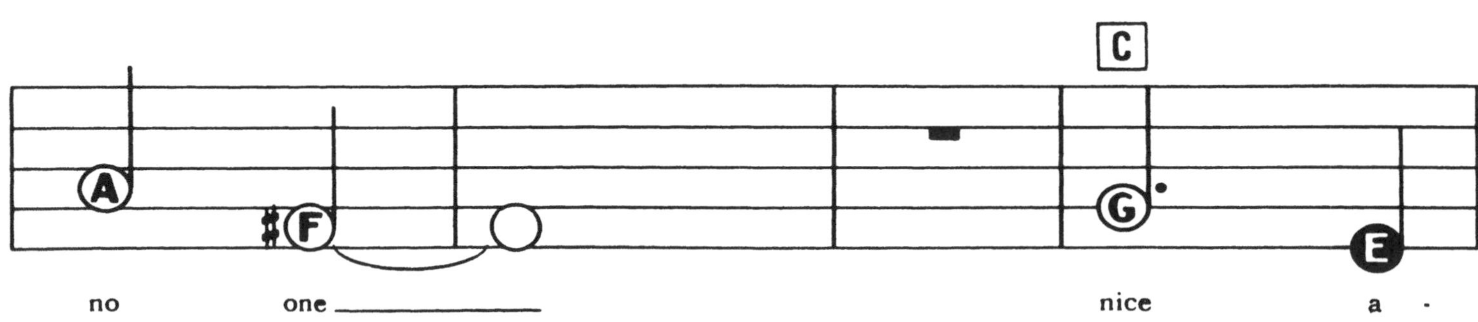

© 1974 (Renewed) PAUL and LINDA McCARTNEY
Administered by MPL COMMUNICATIONS, INC.
All Rights Reserved

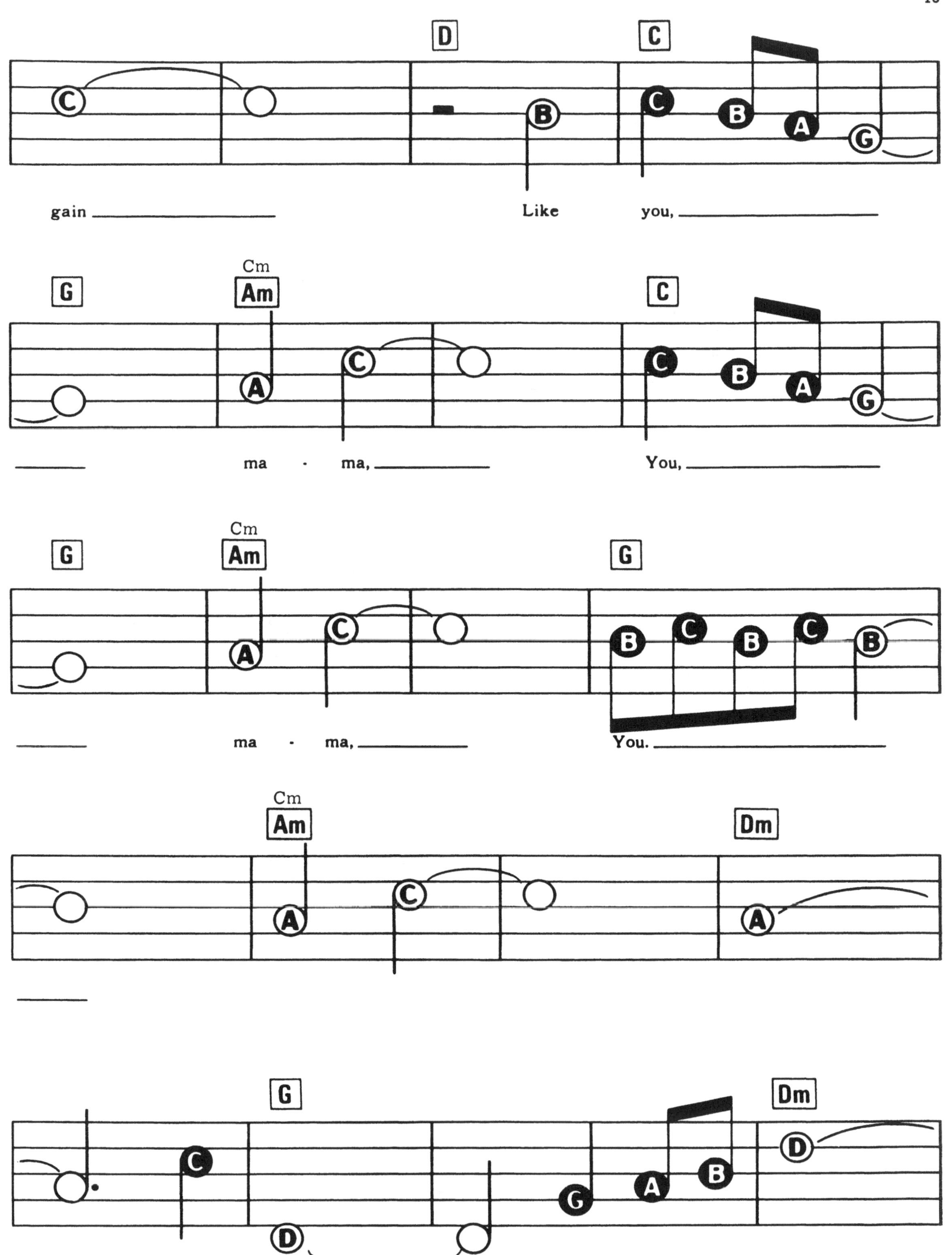

D
C
C
B
C
B
A
G
gain
Like
you,
G
Cm
Am
C
A
C
C
B
A
G
ma - ma,
You,
G
Cm
Am
G
A
C
B
C
B
C
B
ma - ma,
You.
Cm
Am
Dm
A
C
A
G
Dm
C
D
G
A
B
D

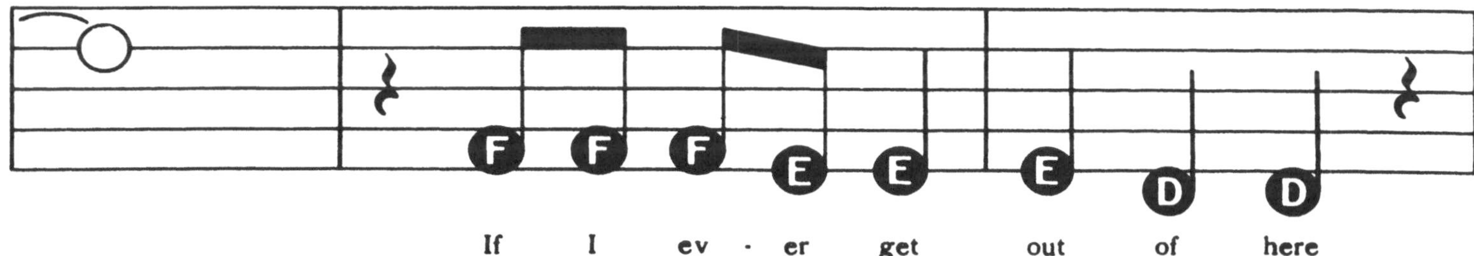
If I ev - er get out of here

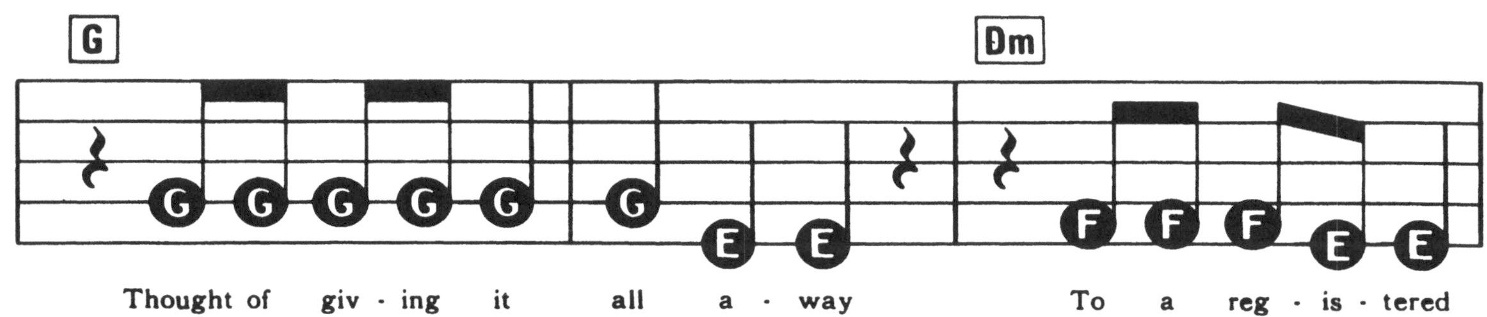
G
Dm
Thought of giv - ing it all a - way To a reg - is - tered

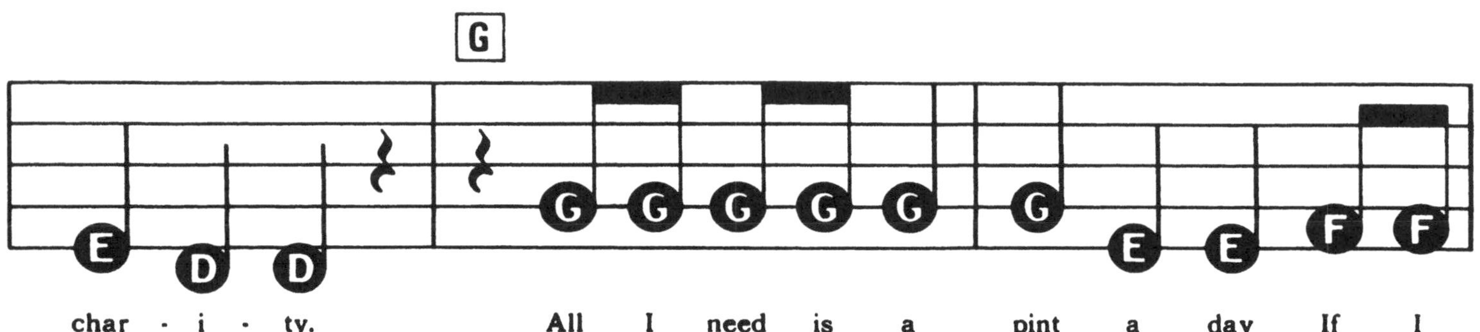
G
char - i - ty. All I need is a pint a day If I

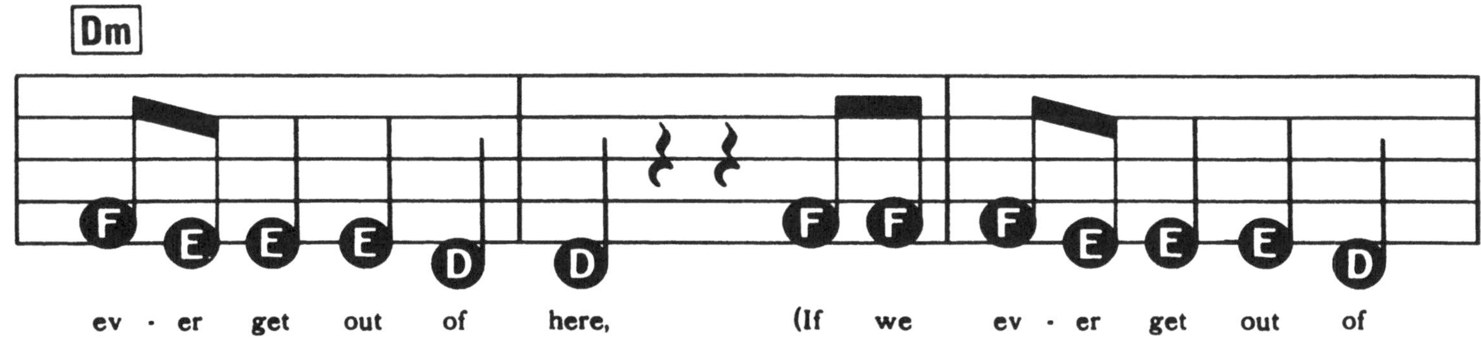
Dm
ev - er get out of here, (If we ev - er get out of

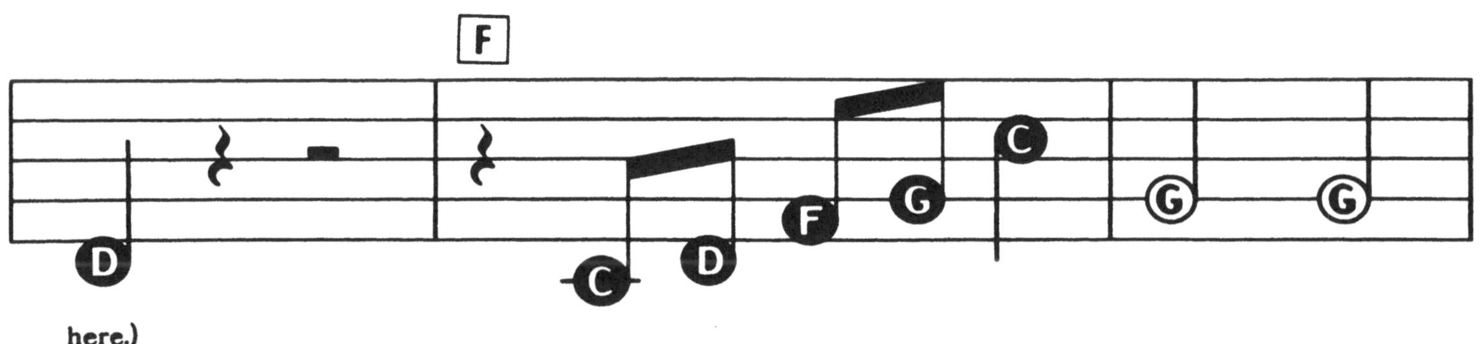
F
here.)

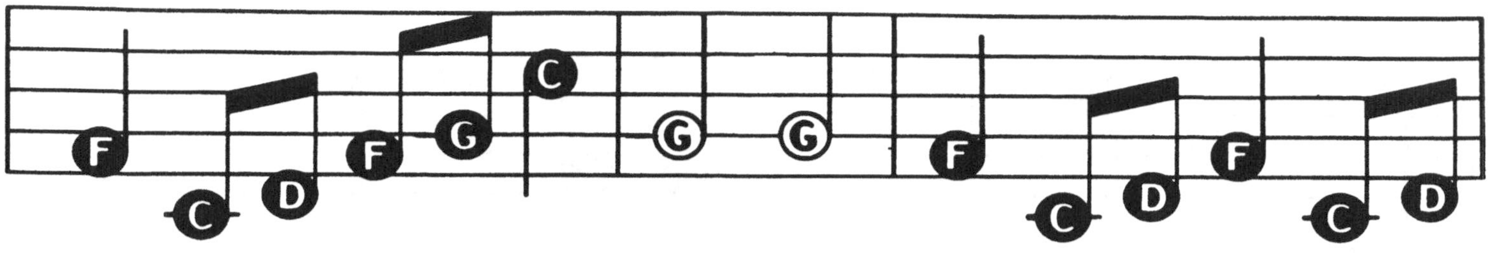

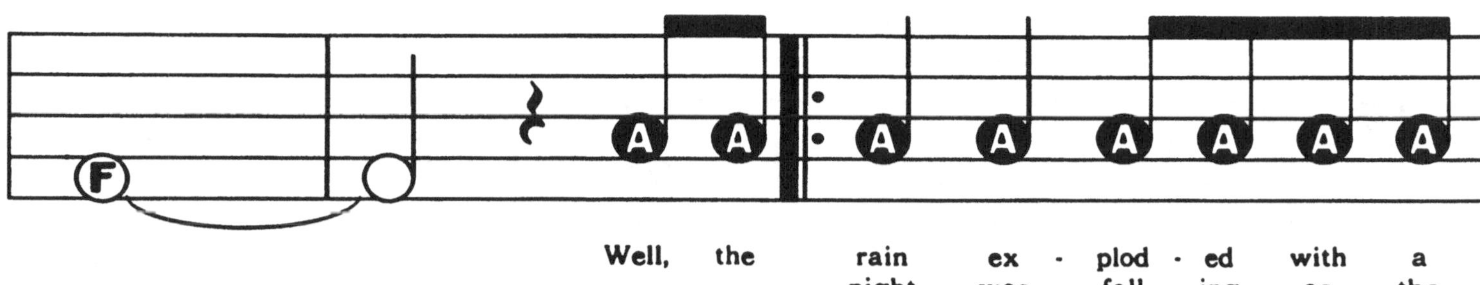
Well, the rain ex - plod - ed with a
night was fall - ing as the

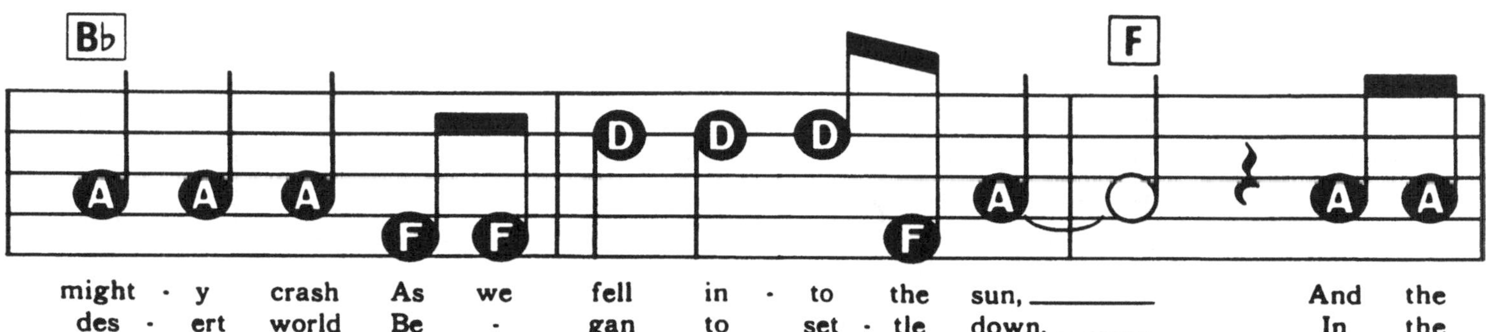
Bb
F
might - y crash As we fell in - to the sun, And the
des - ert world Be - gan to set - tle down. In the

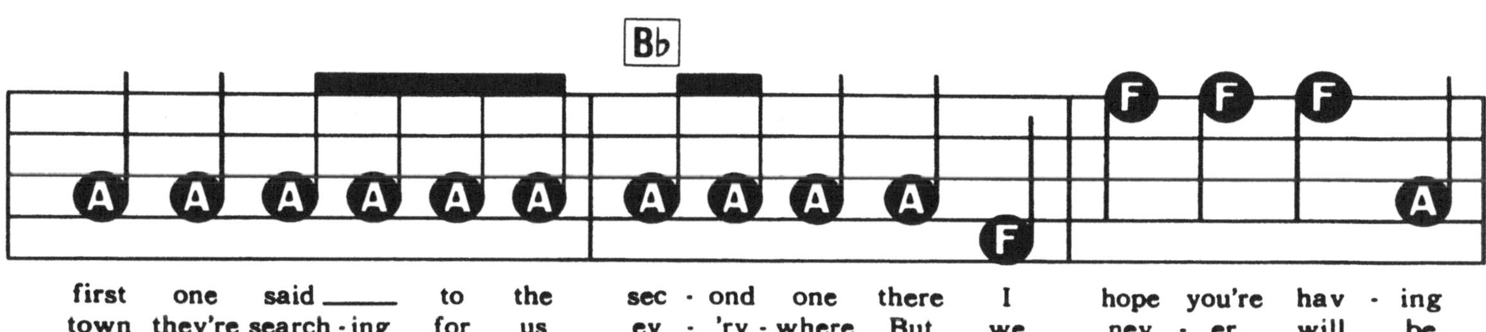
Bb
first one said to the sec - ond one there I hope you're hav - ing
town they're search - ing for us ev - 'ry - where But we nev - er will be

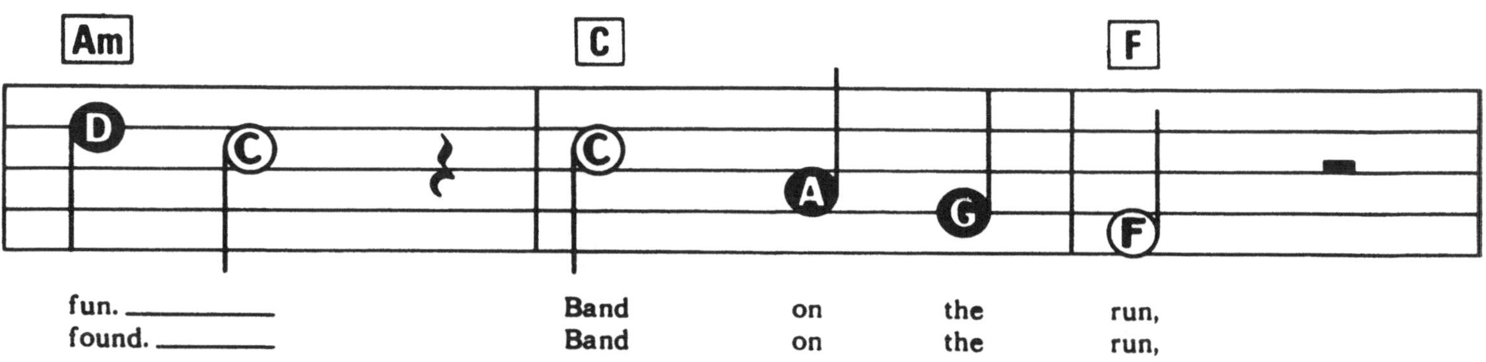
Am
C
F
fun. Band on the run,
found. Band on the run,

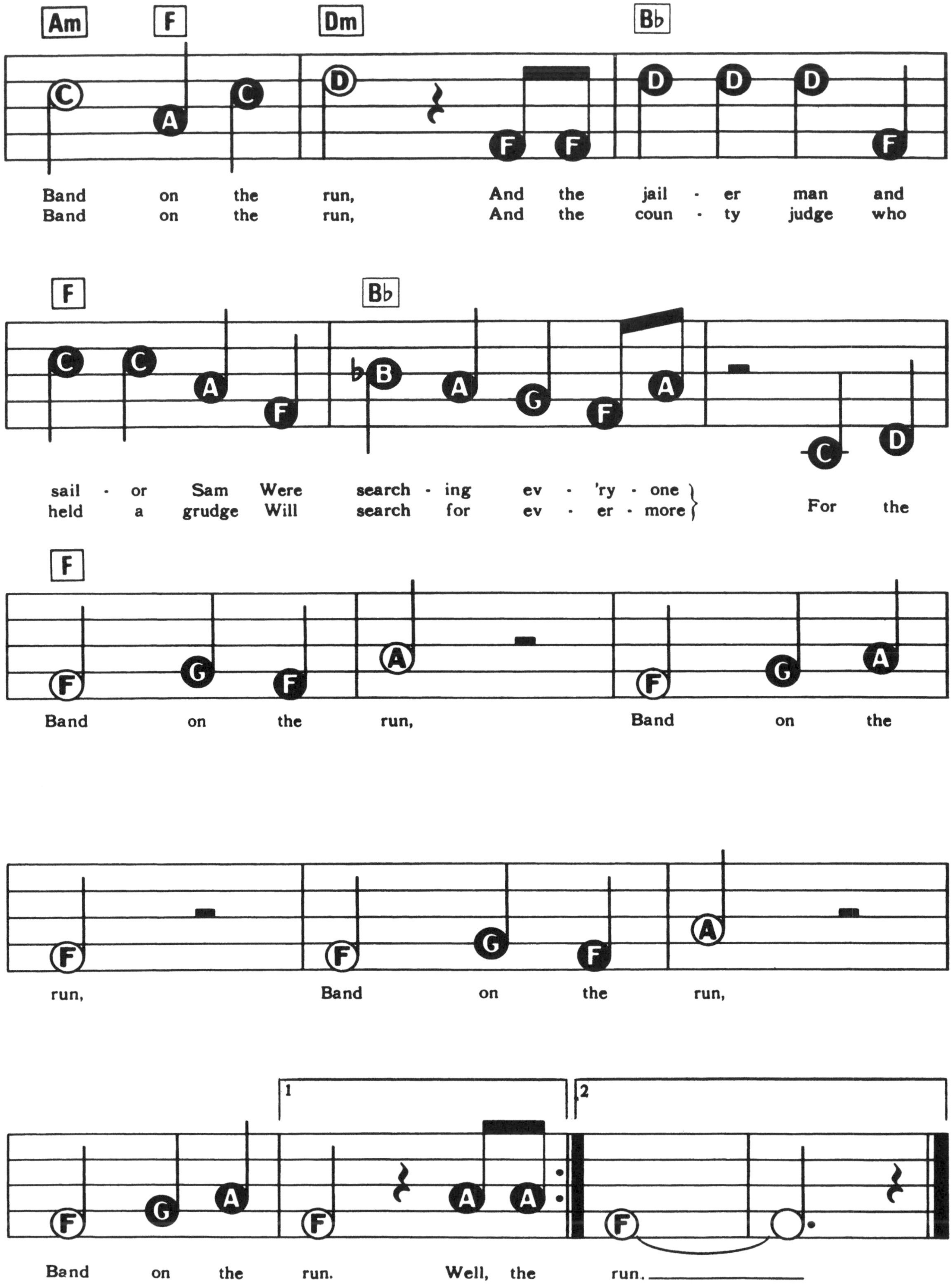

Am F Dm Bb

Band on the run, And the jail - er man and
Band on the run, And the coun - ty judge who

F Bb

sail - or Sam Were search - ing ev - 'ry - one
held a grudge Will search for ev - er - more
For the

F

Band on the run, Band on the

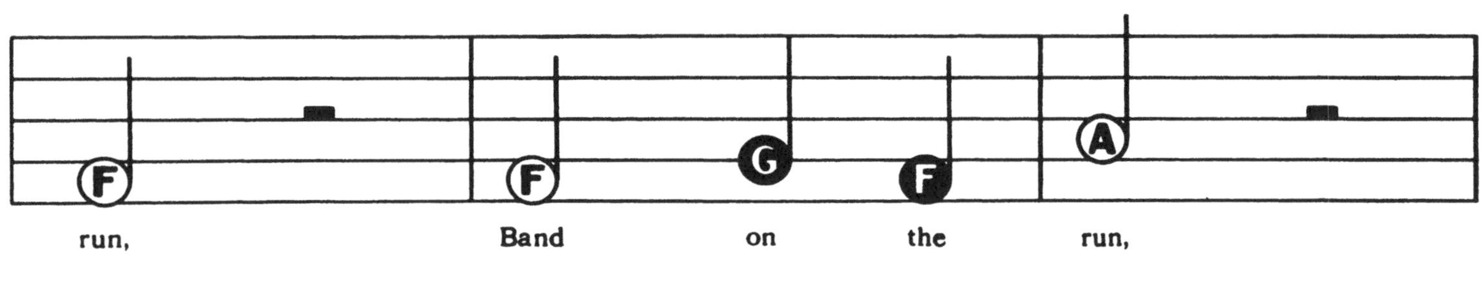

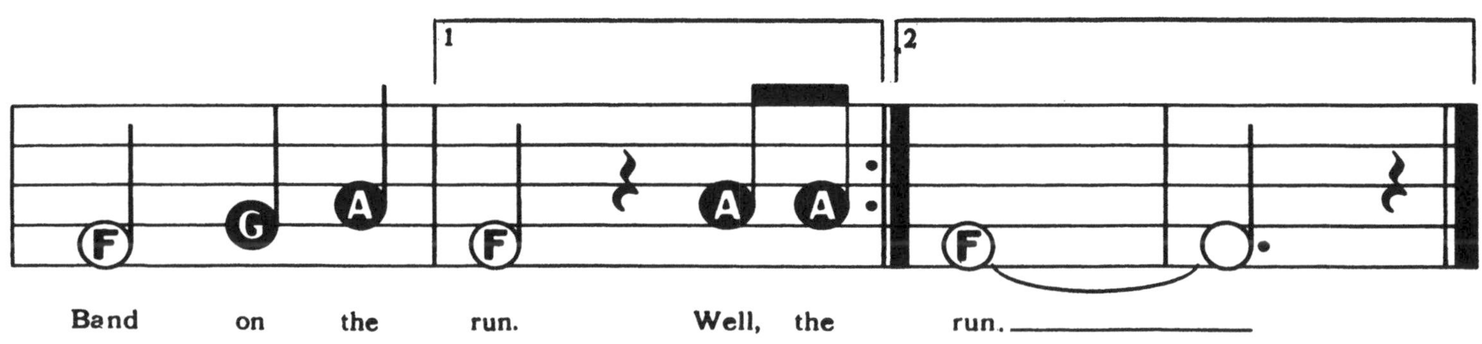

Coming Up

Registration 7
Rhythm: 8-Beat or Rock

Words and Music by
Paul McCartney

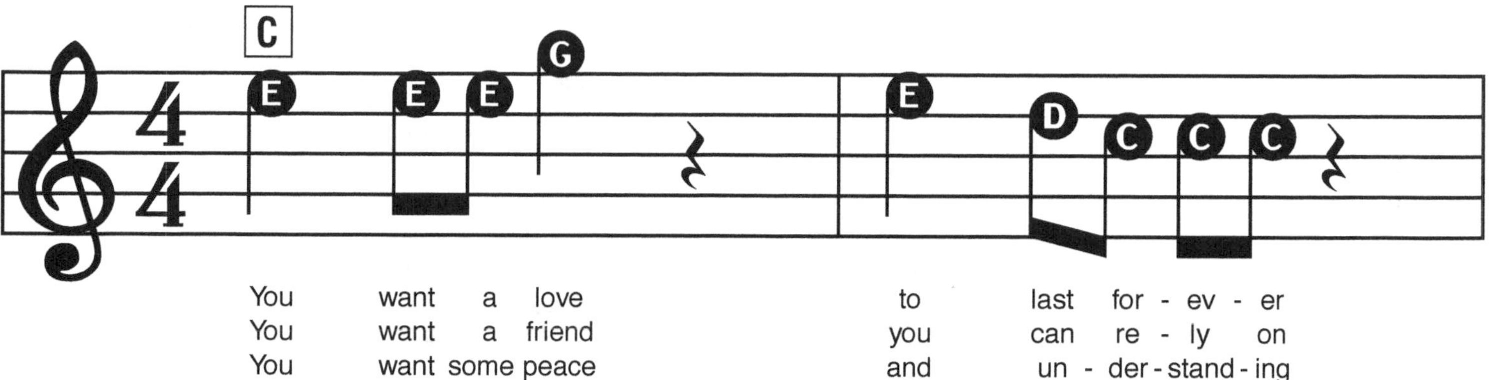

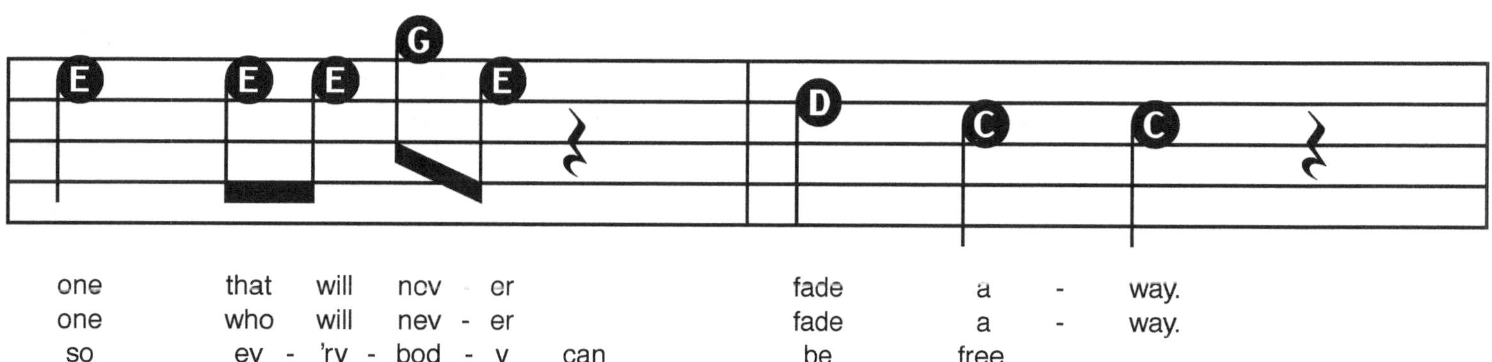

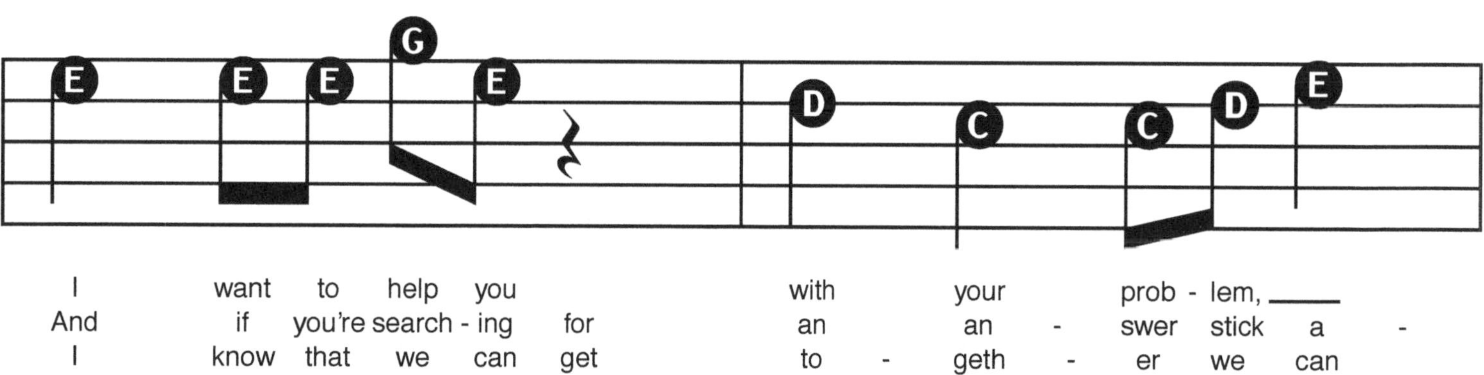

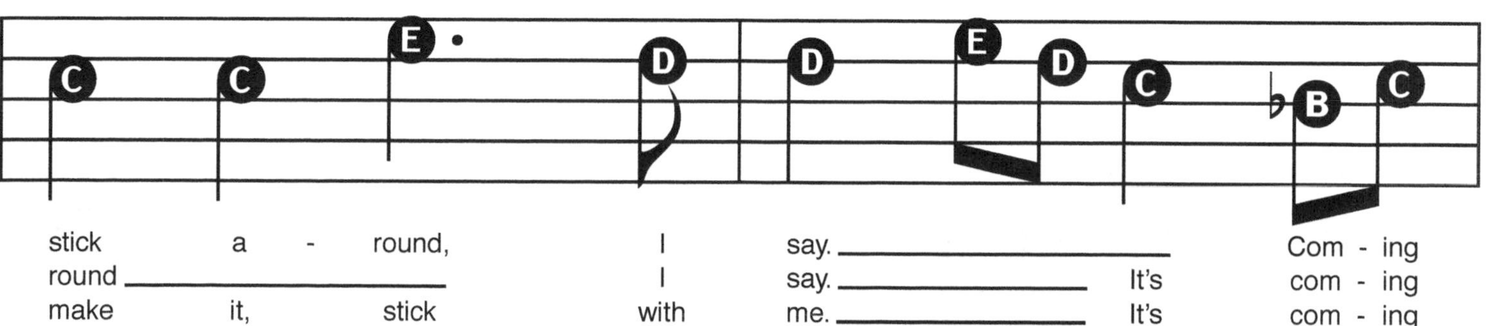

© 1980 MPL COMMUNICATIONS LTD.
Administered by MPL COMMUNICATIONS, INC.
All Rights Reserved

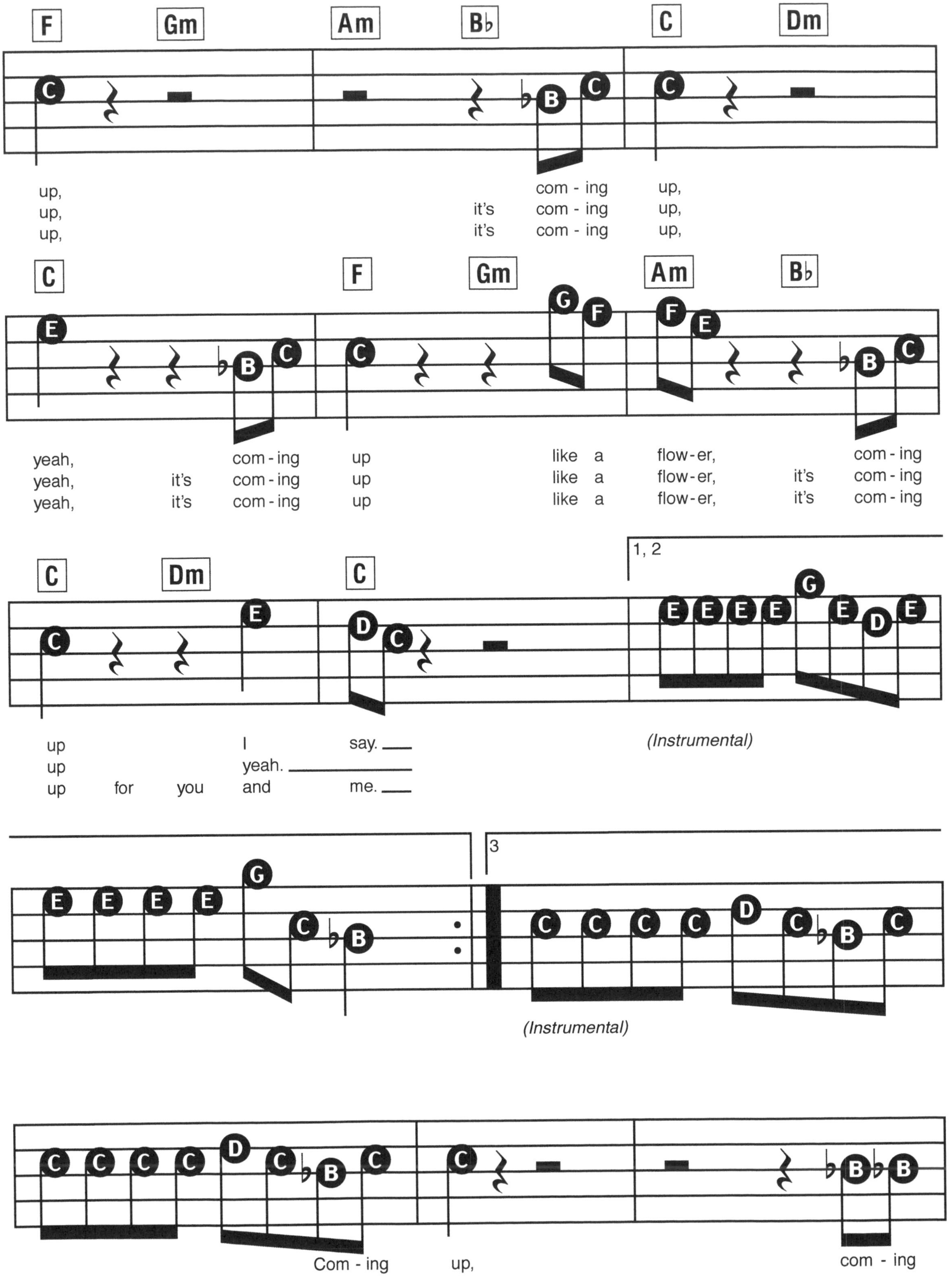

F Gm Am B♭ C Dm
up, com - ing up,
up, it's com - ing up,
up, it's com - ing up,
C F Gm Am B♭
yeah, com - ing up like a flow - er, com - ing
yeah, it's com - ing up like a flow - er, it's com - ing
yeah, it's com - ing up like a flow - er, it's com - ing
C Dm C
1, 2
up I say.
up yeah.
up for you and me.
(Instrumental)
3
(Instrumental)
Com - ing up, com - ing

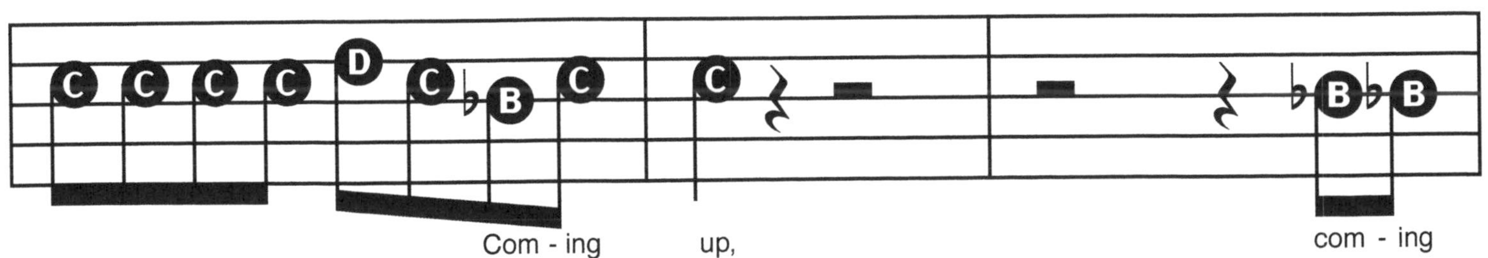

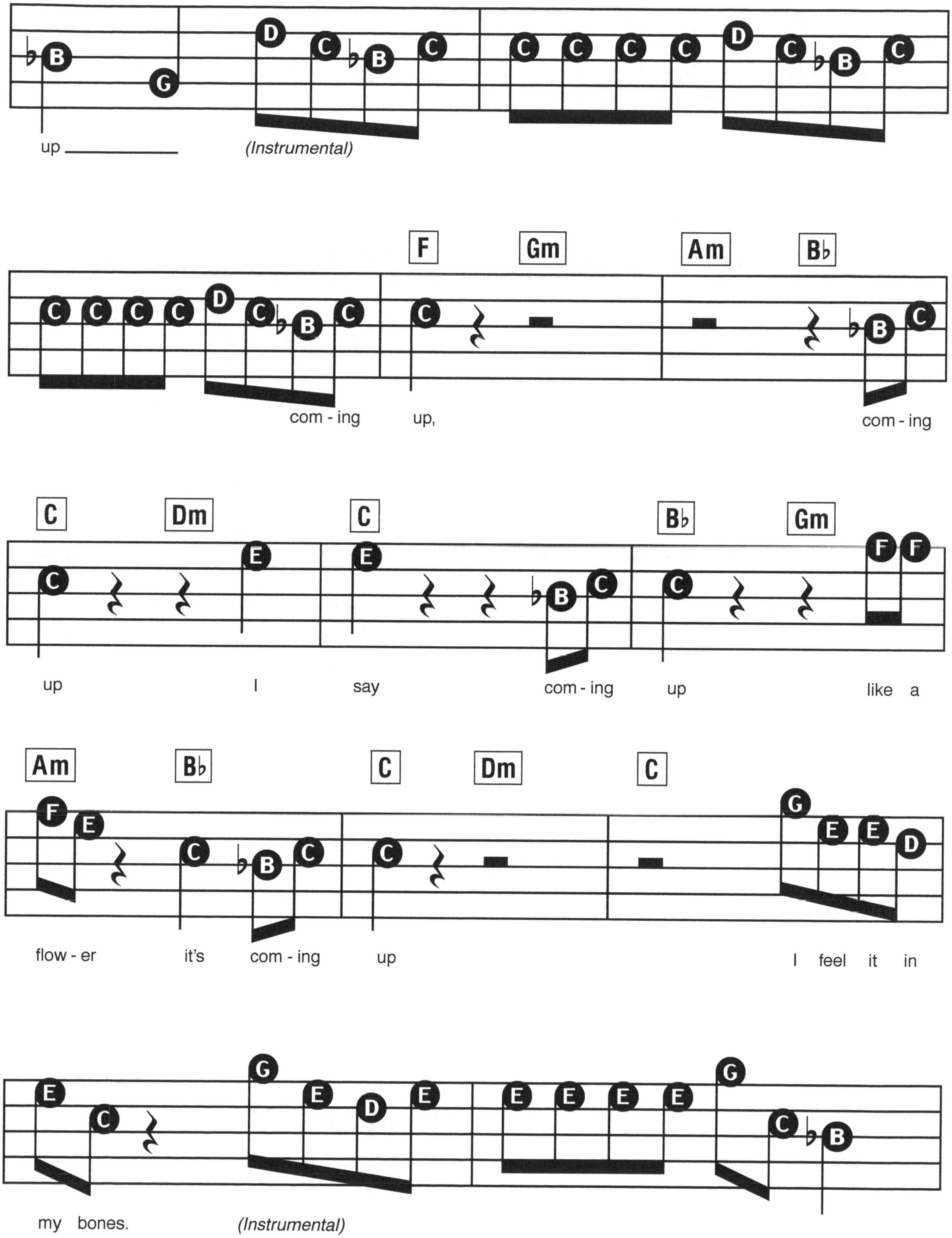

up ______ *(Instrumental)*

F Gm Am B♭

com - ing up, com - ing

C Dm C B♭ Gm

up I say com - ing up like a

Am B♭ C Dm C

flow - er it's com - ing up I feel it in

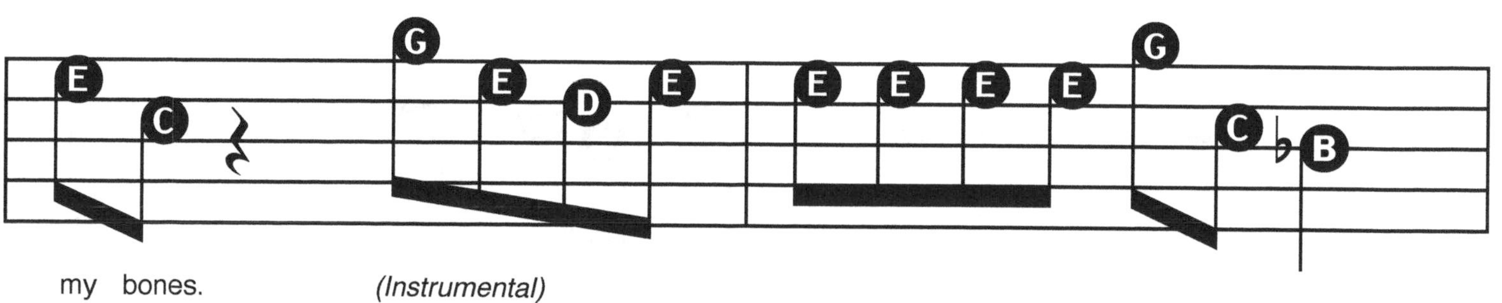

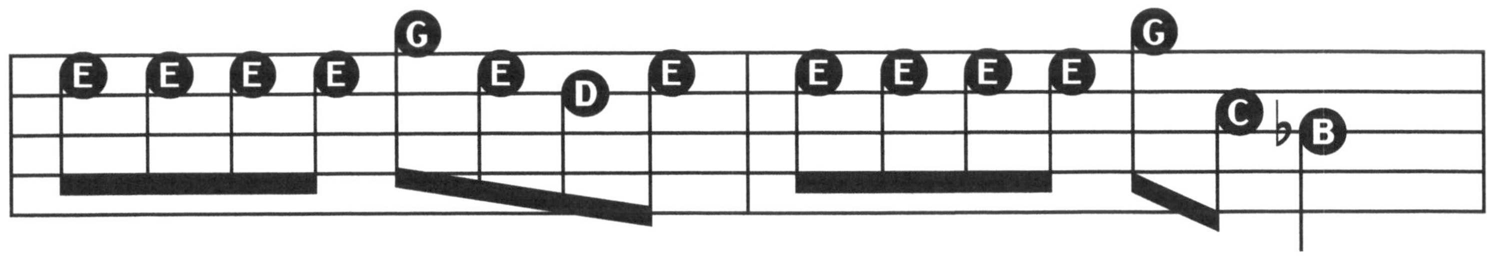
E E E E G E D E E E E E G C B

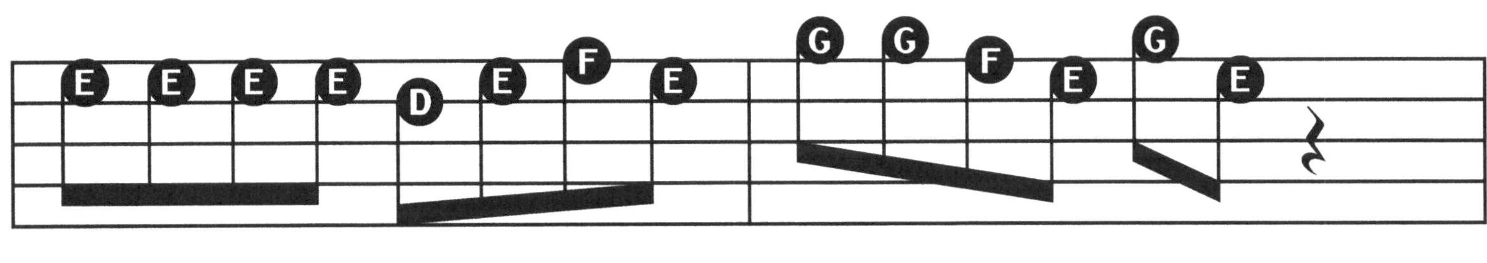
E E E E D E F E G G F E G E
You want a bet - ter kind of fu - ture

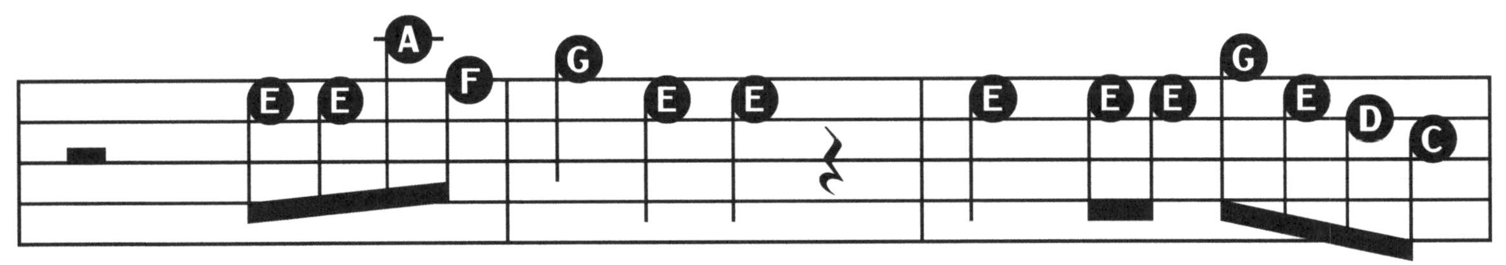
E E A F G E E E E E G E D C
one that ev - 'ry - one can share. You're not a - lone, we all could

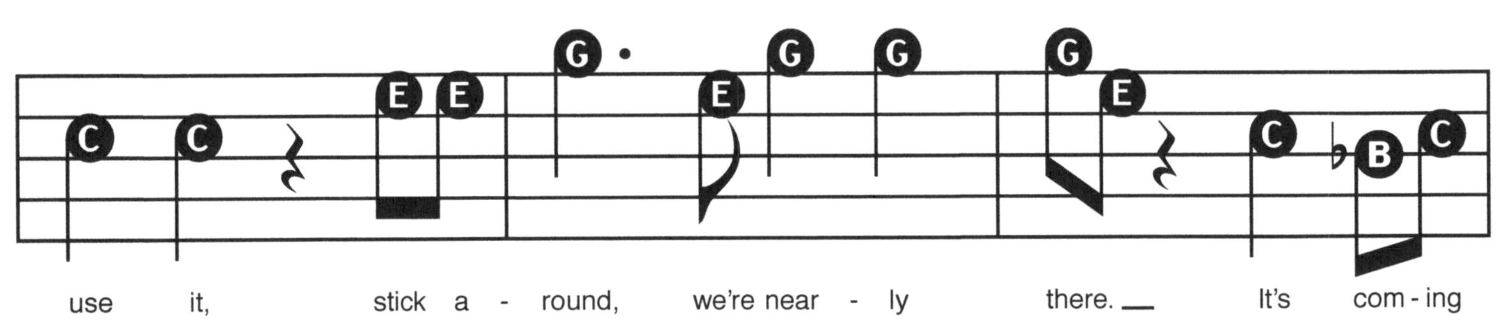
C C E E G E G G G E C B C
use it, stick a - round, we're near - ly there. It's com - ing

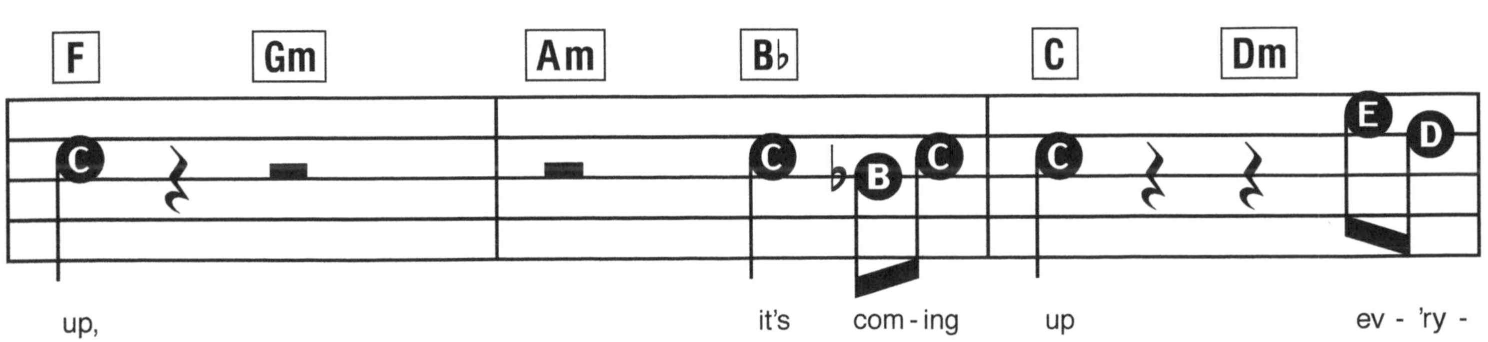
F Gm Am B♭ C Dm
C C B C C E D
up, it's com - ing up ev - 'ry -

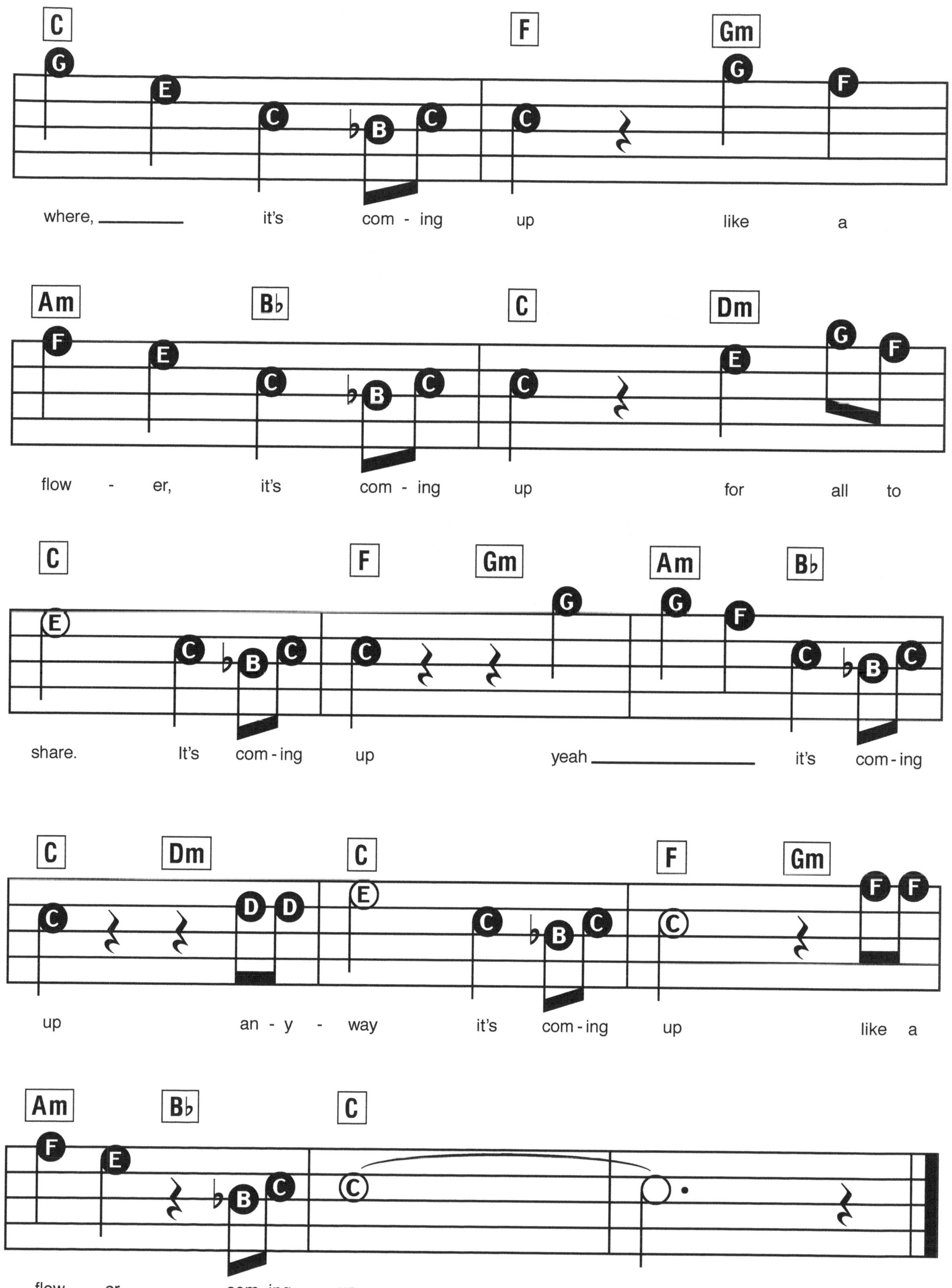
C
F
Gm
where,
it's
com - ing
up
like
a
Am
B♭
C
Dm
flow - er,
it's
com - ing
up
for
all
to
C
F
Gm
Am
B♭
share.
It's
com - ing
up
yeah
it's
com - ing
C
Dm
C
F
Gm
up
an - y - way
it's
com - ing
up
like
a
Am
B♭
C
flow - er,
com - ing
up.

Dance Tonight

Registration 4
Rhythm: 8-Beat or Rock

Words and Music by
Paul McCartney

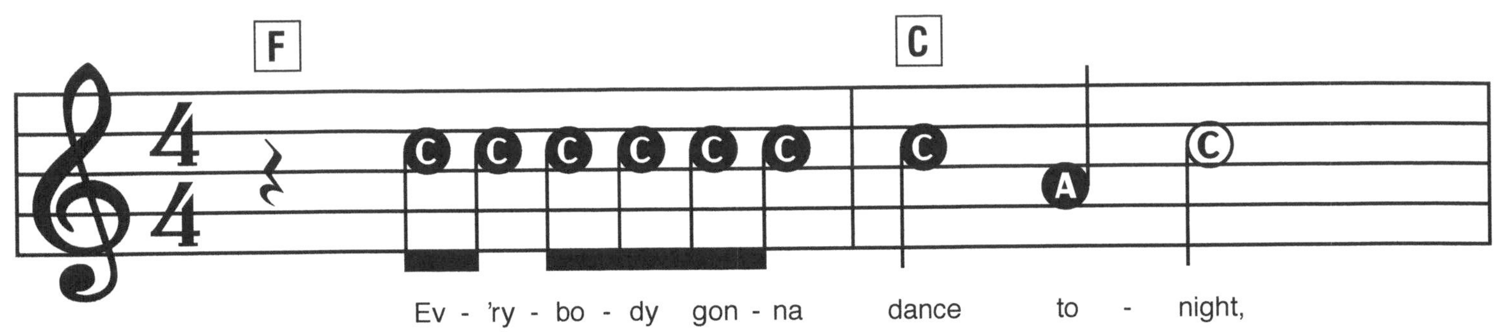

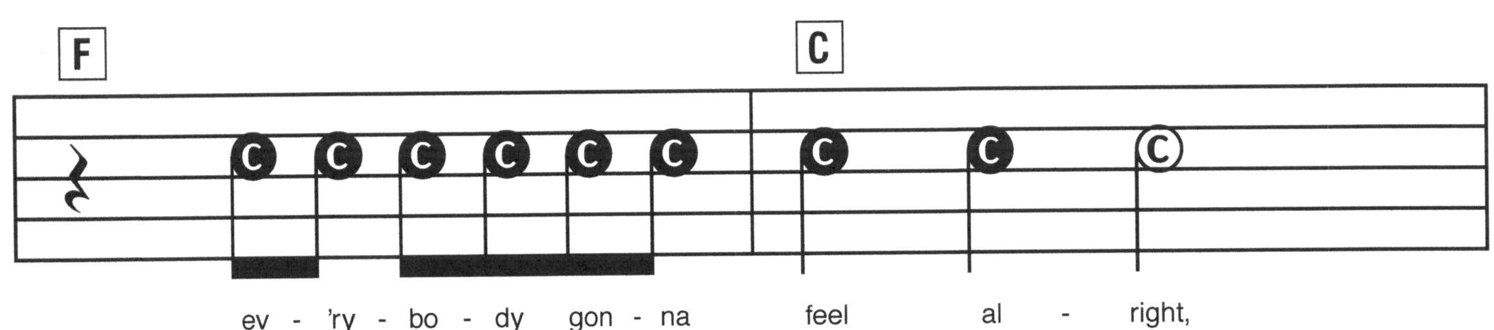

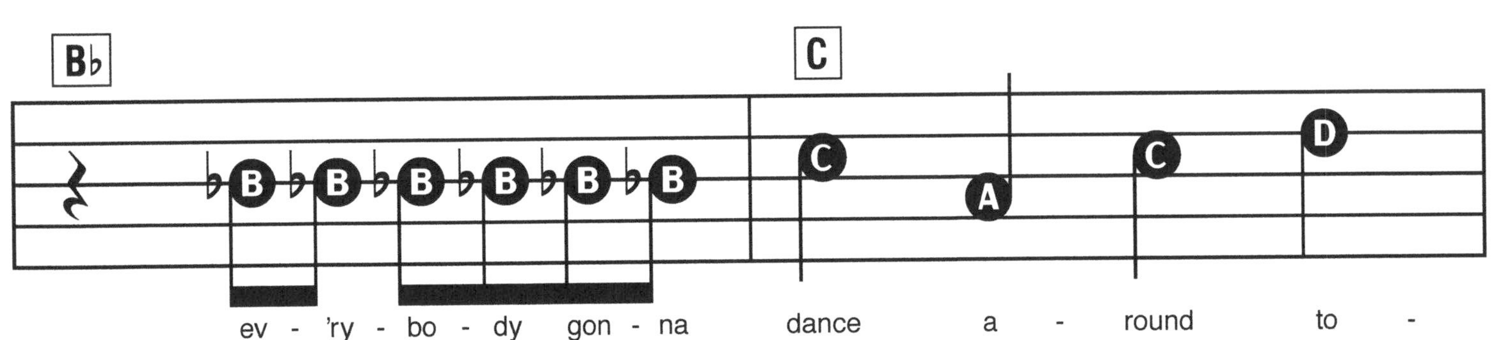

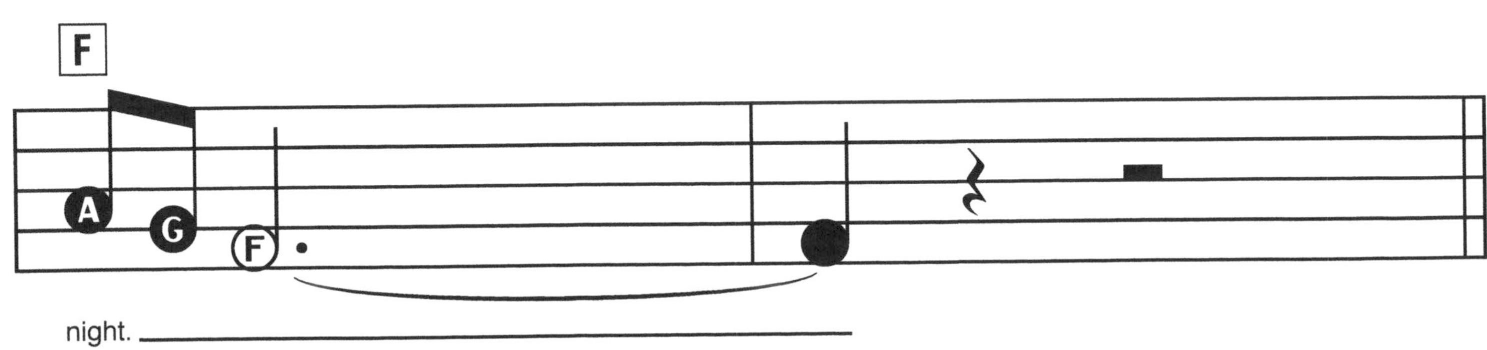

© 2007 MPL COMMUNICATIONS LTD.
Administered by MPL COMMUNICATIONS, INC.
All Rights Reserved

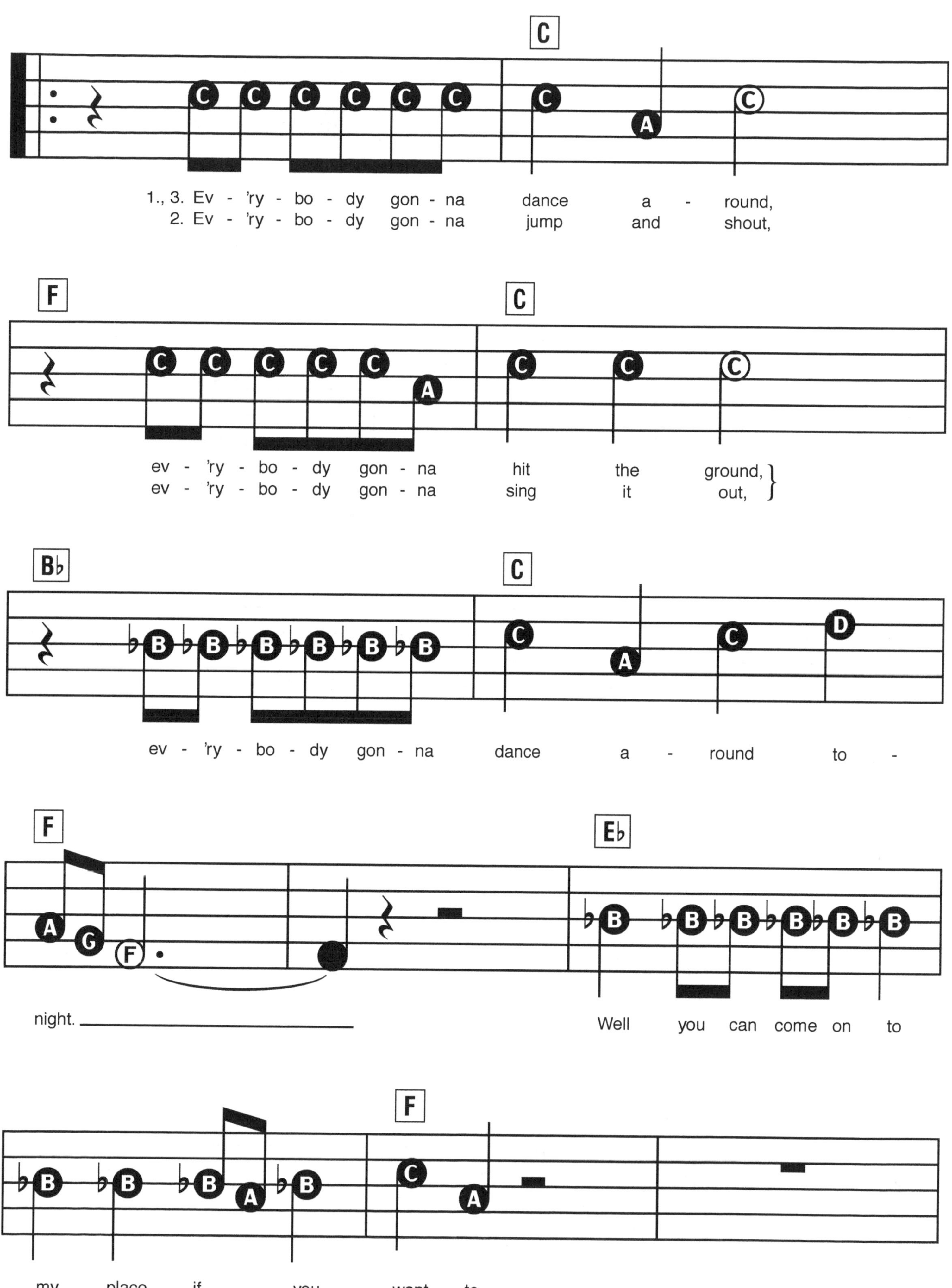
C
C C C C C C
C A C
1., 3. Ev - 'ry - bo - dy gon - na dance a - round,
2. Ev - 'ry - bo - dy gon - na jump and shout,
F
C C C C C A
C
C C C
ev - 'ry - bo - dy gon - na hit the ground,
ev - 'ry - bo - dy gon - na sing it out,
B♭
B B B B B B
C
C A C D
ev - 'ry - bo - dy gon - na dance a - round to -
F
A G F
E♭
B B B B B B
night.
Well you can come on to
B B B A B
F
C A
my place if you want to,

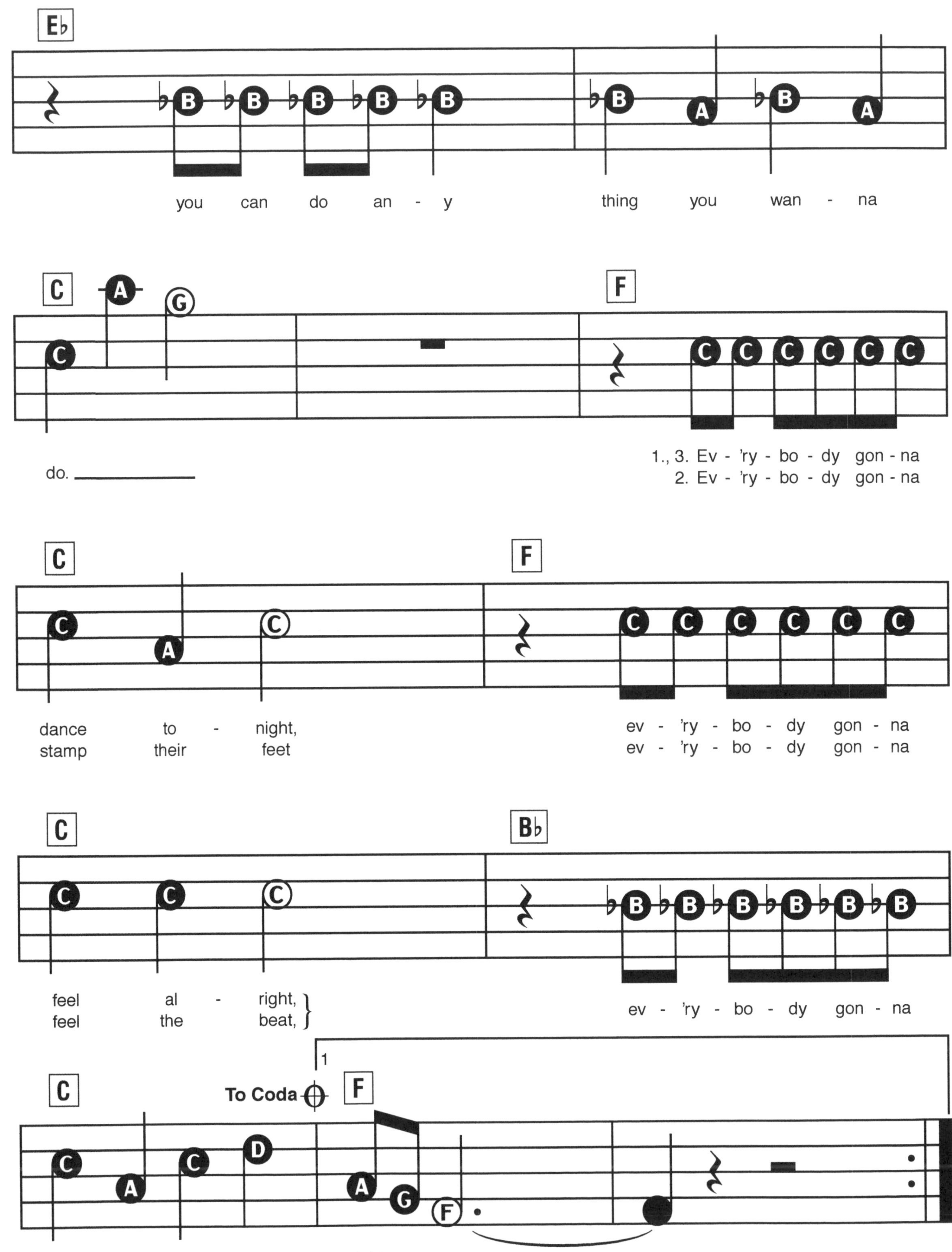

E♭
B B B B B B A B A
you can do an - y thing you wan - na
C
C A G
do.
F
C C C C C C
1., 3. Ev - 'ry - bo - dy gon - na
2. Ev - 'ry - bo - dy gon - na
C
C A C
dance to - night,
stamp their feet
F
C C C C C C
ev - 'ry - bo - dy gon - na
ev - 'ry - bo - dy gon - na
C
C C C
feel al - right,
feel the beat,
B♭
B B B B B B
ev - 'ry - bo - dy gon - na
C
C A C D
To Coda
1
F
A G F
dance a - round to - night.

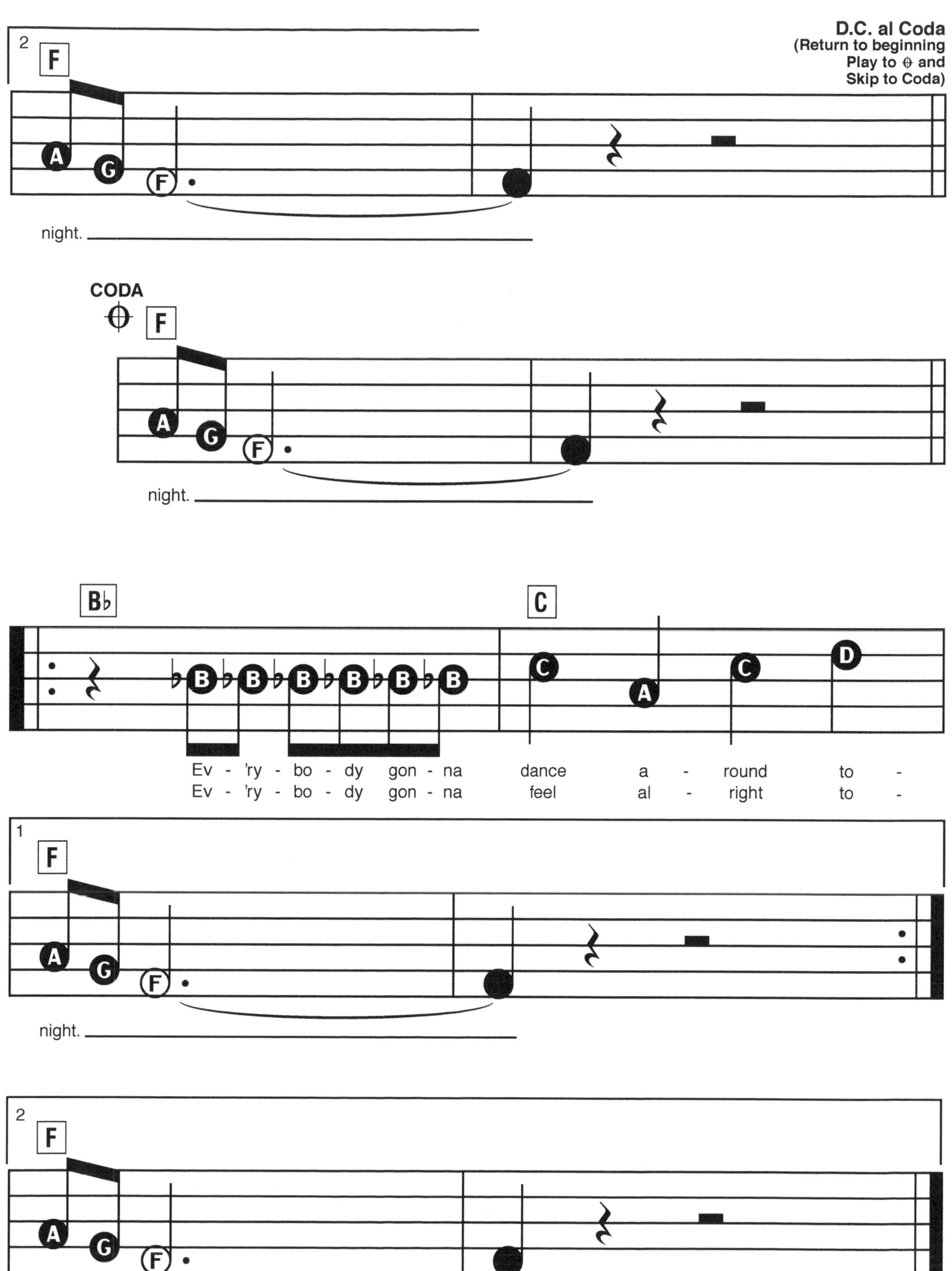

2
F
A G F
night.
D.C. al Coda
(Return to beginning
Play to ⊕ and
Skip to Coda)
CODA
F
A G F
night.
B♭
B B B B B B
Ev - 'ry - bo - dy gon - na
Ev - 'ry - bo - dy gon - na
C
C A C D
dance a - round to -
feel al - right to -
1
F
A G F
night.
2
F
A G F
night.

Ebony and Ivory

Registration 1
Rhythm: Rock or 8-Beat

Words and Music by
Paul McCartney

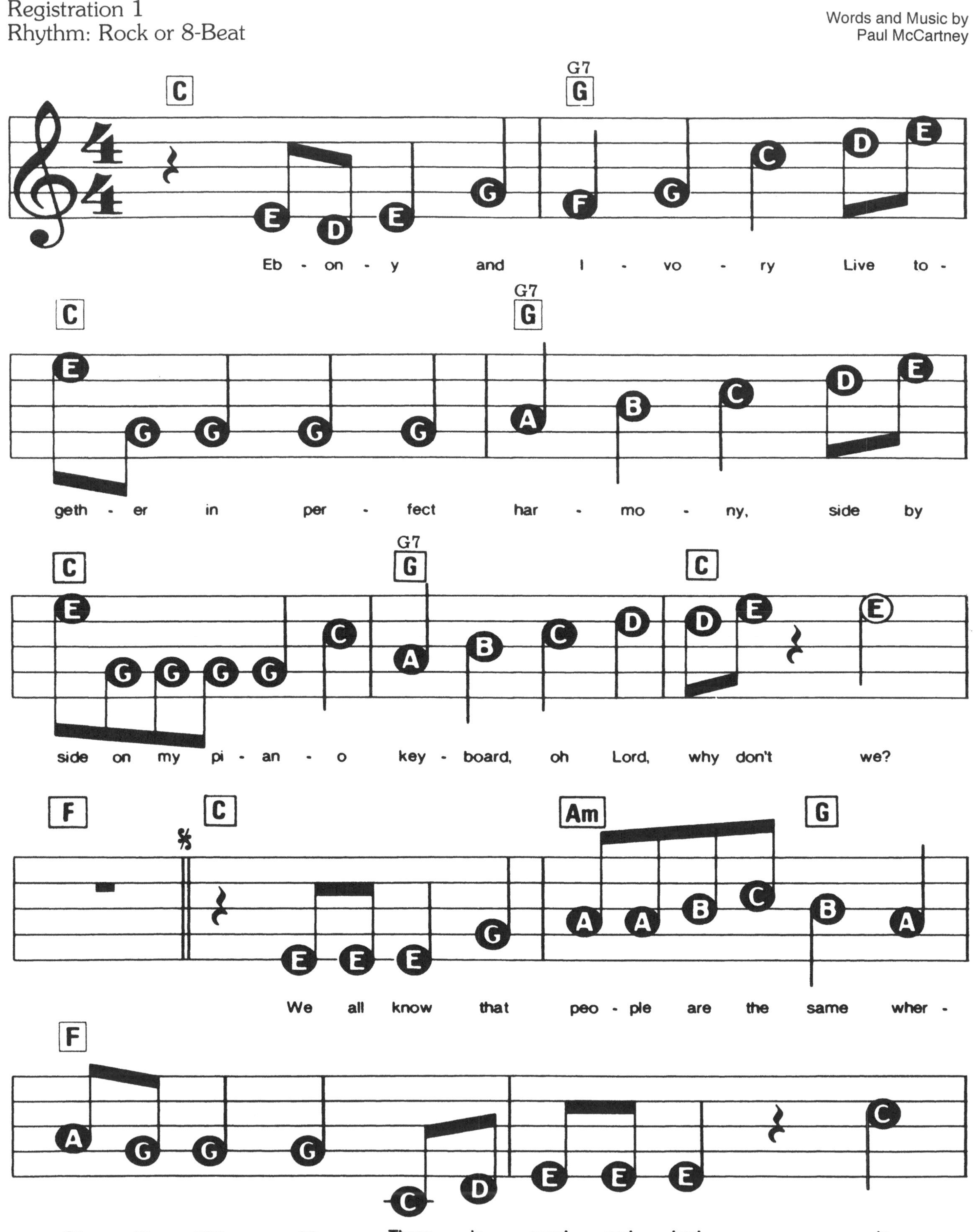

© 1982 MPL COMMUNICATIONS, INC.
All Rights Reserved

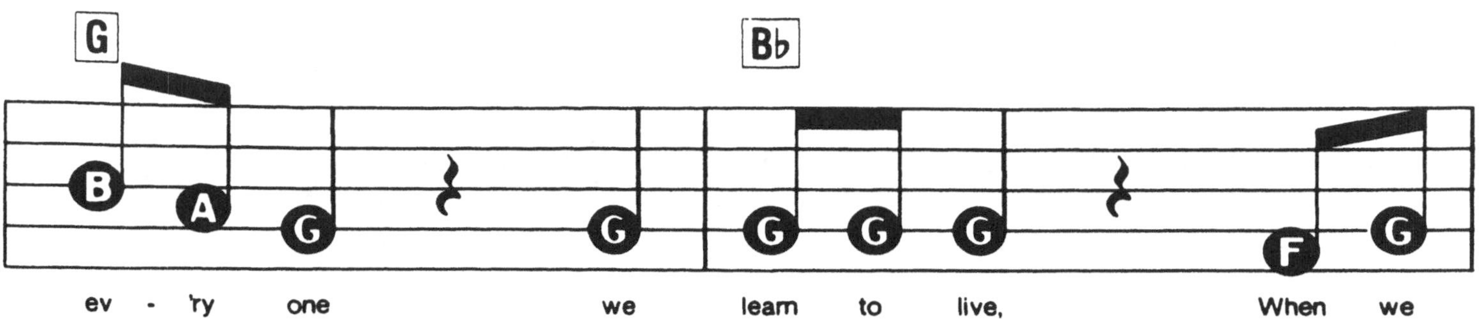
G
Bb
B A G G G G G F G
ev - 'ry one we learn to live, When we

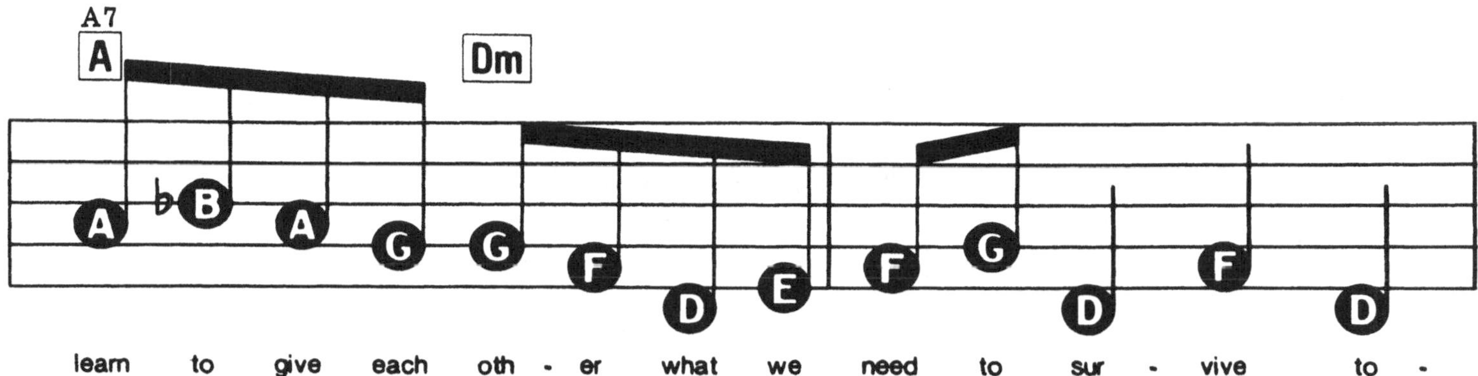
A7
A
Dm
A B A G G F D E F G D F D
learn to give each oth - er what we need to sur - vive to -

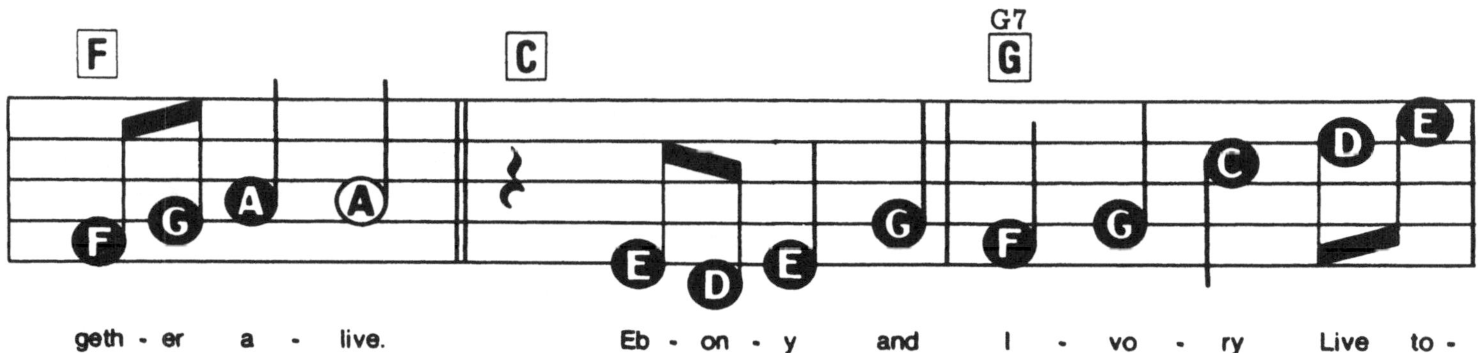
F
C
G7
G
F G A A E D E G F G C D E
geth - er a - live. Eb - on - y and I - vo - ry Live to -

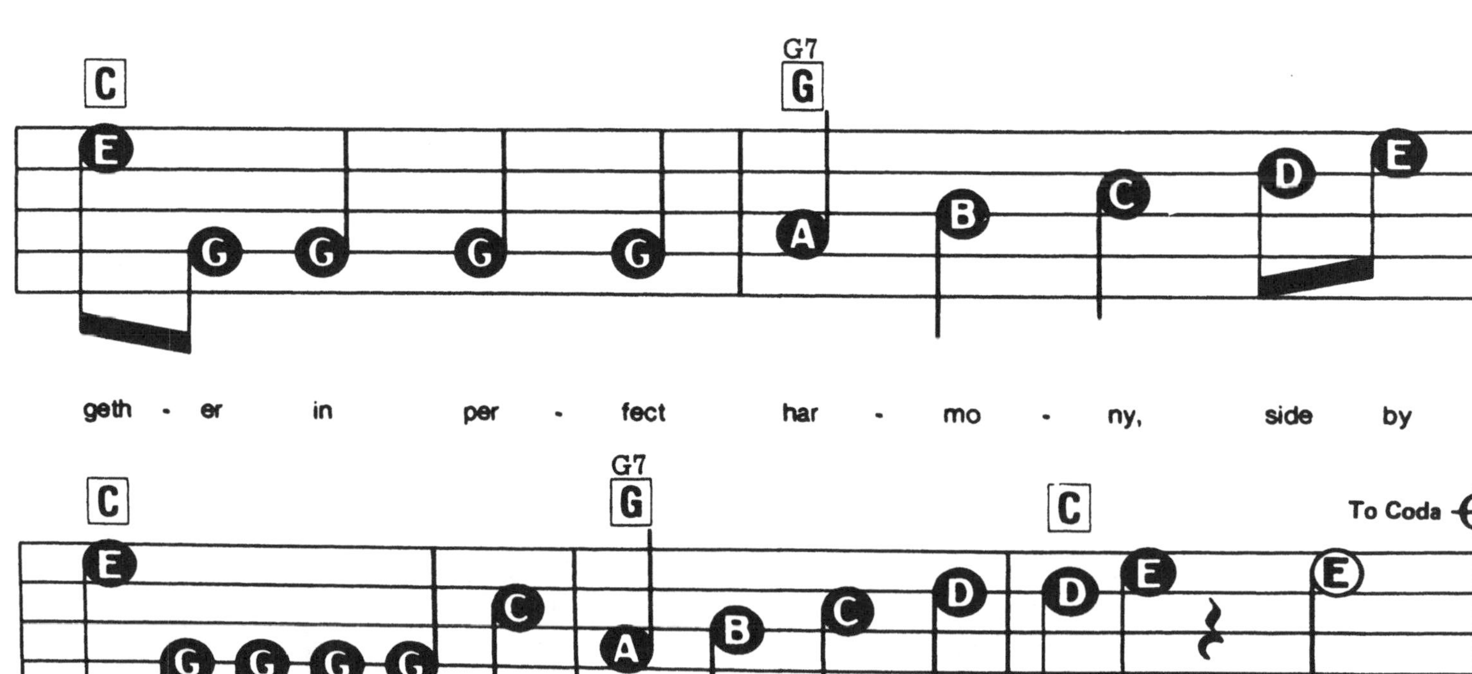
C
G7
G
E G G G G A B C D E
geth - er in per - fect har - mo - ny, side by
C
G7
G
C
To Coda
E G G G G C A B C D D E E
side on my pi - an - o key - board, Oh Lord, why don't we?

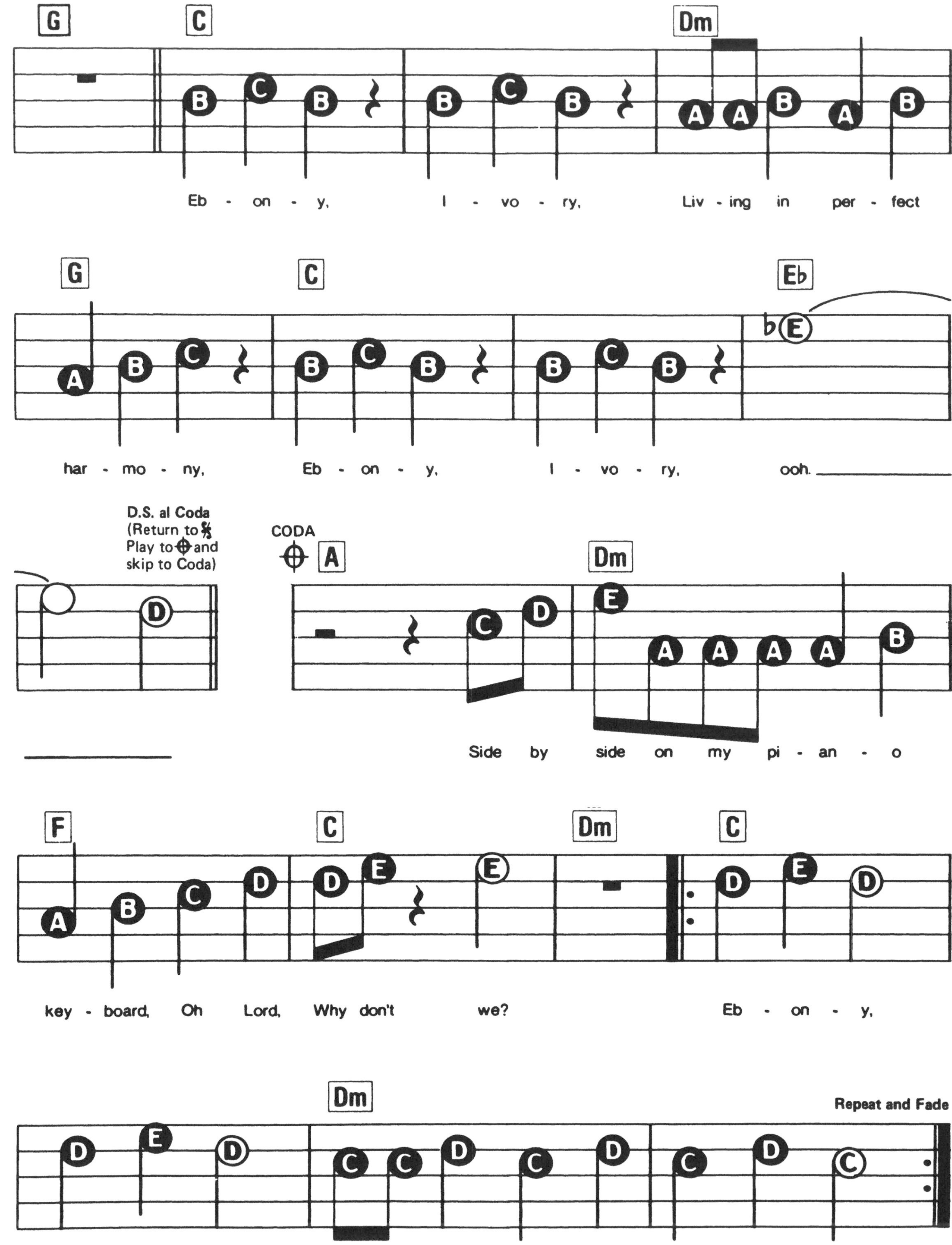
G C Dm
Eb - on - y, I - vo - ry, Liv - ing in per - fect
G C Eb
har - mo - ny, Eb - on - y, I - vo - ry, ooh.
D.S. al Coda
(Return to 𝄋
Play to ⊕ and
skip to Coda)
CODA
A Dm
Side by side on my pi - an - o
F C Dm C
key - board, Oh Lord, Why don't we? Eb - on - y,
Dm
Repeat and Fade
I - vo - ry, Liv - ing in per - fect har - mo - ny

Hi, Hi, Hi

Registration 4
Rhythm: 8-Beat or Rock

Words and Music by Paul McCartney
and Linda McCartney

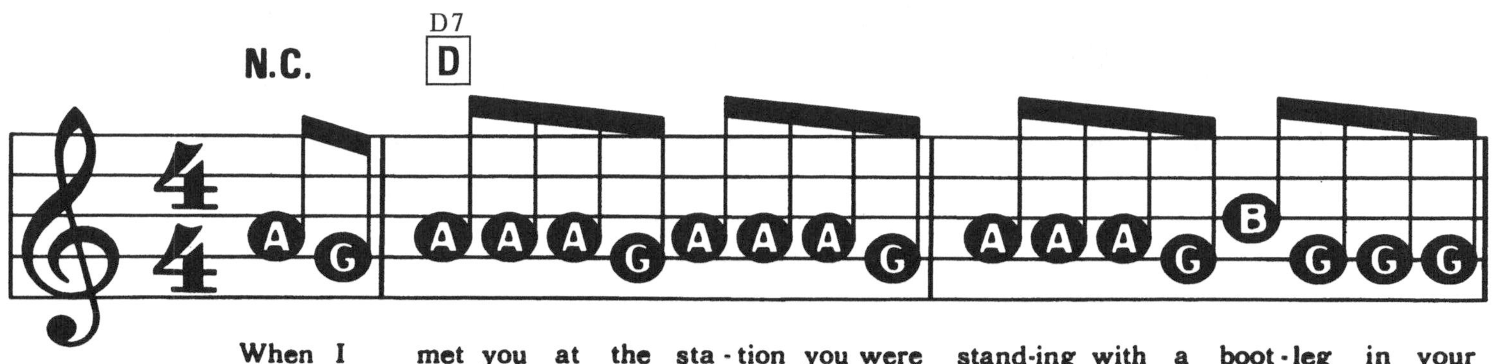

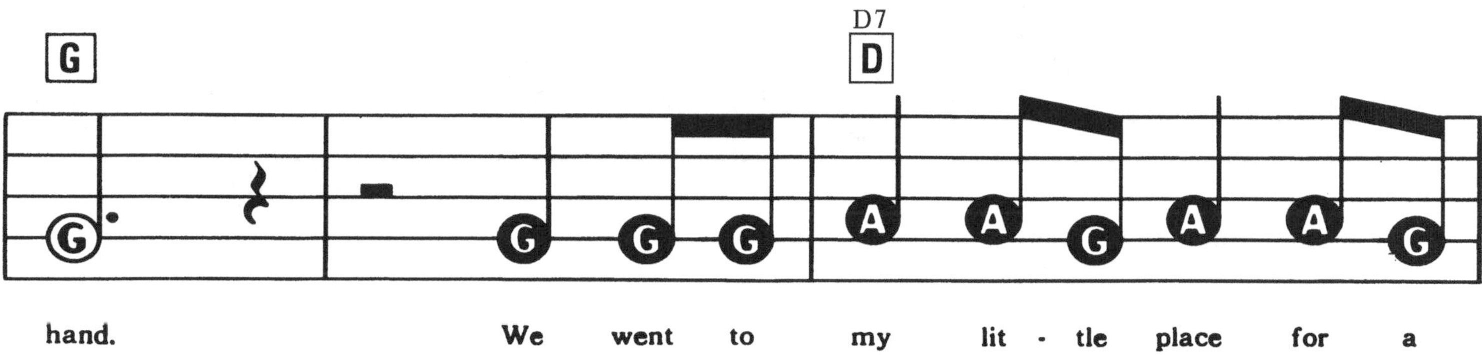

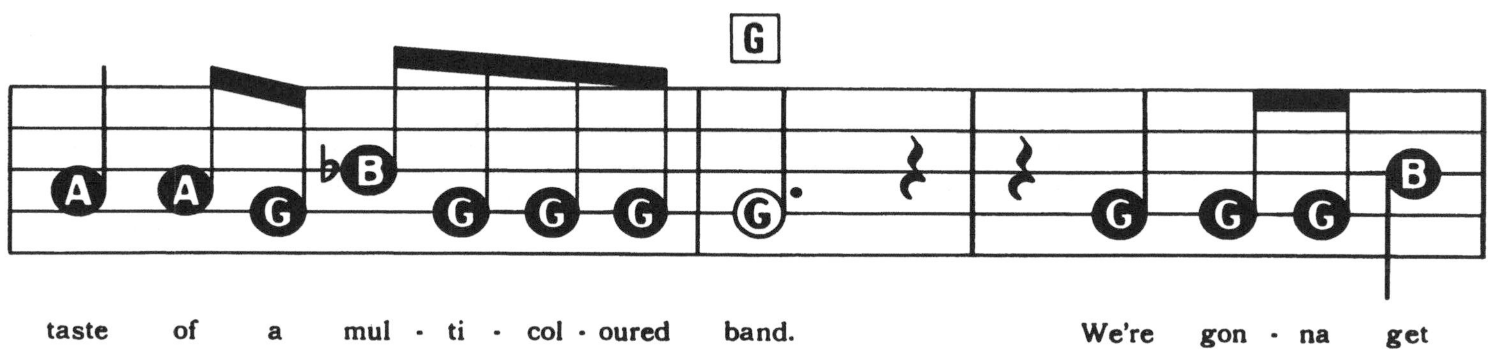

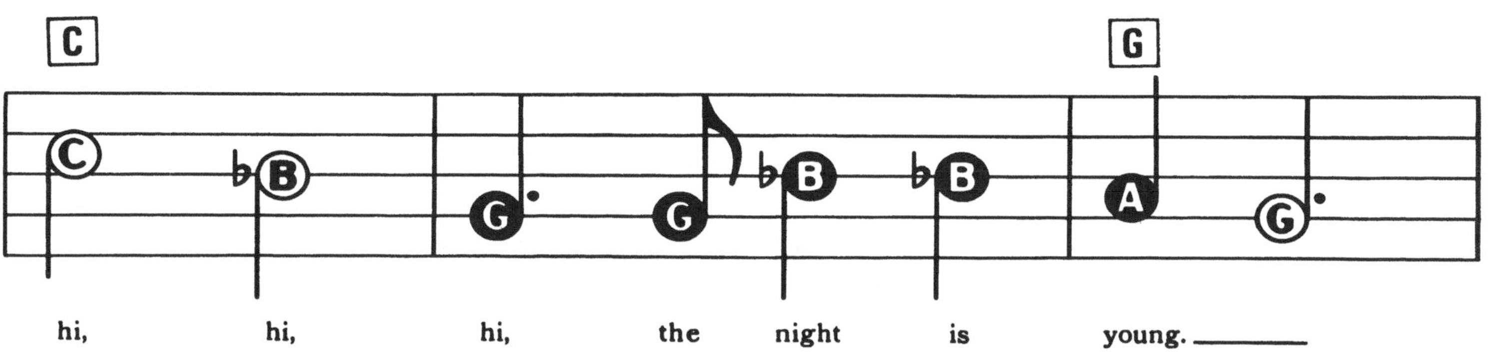

© 1972 (Renewed) PAUL and LINDA McCARTNEY
Administered by MPL COMMUNICATIONS, INC.
All Rights Reserved

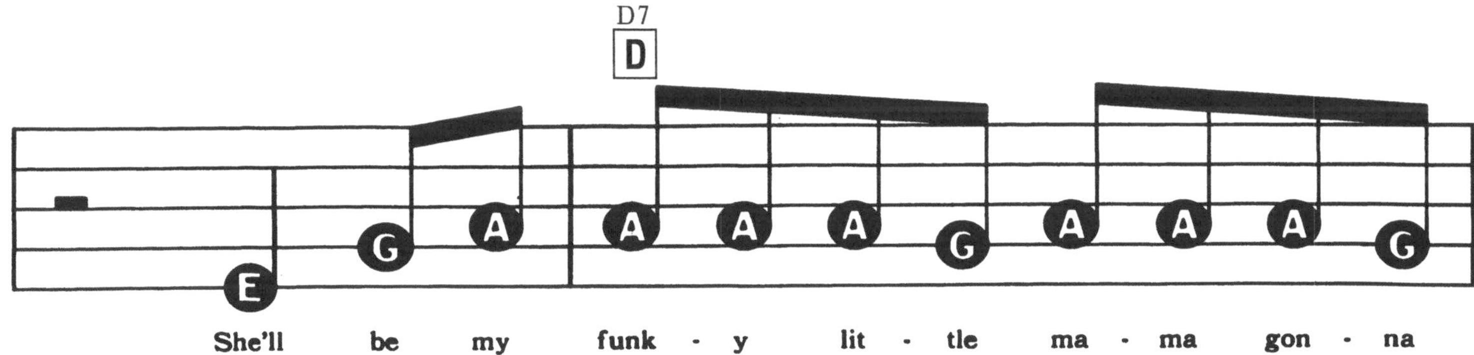
D7
D
E
G
A
A
A
A
G
A
A
A
G
She'll be my funk - y lit - tle ma - ma gon - na

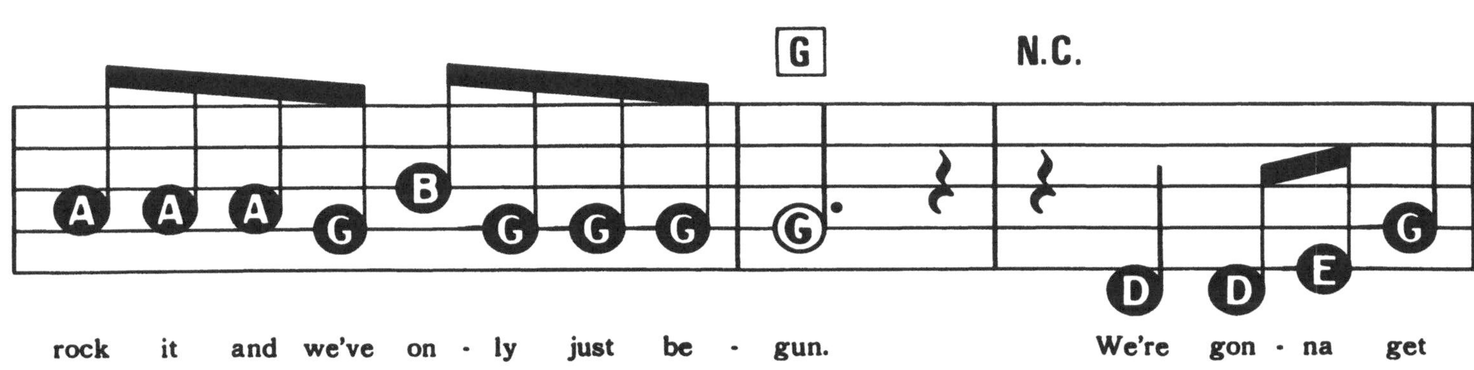
G
N.C.
A
A
A
G
B
G
G
G
G
D
D
E
G
rock it and we've on - ly just be - gun. We're gon - na get

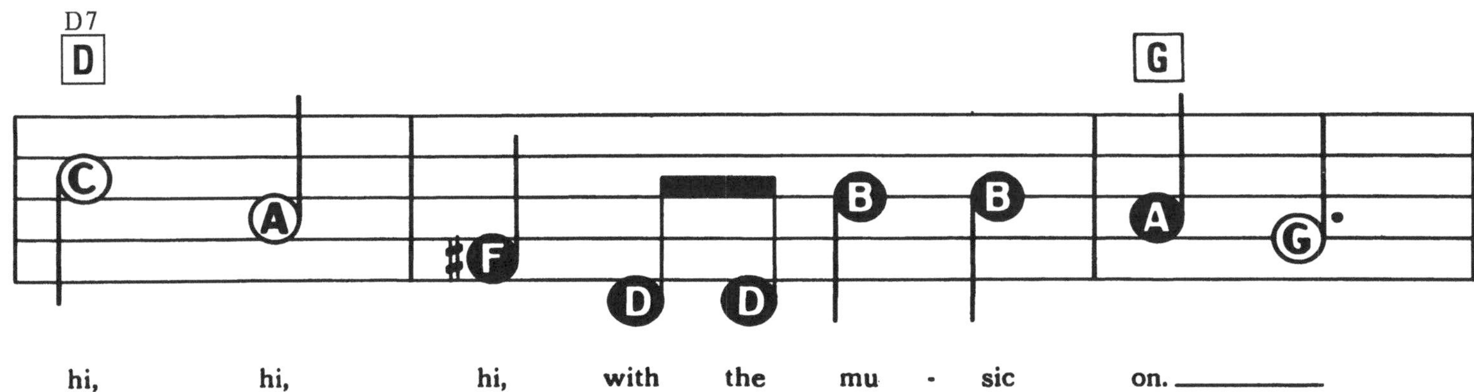
D7
D
G
C
A
F
D
D
B
B
A
G
hi, hi, hi, with the mu - sic on.

D7
D
D
E
G
A
A
A
A
A
A
A
A
G
B
G
Won't say bye - bye, bye - bye, bye - bye, bye - bye 'til the night has

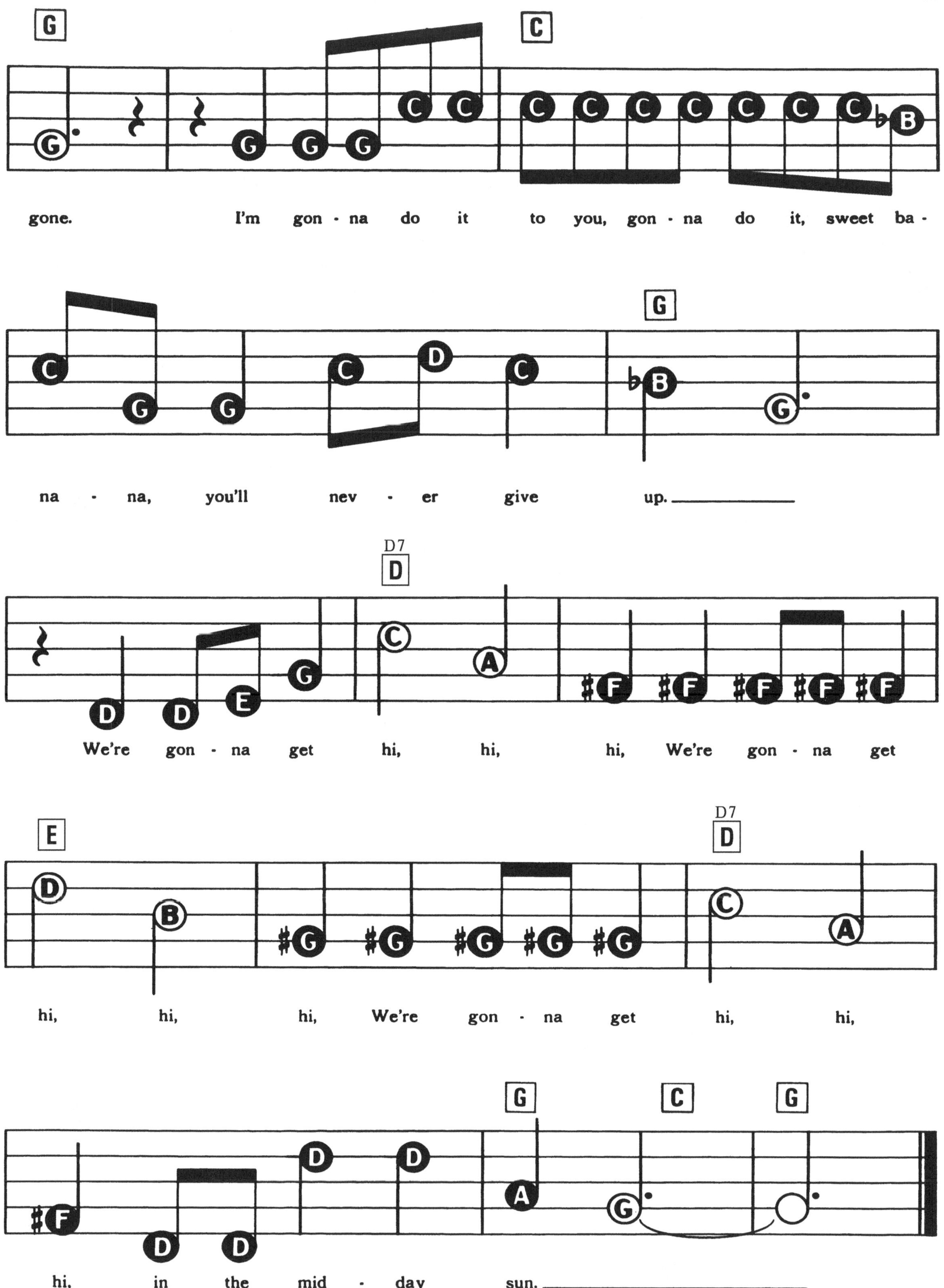
G
C
gone. I'm gon - na do it to you, gon - na do it, sweet ba -
G
na - na, you'll nev - er give up.
D7
D
We're gon - na get hi, hi, hi, We're gon - na get
E
D7
D
hi, hi, hi, We're gon - na get hi, hi,
G
C
G
hi, in the mid - day sun.

Goodnight Tonight

Registration 4
Rhythm: 8-Beat or Rock

Words and Music by
Paul McCartney

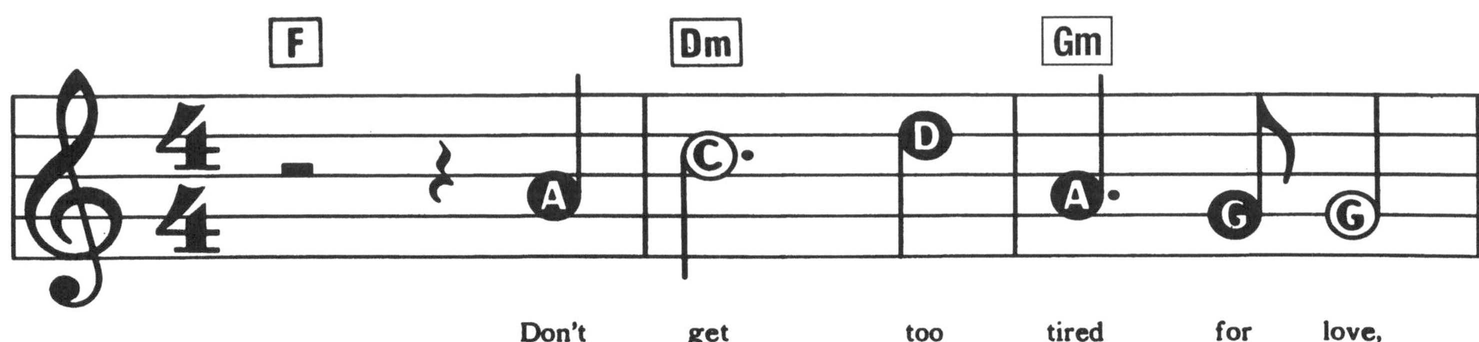

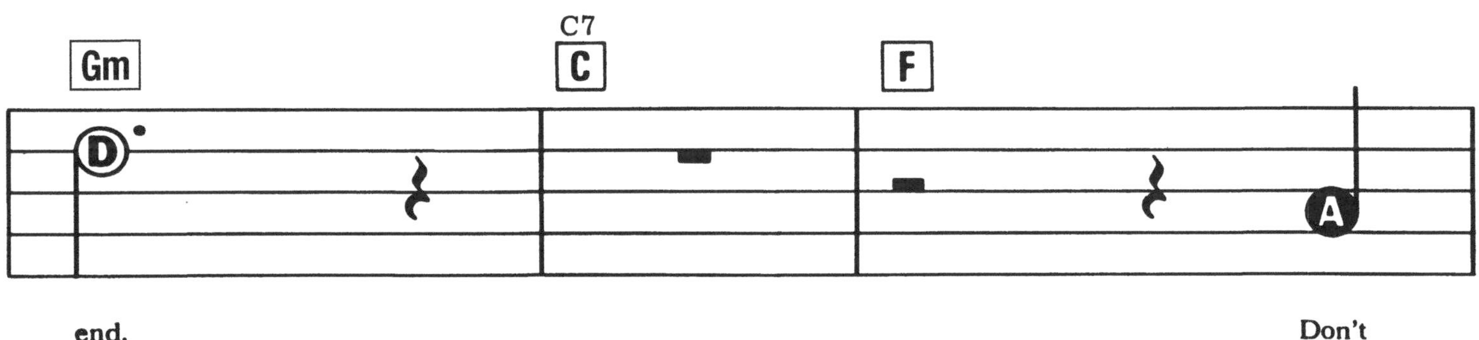

© 1979 MPL COMMUNICATIONS LTD.
Administered by MPL COMMUNICATIONS, INC.
All Rights Reserved

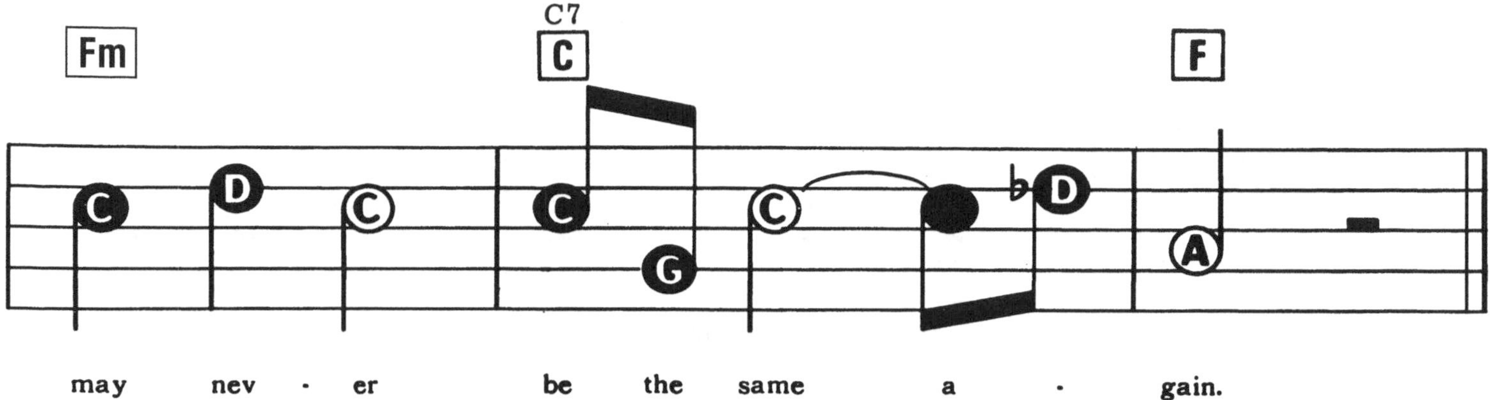
Fm
C7
C
F
C D C C G C D A
may nev - er be the same a - gain.

Dm
Gm
F F G F F G F G F D A
Don't say it! Don't say it! Say an - y - thing but

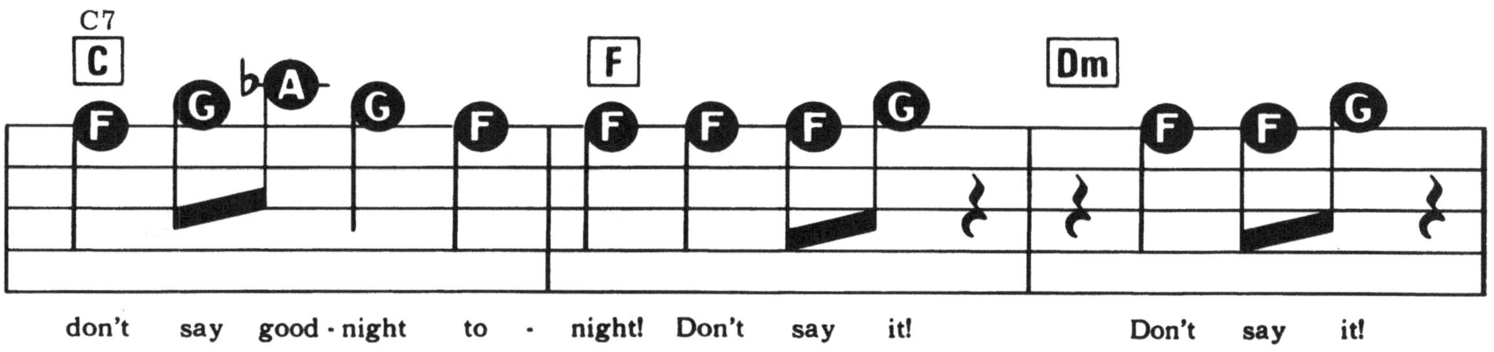
C7
C
F
Dm
F G A G F F F F G F F G
don't say good - night to - night! Don't say it! Don't say it!

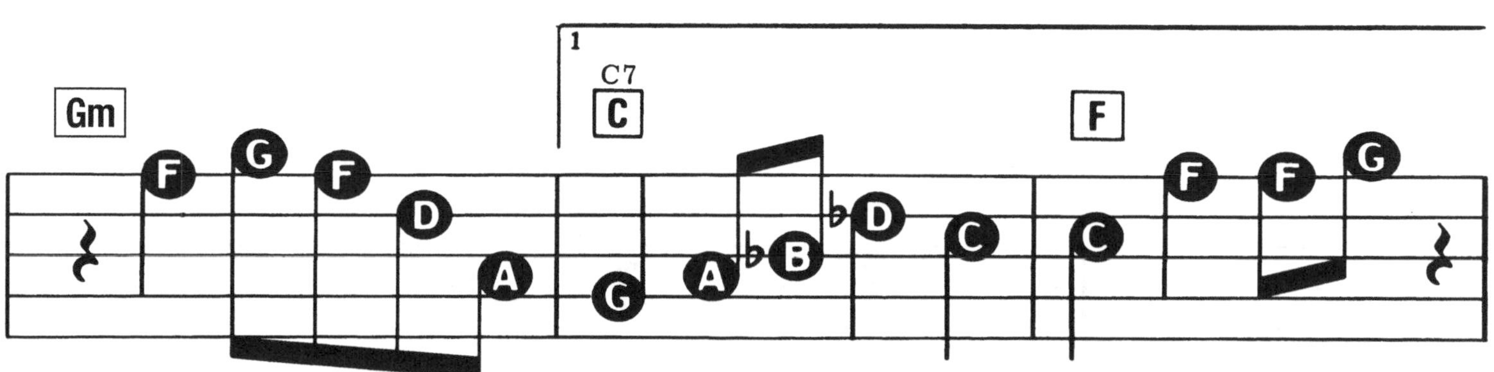
Gm
1
C7
C
F
F G F D A G A B D C C F F G
Say an - y - thing but don't say good - night to - night! Don't say it!

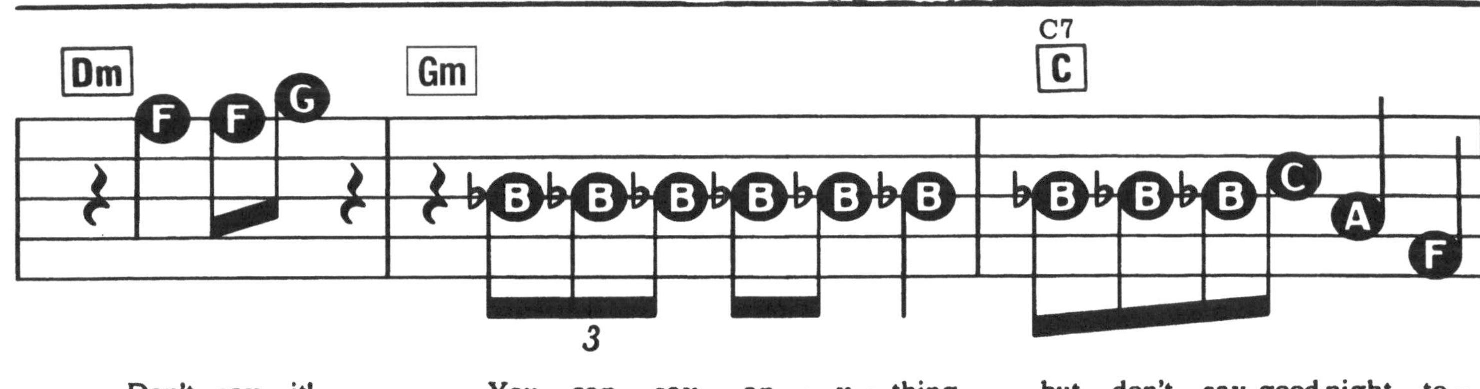
Dm
F F G
Gm
B B B B B B
3
C7
C
B B B C A F
Don't say it! You can say an - y - thing, but don't say good-night to -

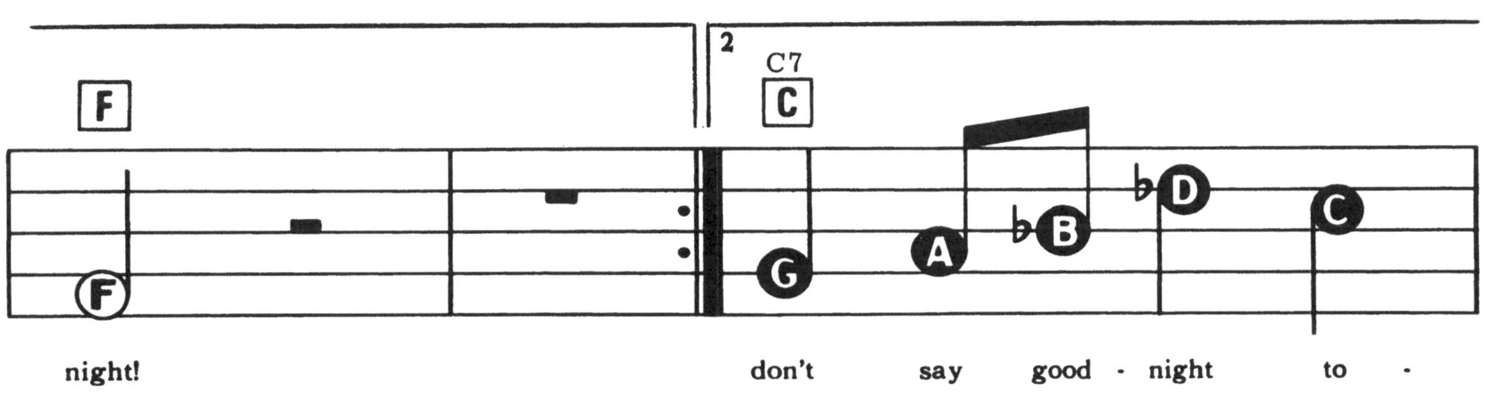
F
F
2
C7
C
G A B D C
night! don't say good - night to -

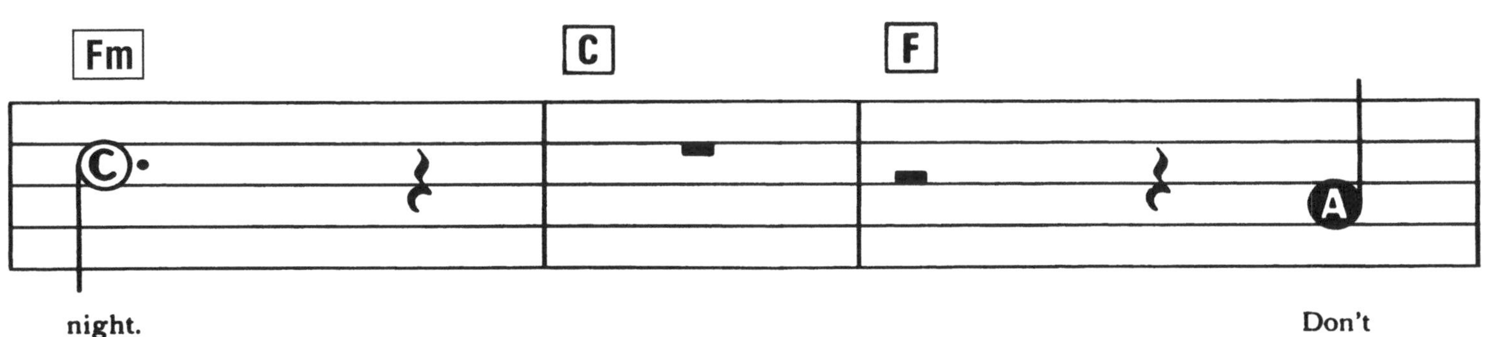
Fm
C
C
F
A
night. Don't

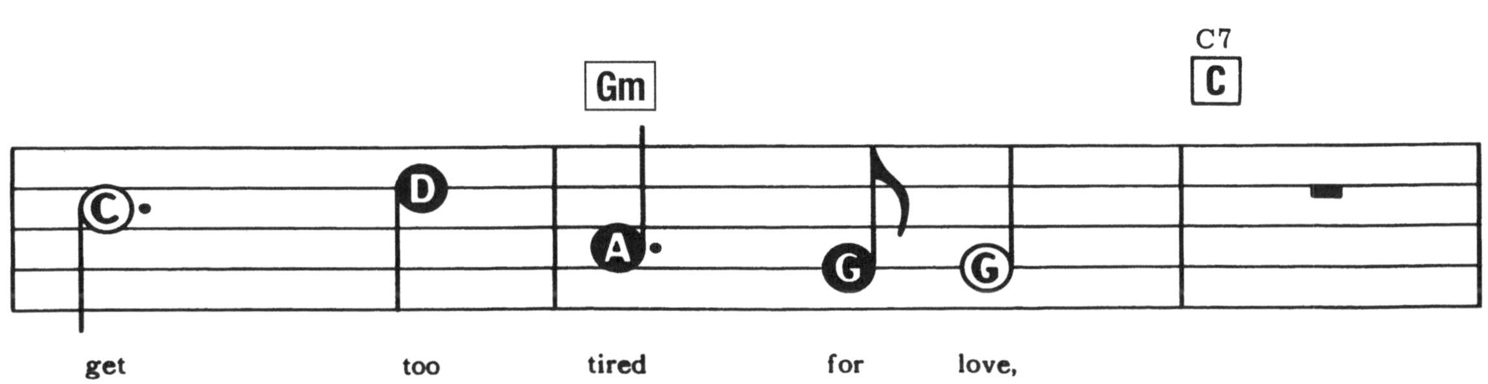
C D
Gm
A G G
C7
C
get too tired for love,

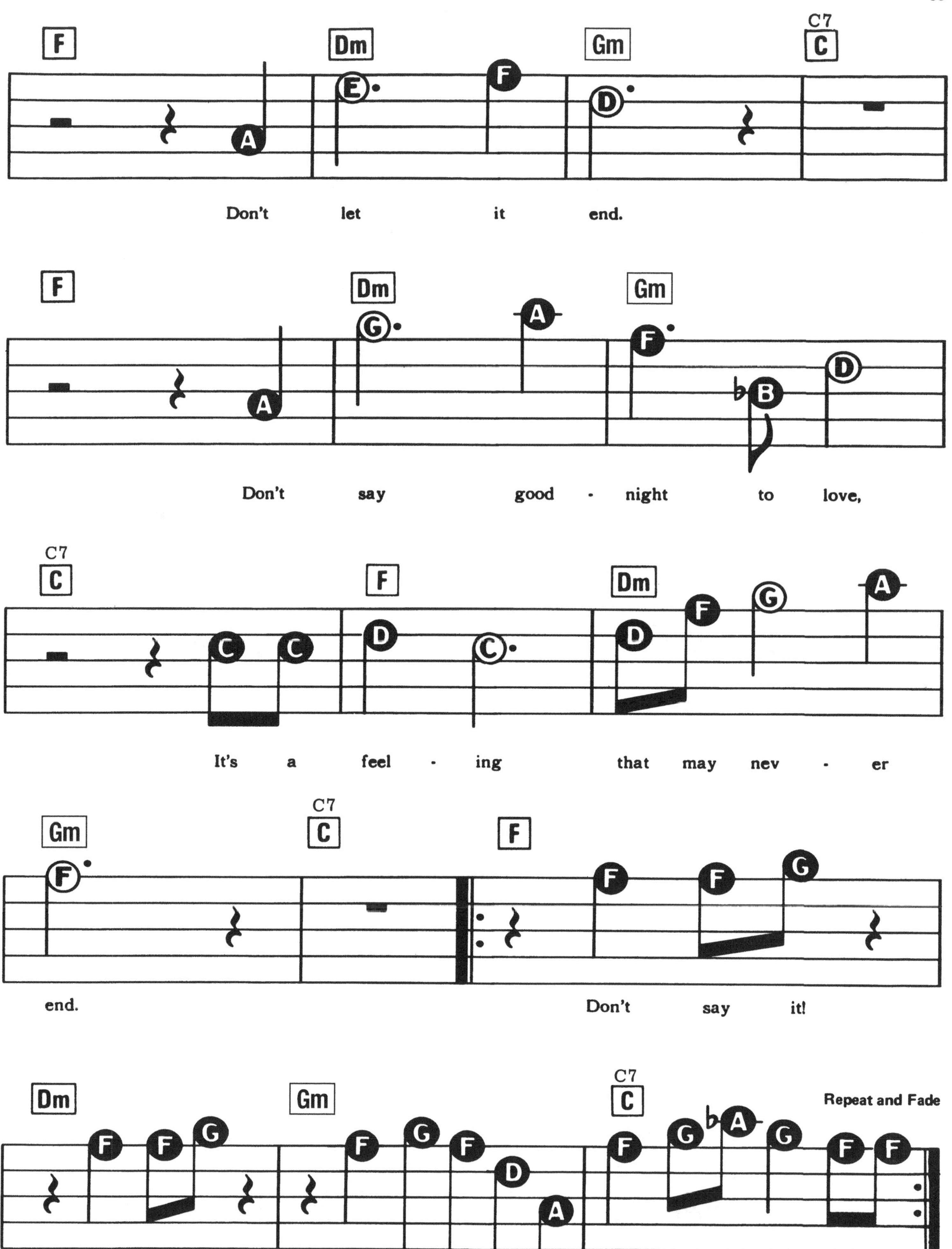
F
Dm
Gm
C7
C
Don't let it end.
F
Dm
Gm
Don't say good - night to love,
C7
C
F
Dm
It's a feel - ing that may nev - er
Gm
C7
C
F
end.
Don't say it!
Dm
Gm
C7
C
Repeat and Fade
Don't say it! Say an - y - thing but don't say good-night to - night!

Helen Wheels

Registration 4
Rhythm: 8-Beat or Rock

Words and Music by Paul McCartney
and Linda McCartney

© 1974 (Renewed) PAUL and LINDA McCARTNEY
Administered by MPL COMMUNICATIONS, INC.
All Rights Reserved

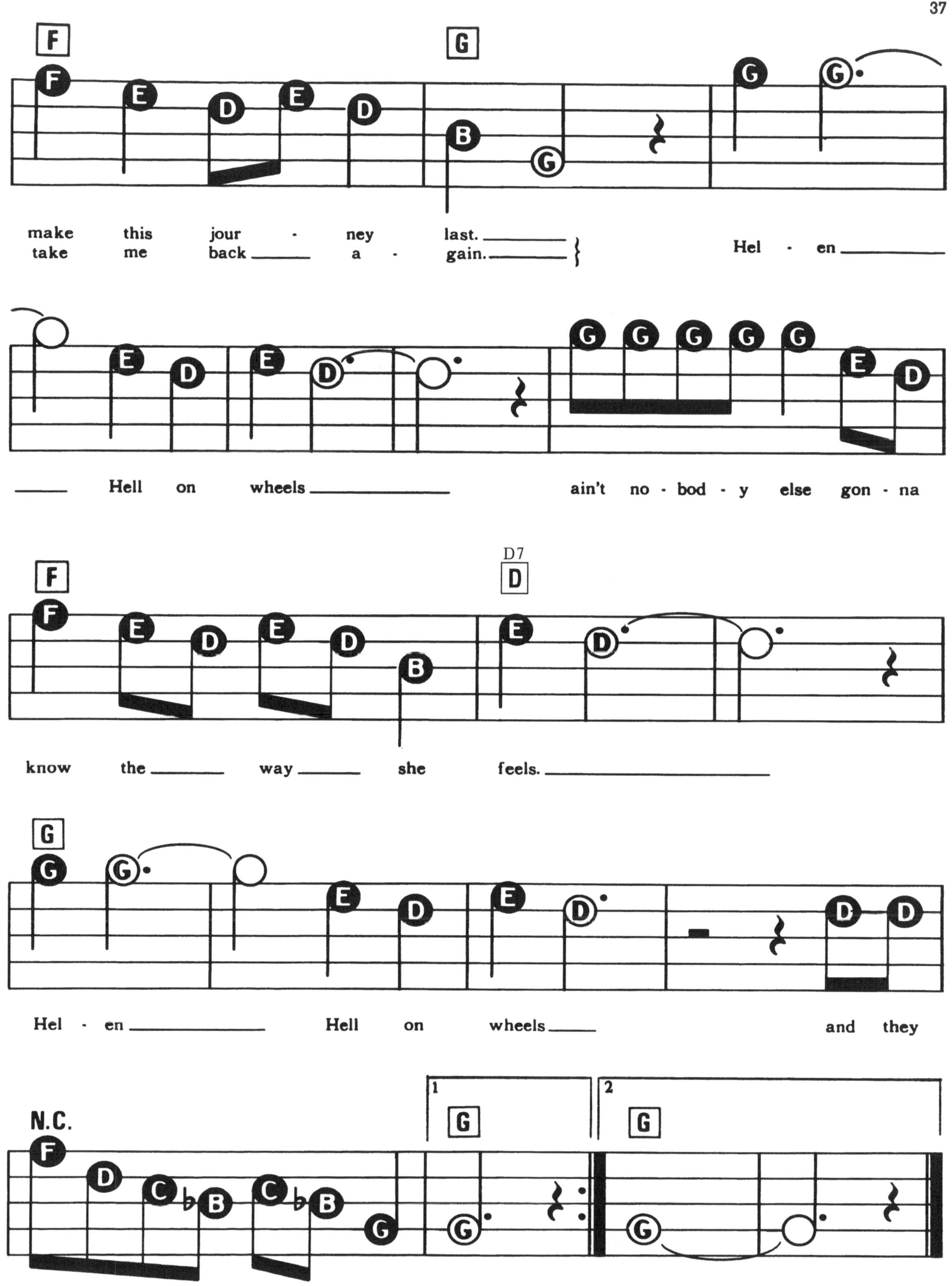
F
G
make this jour - ney last.
take me back a - gain.
Hel - en
Hell on wheels
ain't no - bod - y else gon - na
F
D7
D
know the way she feels.
G
Hel - en
Hell on wheels
and they
N.C.
1
G
2
G
nev - er gon - na take her a - way.
way.

Jet

Registration 4
Rhythm: 8-Beat or Rock

Words and Music by Paul McCartney
and Linda McCartney

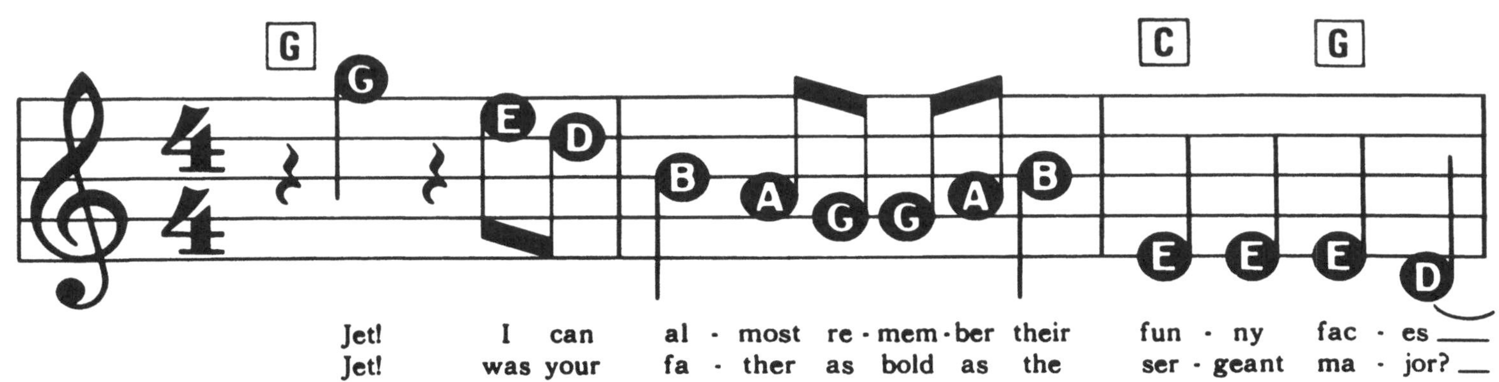

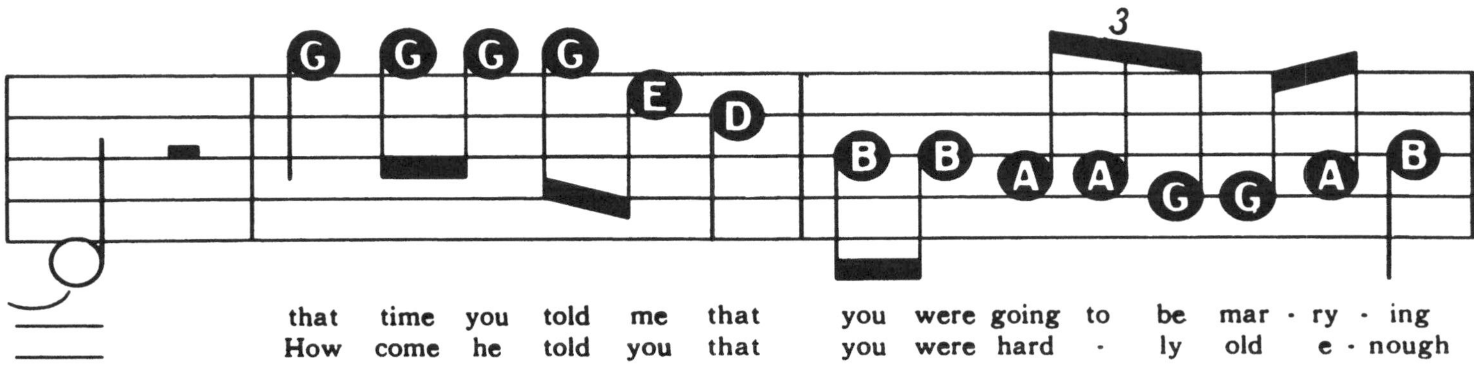

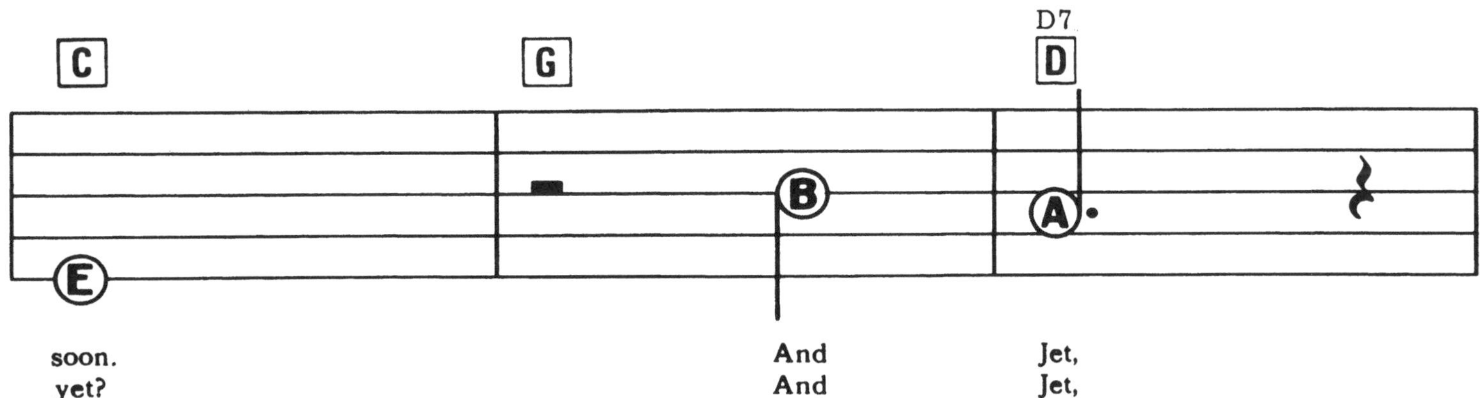

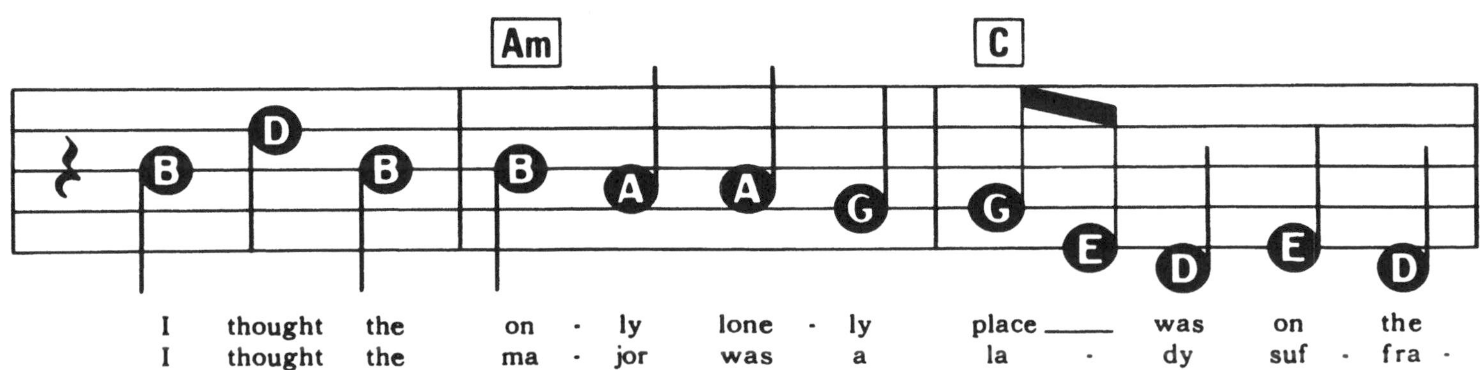

© 1974 (Renewed) PAUL and LINDA McCARTNEY
Administered by MPL COMMUNICATIONS, INC.
All Rights Reserved

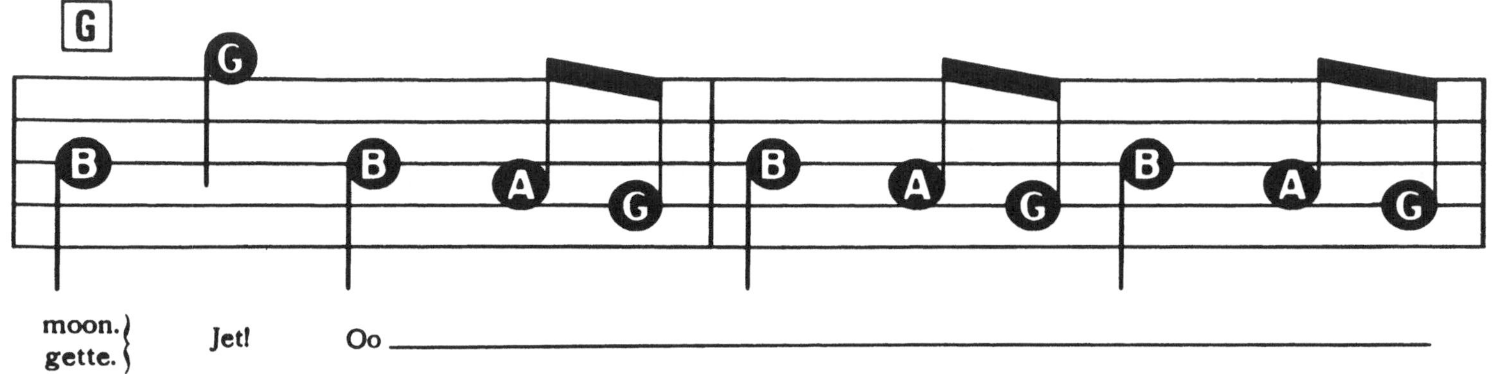
G
G
B
B
A
G
B
A
G
B
A
G
moon.
gette.
Jet!
Oo

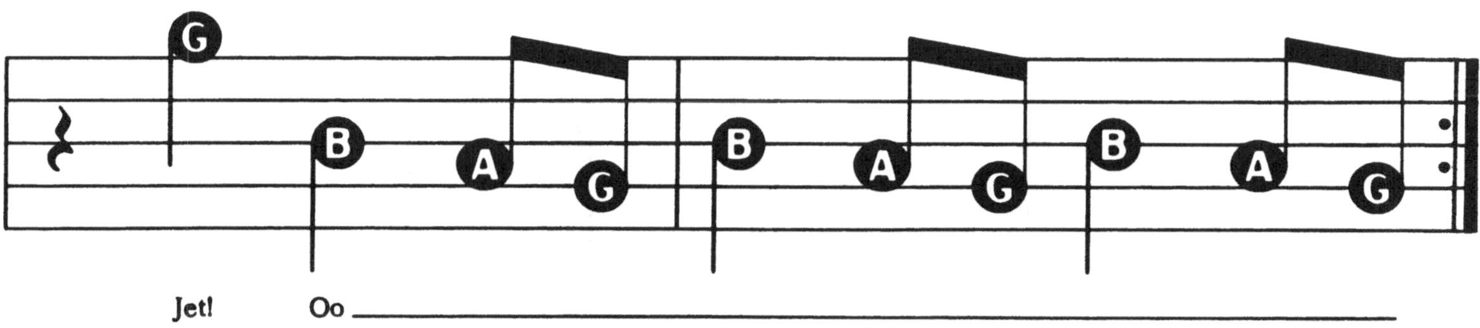
G
B
A
G
B
A
G
B
A
G
Jet!
Oo

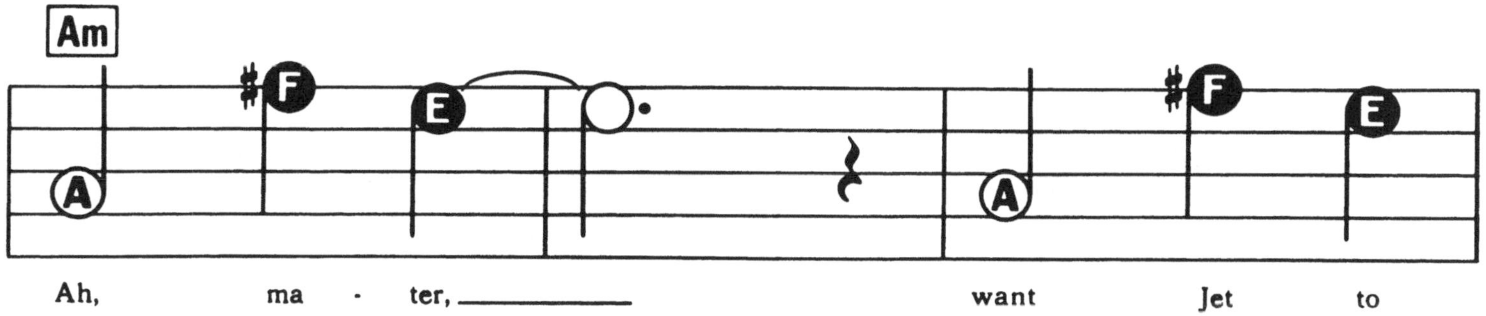
Am
A
♯F
E
A
♯F
E
Ah,
ma - ter,
want
Jet
to

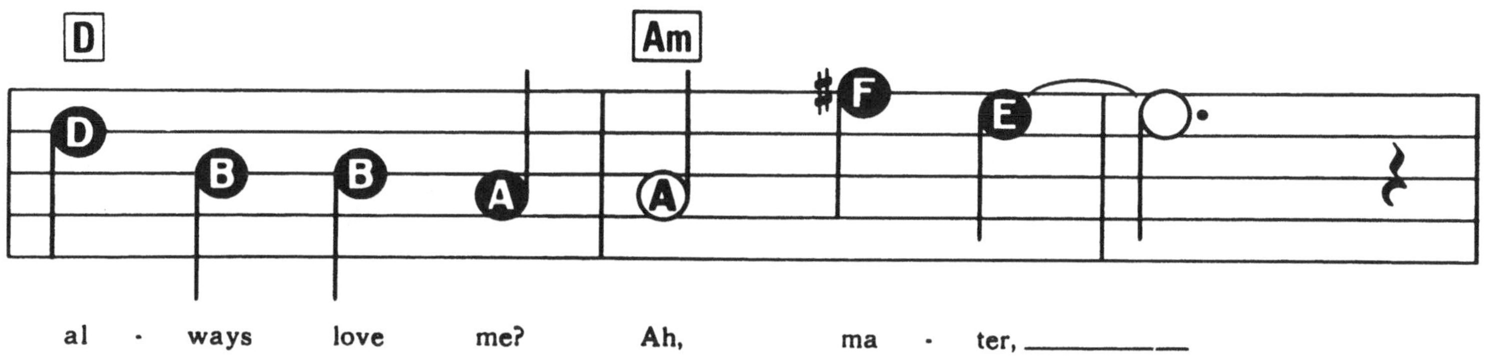
D
Am
D
B
B
A
A
♯F
E
al - ways
love
me?
Ah,
ma - ter,

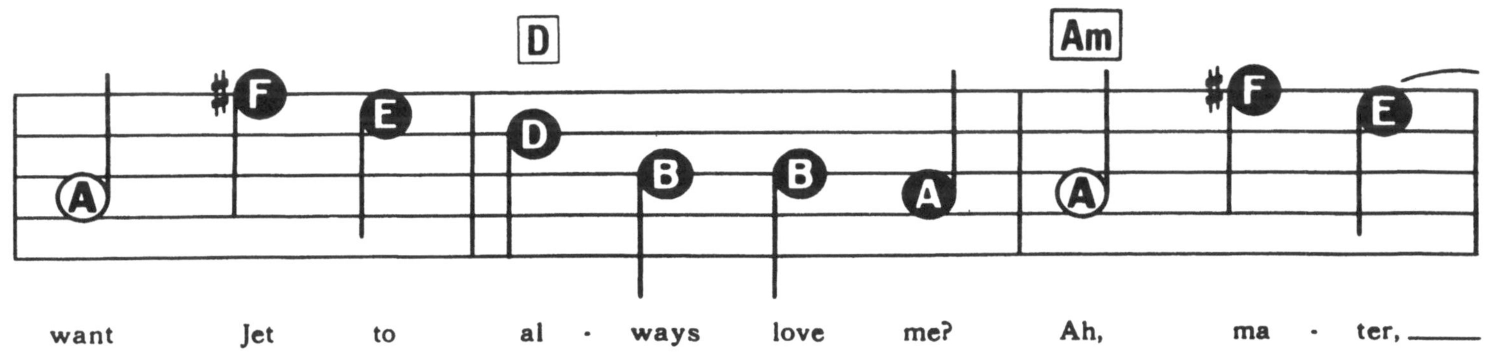
D
Am
A
#F
E
D
B
B
A
A
#F
E
want Jet to al - ways love me? Ah, ma - ter,

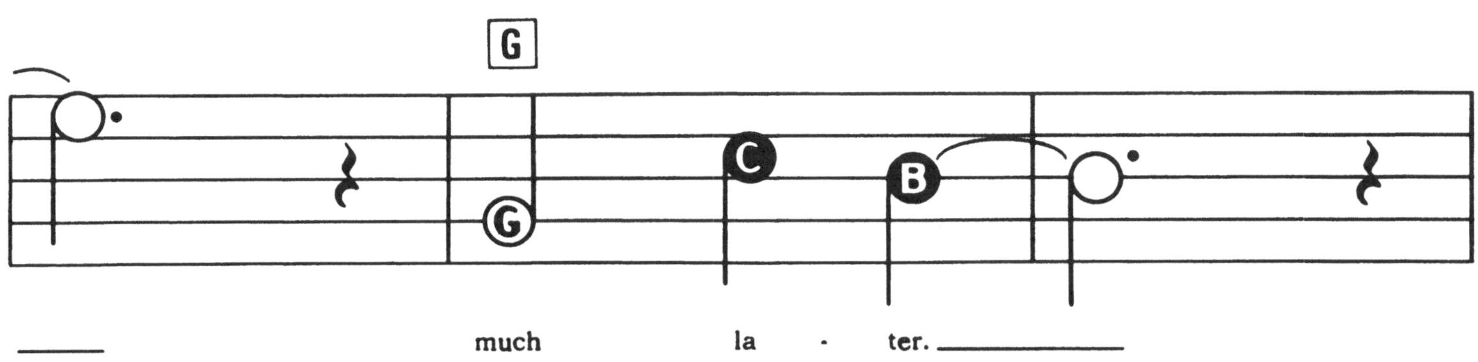
G
G
C
B
much la - ter.

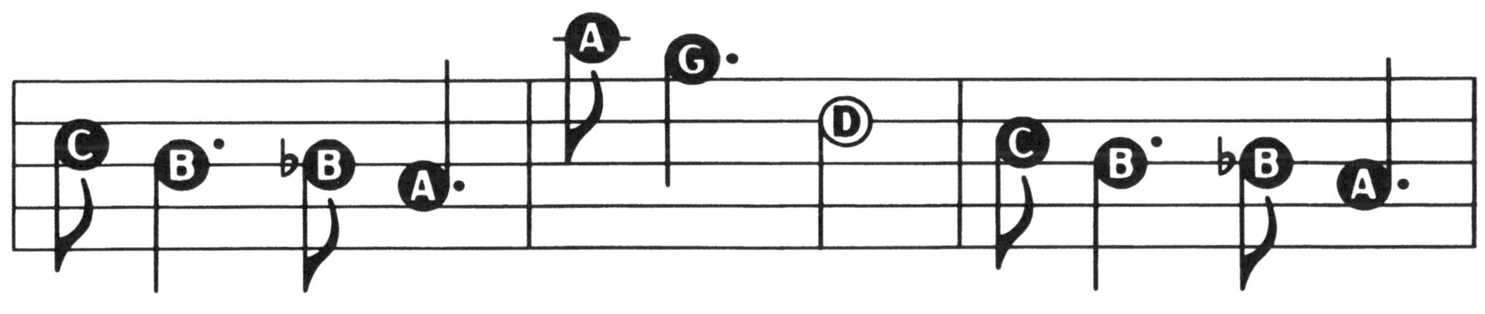
C
B
♭B
A
A
G
D
C
B
♭B
A

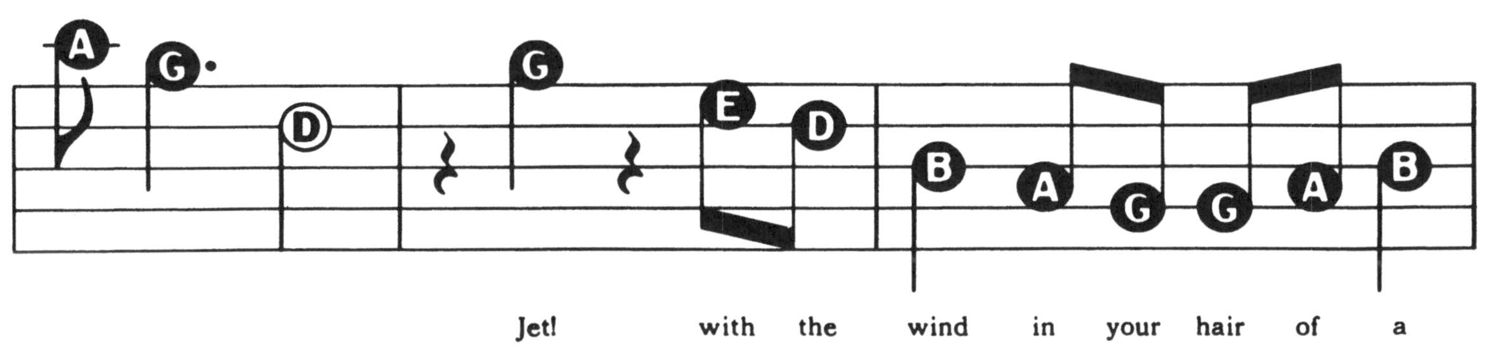
A
G
D
G
E
D
B
A
G
G
A
B
Jet! with the wind in your hair of a

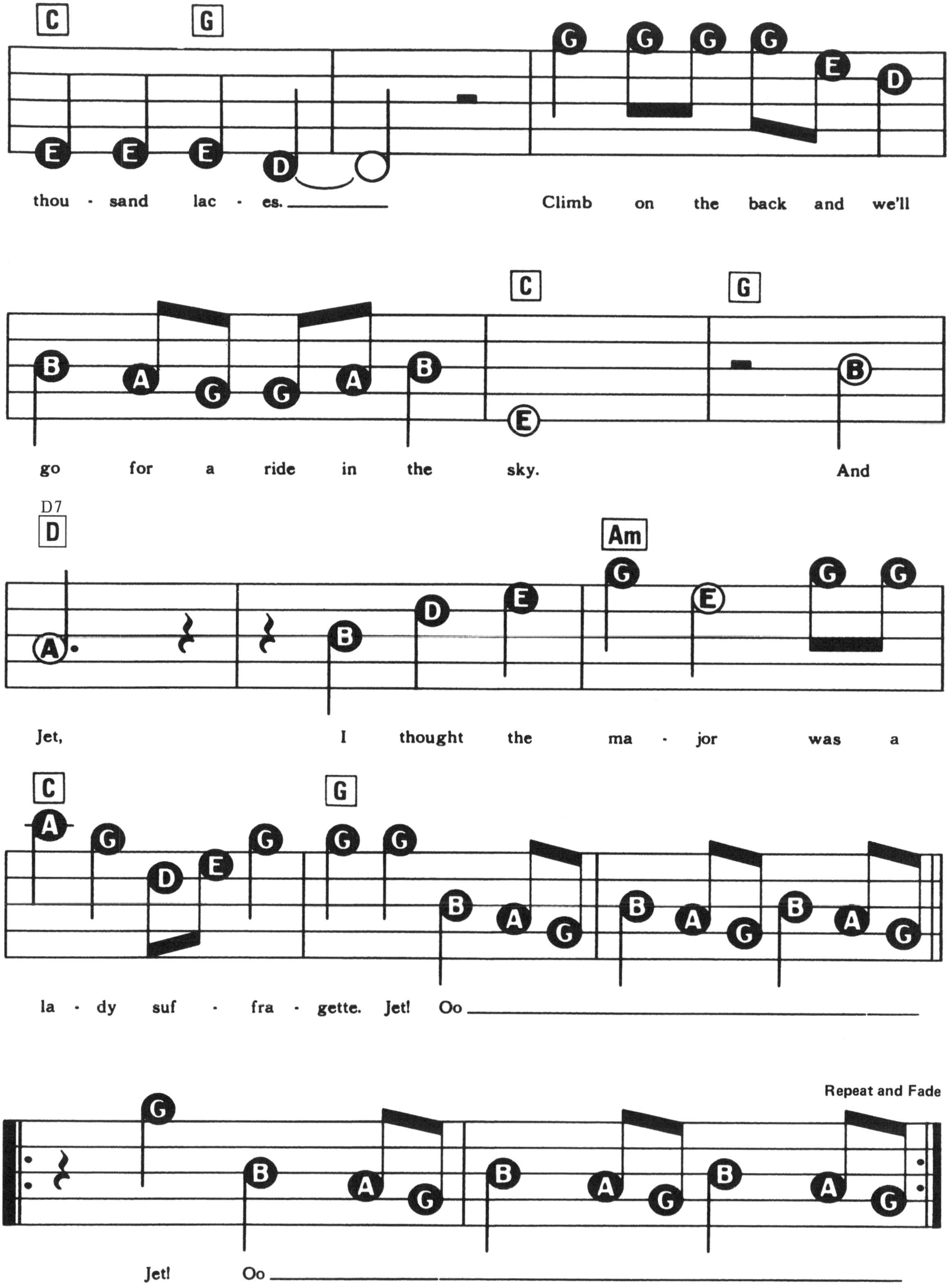

C G

thou - sand lac - es. ______ Climb on the back and we'll

C G

go for a ride in the sky. And

D7
D Am

Jet, I thought the ma - jor was a

C G

la - dy suf - fra - gette. Jet! Oo ______________________________

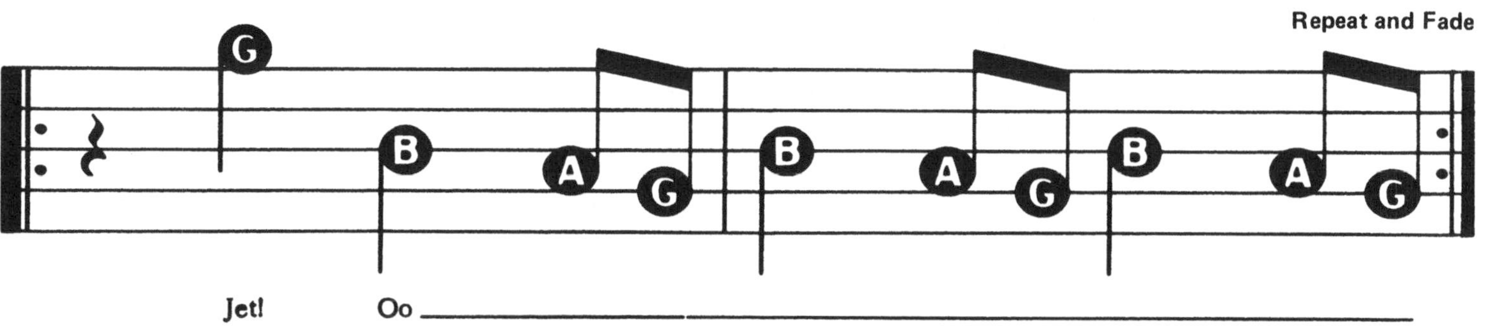

Junior's Farm

Registration 1
Rhythm: 8-Beat or Rock

Words and Music by Paul McCartney
and Linda McCartney

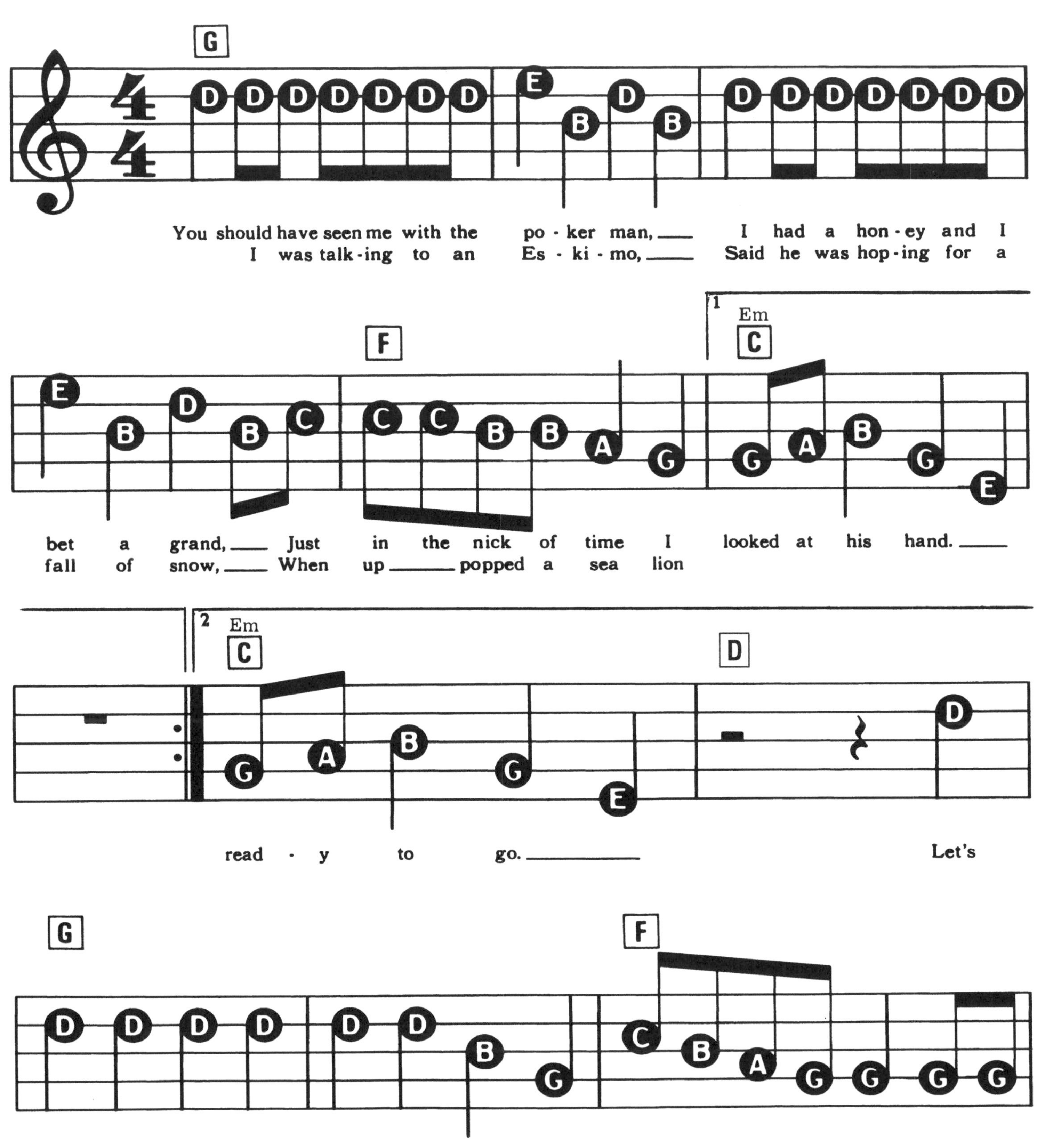

© 1974 (Renewed) PAUL and LINDA McCARTNEY
Administered by MPL COMMUNICATIONS, INC.
All Rights Reserved

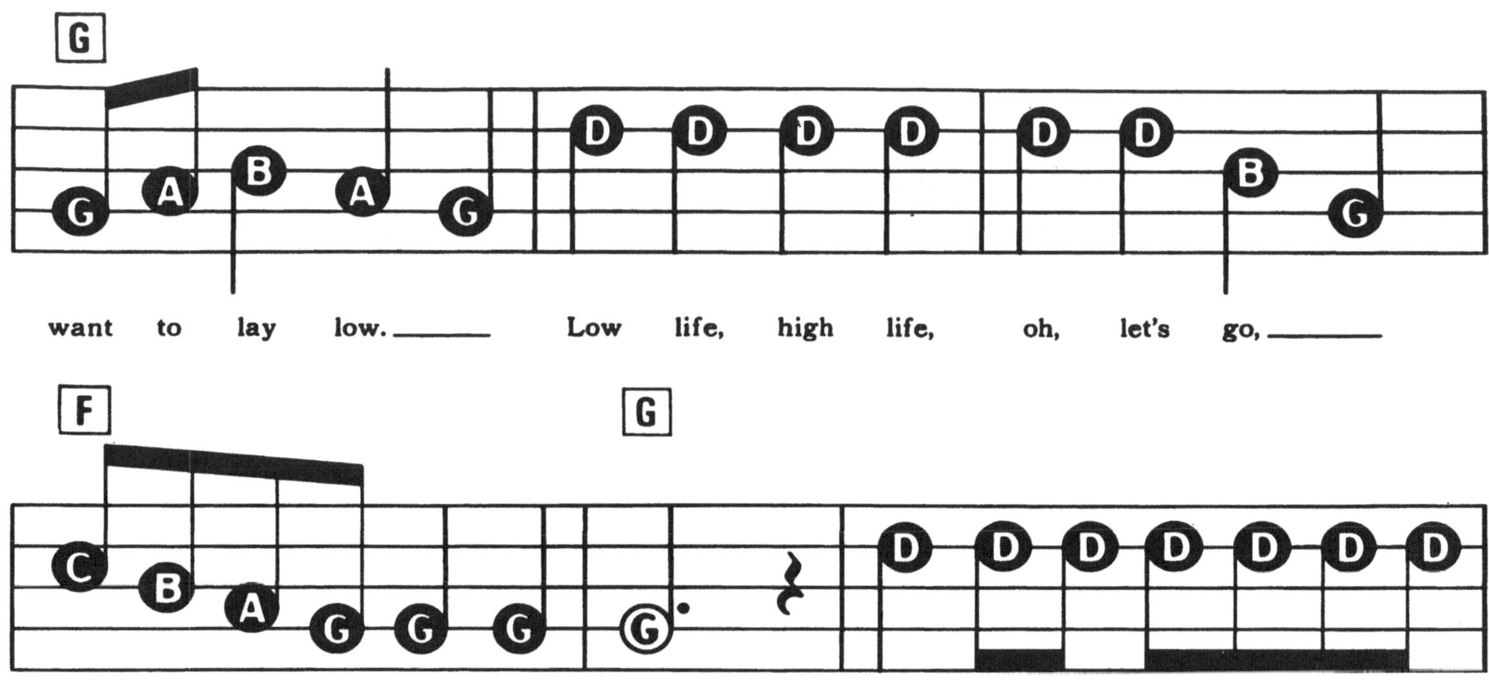
G
want to lay low.
Low life, high life, oh, let's go,
F
G
Take me down to Ju - nior's Farm.
I took my bag in - to a

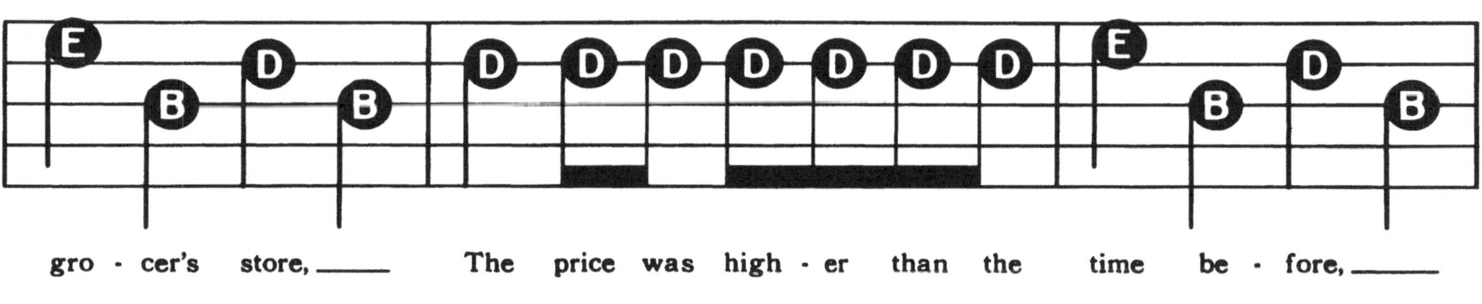
gro - cer's store,
The price was high - er than the time be - fore,

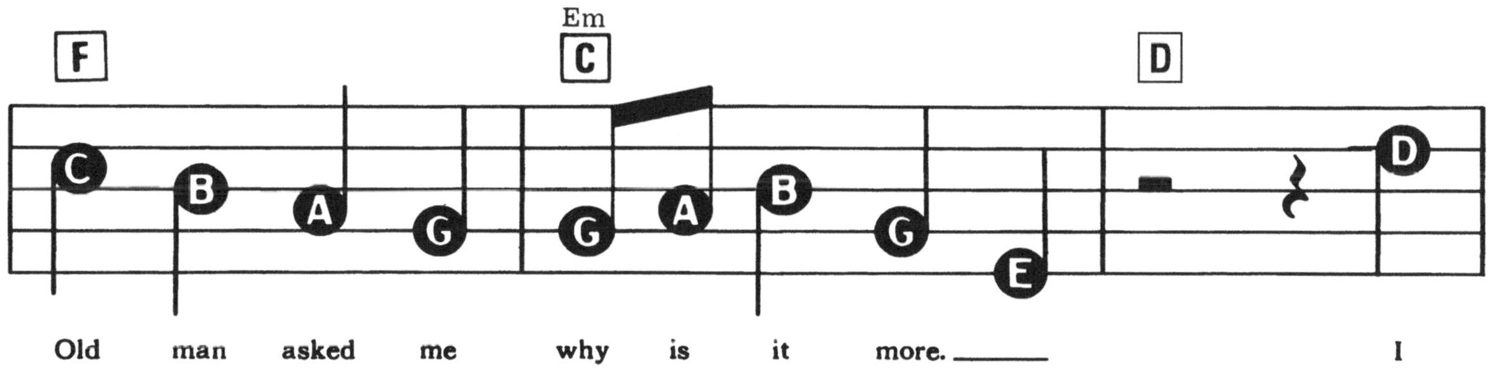
F
Em
C
D
Old man asked me why is it more.
I

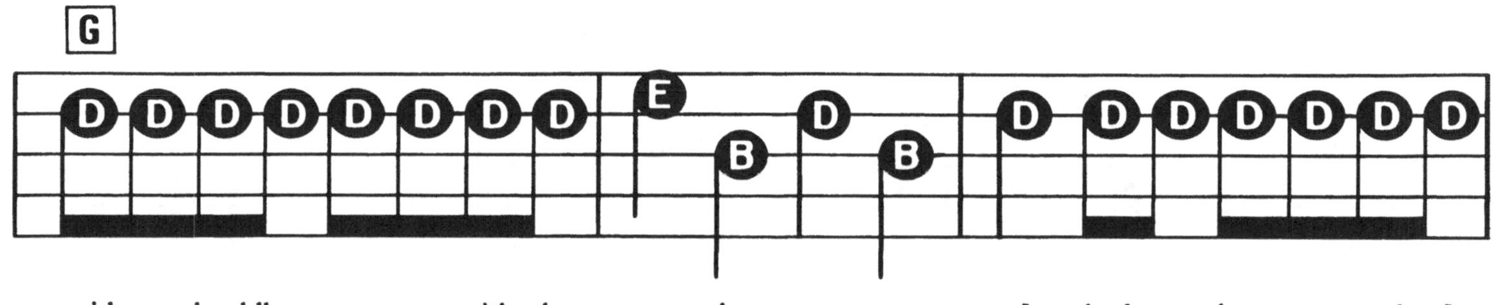
G
said youshouldhaveseen me with the po - ker man,
I had a hon - ey and I

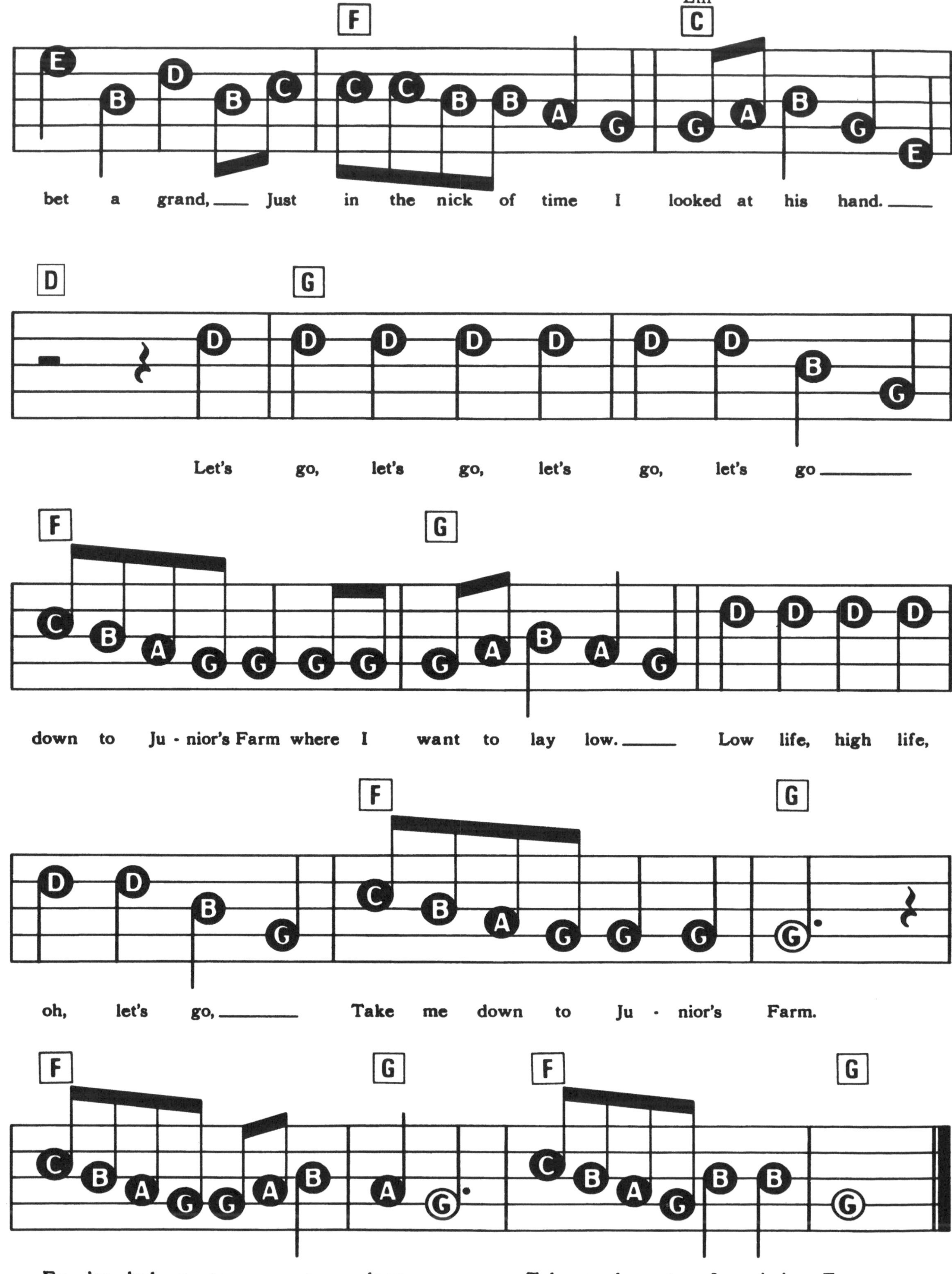
F
Em
C
E B D B C C C B B A G G A B G E
bet a grand, Just in the nick of time I looked at his hand.
D
G
D D D D D D D B G
Let's go, let's go, let's go, let's go
F
G
C B A G G G G G A B A G D D D D
down to Ju - nior's Farm where I want to lay low. Low life, high life,
F
G
D D B G C B A G G G G
oh, let's go, Take me down to Ju - nior's Farm.
F
G
F
G
C B A G G A B A G C B A G B B G
Ev - 'ry - bod - y tag a - long. Take me down to Ju - nior's Farm.

Listen to What the Man Said

Registration 1
Rhythm: Rock

Words and Music by Paul McCartney
and Linda McCartney

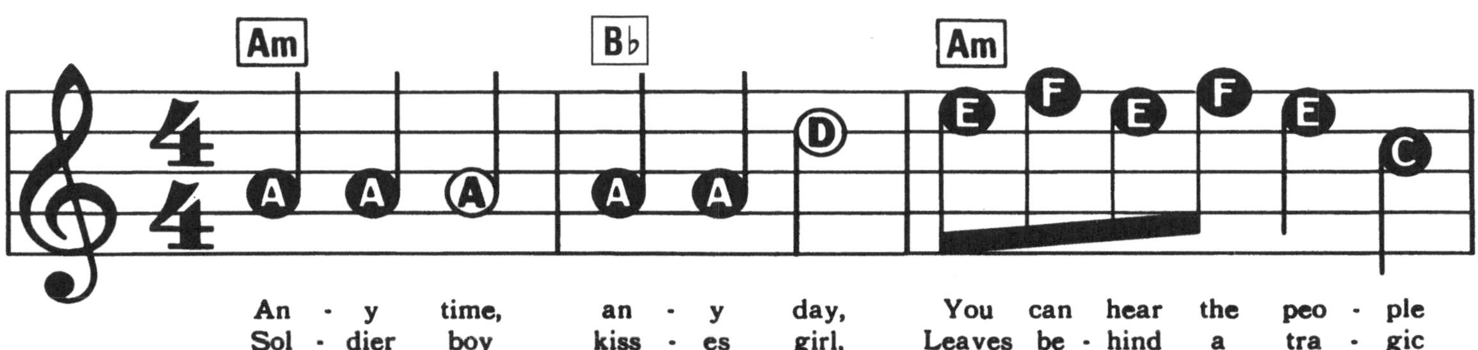

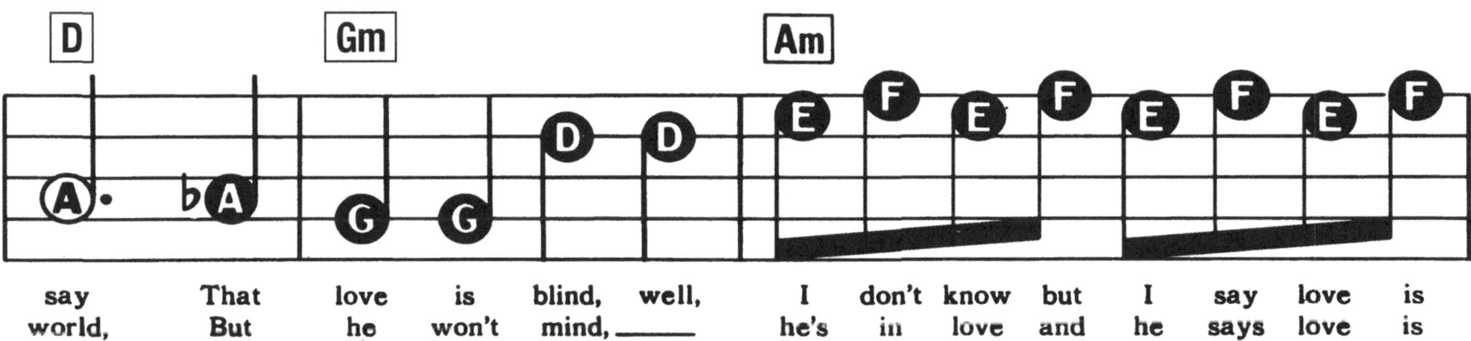

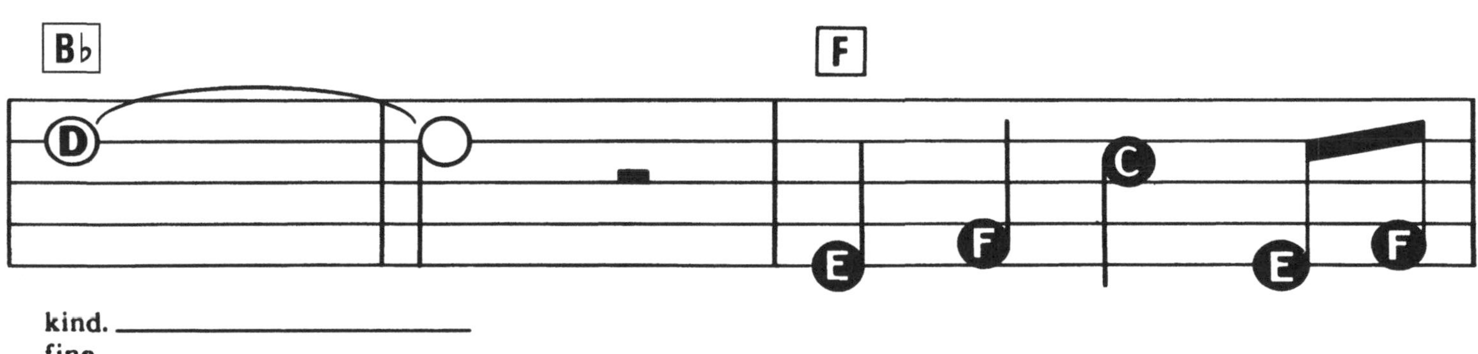

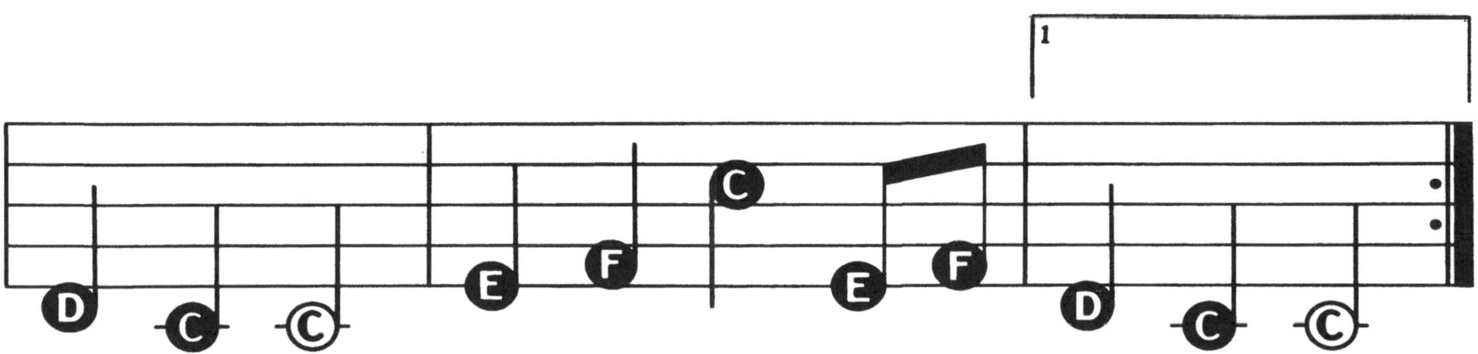

© 1975 (Renewed) MPL COMMUNICATIONS, INC.
All Rights Reserved

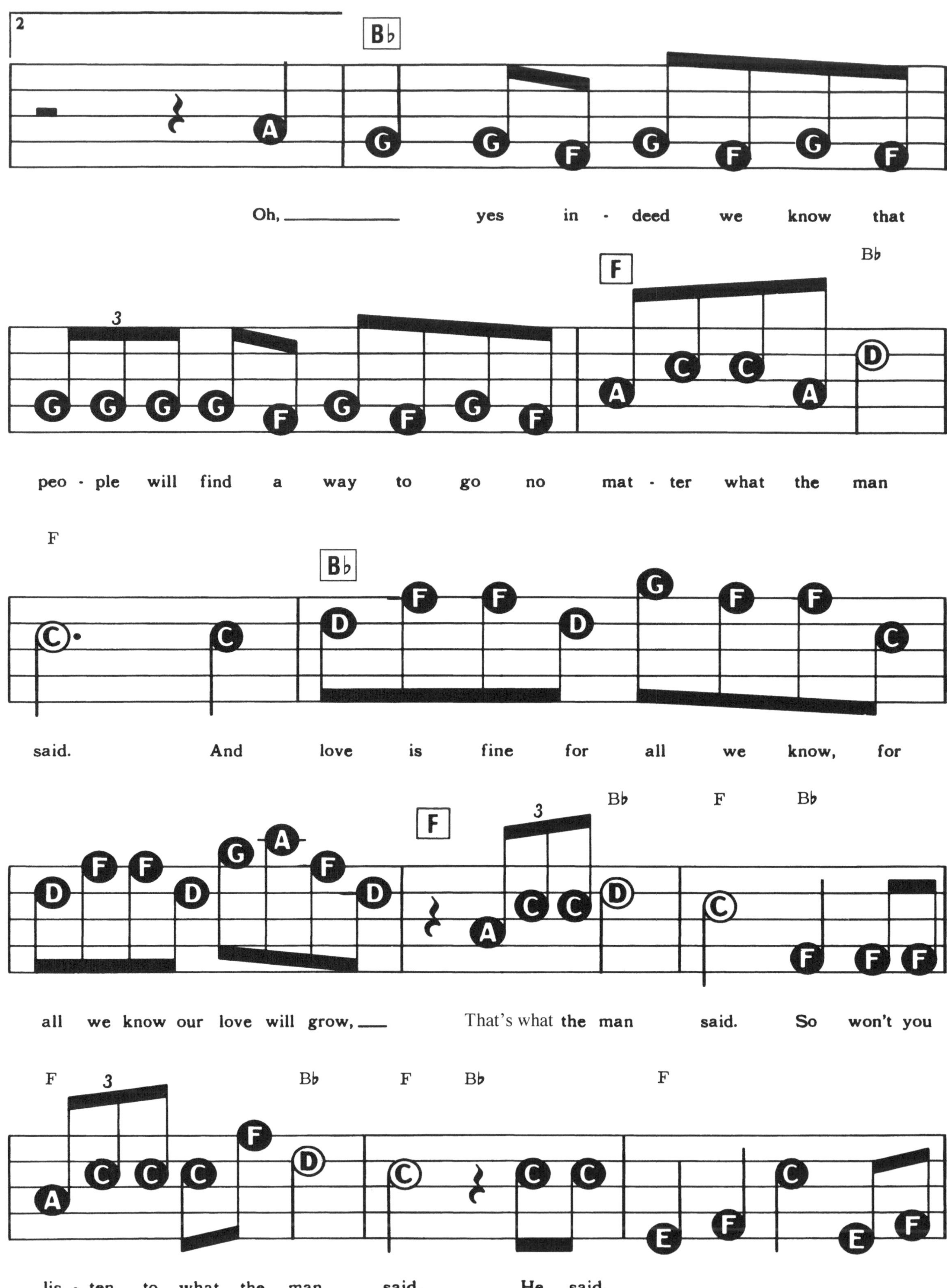
2
B♭
Oh, ___ yes in - deed we know that
F
B♭
peo - ple will find a way to go no mat - ter what the man
F
B♭
said. And love is fine for all we know, for
F
B♭ F B♭
all we know our love will grow, ___ That's what the man said. So won't you
F B♭ F B♭ F
lis - ten to what the man said. He said.

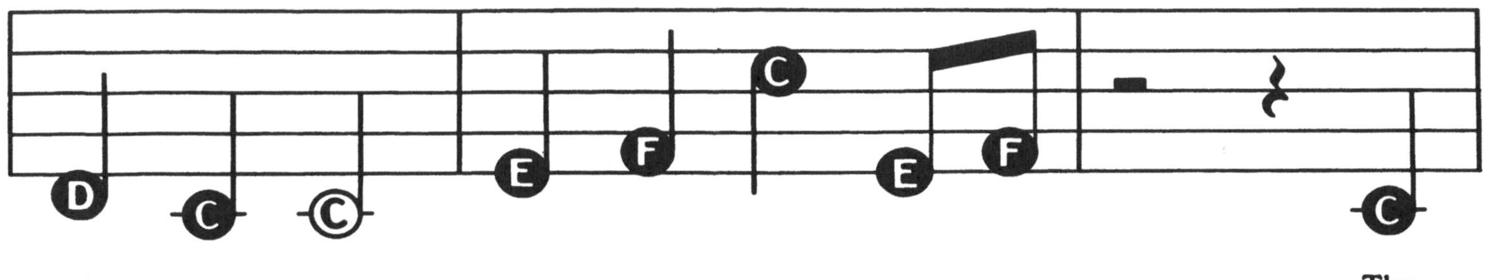

The

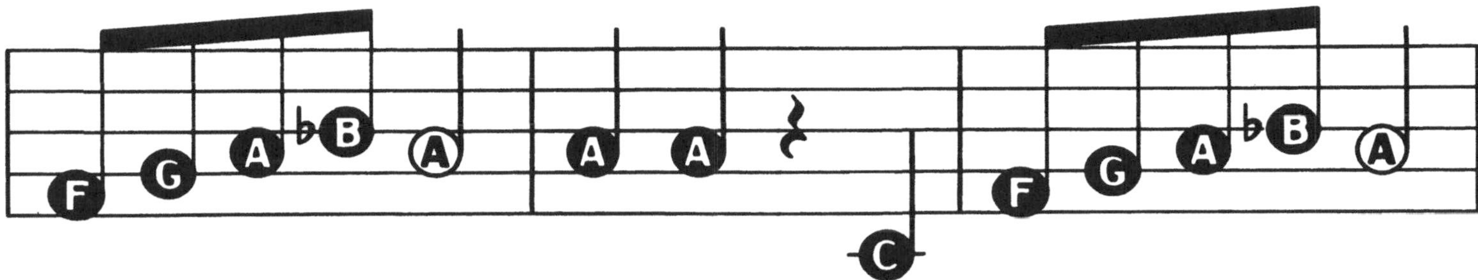

won - der of it all, ba - by, The won - der of it all,

C

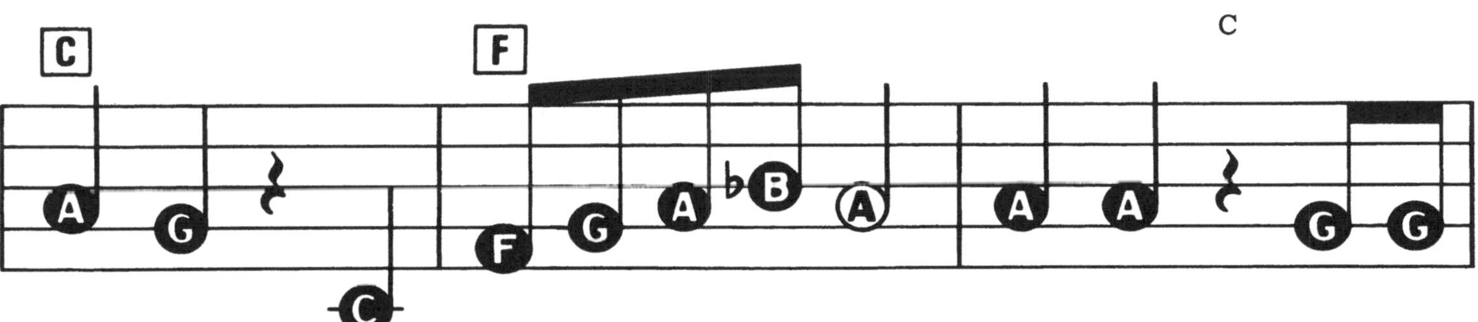

ba - by, The won - der of it all, ba - by, Yeah, yeah,

F

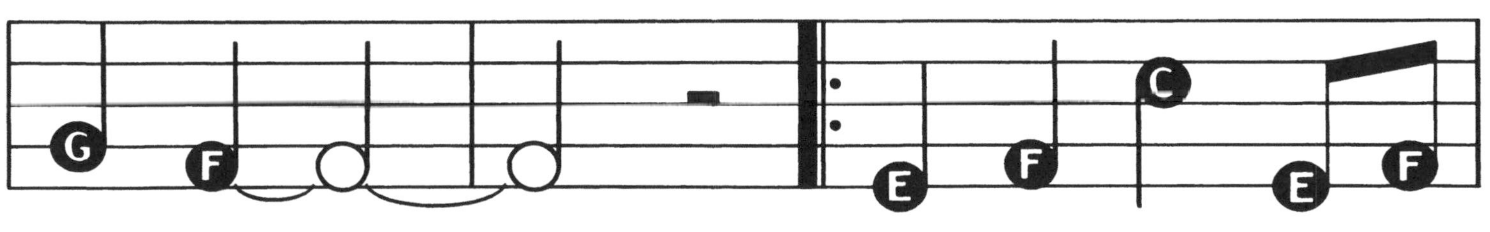

yeah. ______________________

Repeat and Fade

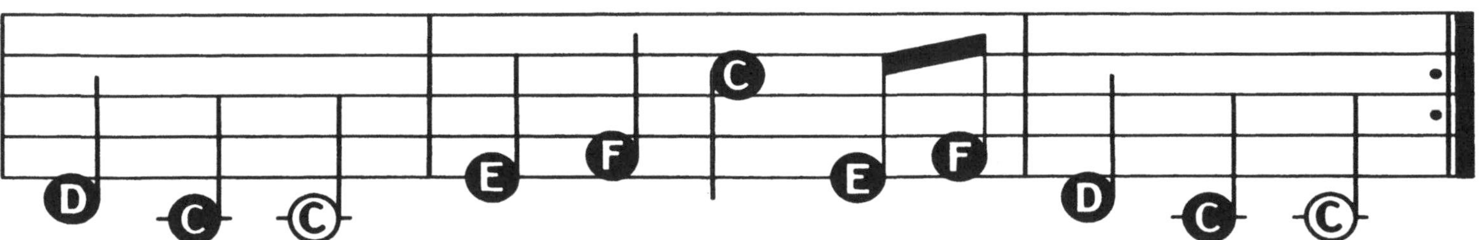

Let 'Em In

Registration 4
Rhythm: Rock

Words and Music by Paul McCartney
and Linda McCartney

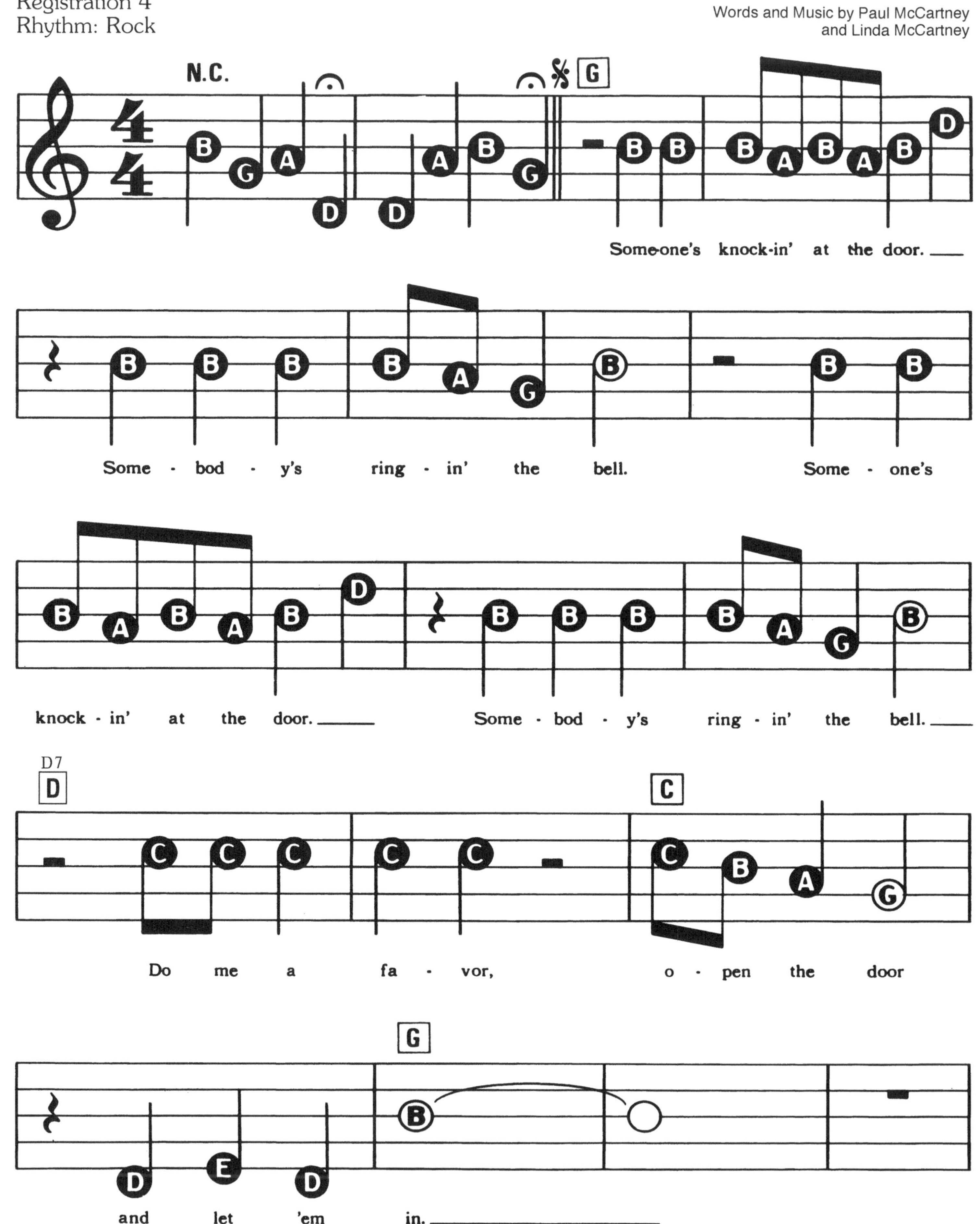

© 1976 (Renewed) MPL COMMUNICATIONS LTD.
Administered by MPL COMMUNICATIONS, INC.
All Rights Reserved

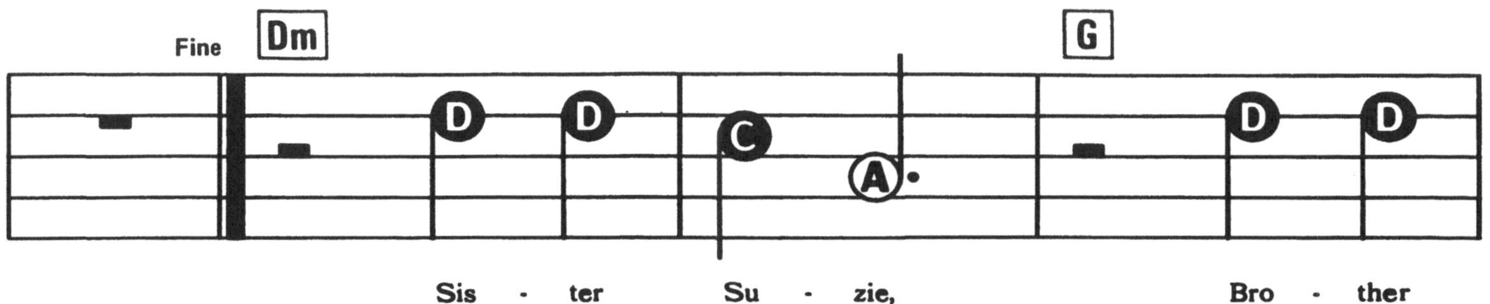
Fine
Dm
G
D D C A D D
Sis - ter Su - zie, Bro - ther

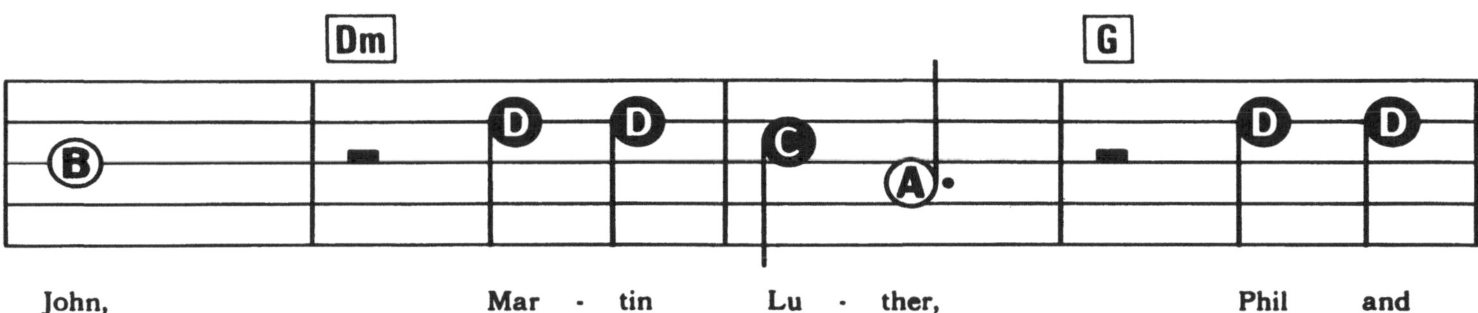
Dm
G
B D D C A D D
John, Mar - tin Lu - ther, Phil and

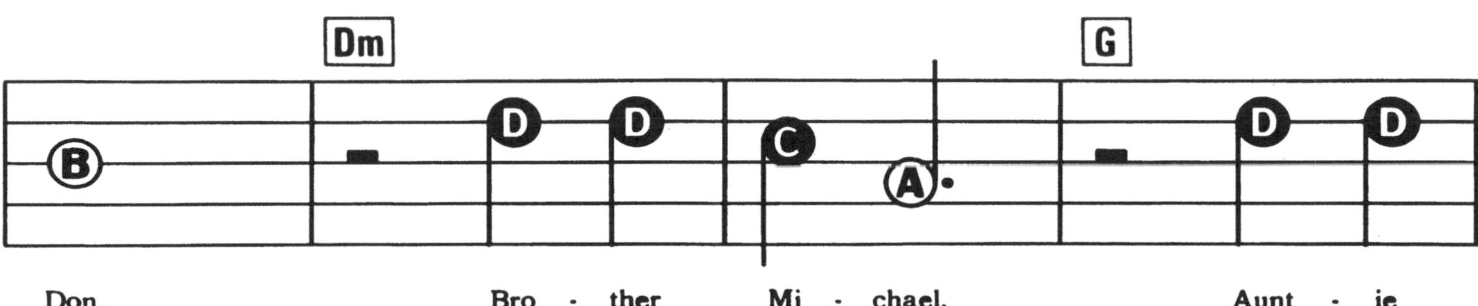
Dm
G
B D D C A D D
Don, Bro - ther Mi - chael, Aunt - ie

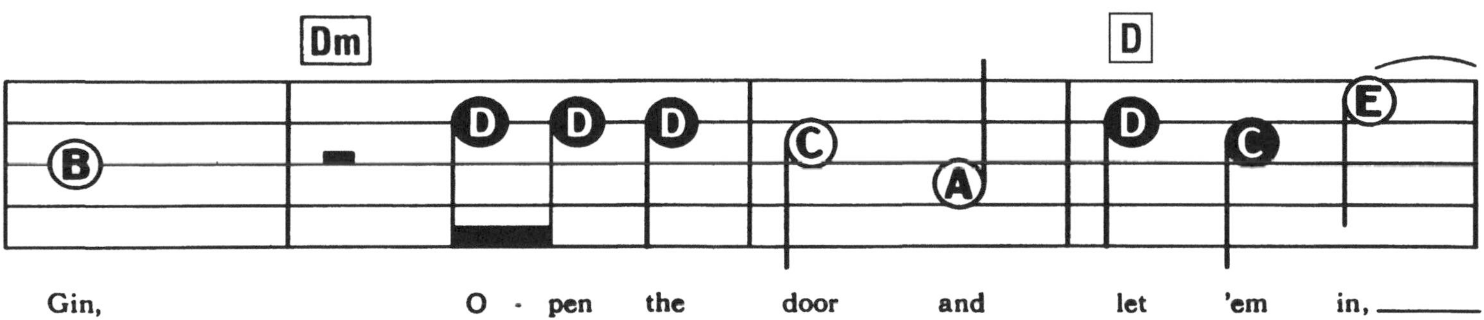
Dm
D
B D D D C A D C E
Gin, O - pen the door and let 'em in,

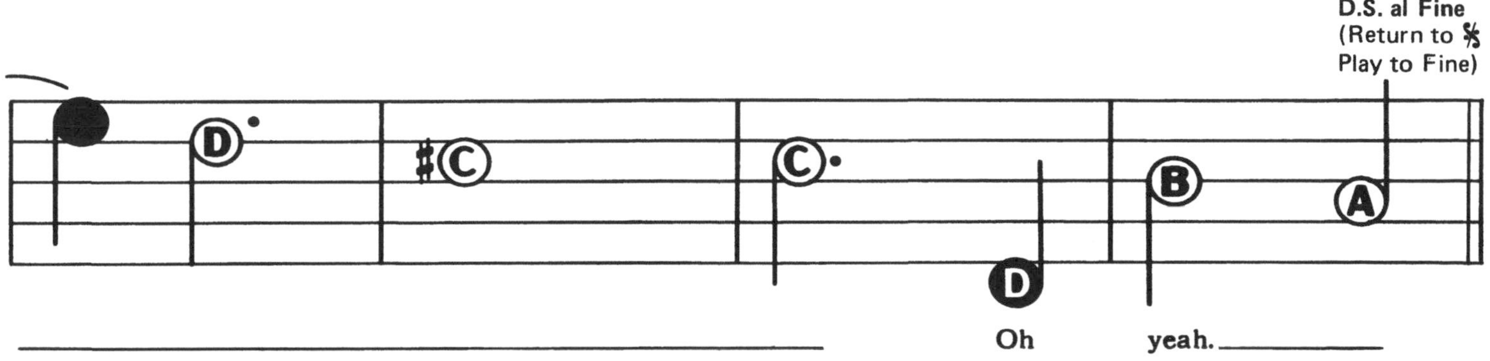
D.S. al Fine
(Return to 𝄋
Play to Fine)
D ♯C C D B A
Oh yeah.

Live and Let Die

Registration 7
Rhythm: Rock

Words and Music by Paul McCartney
and Linda McCartney

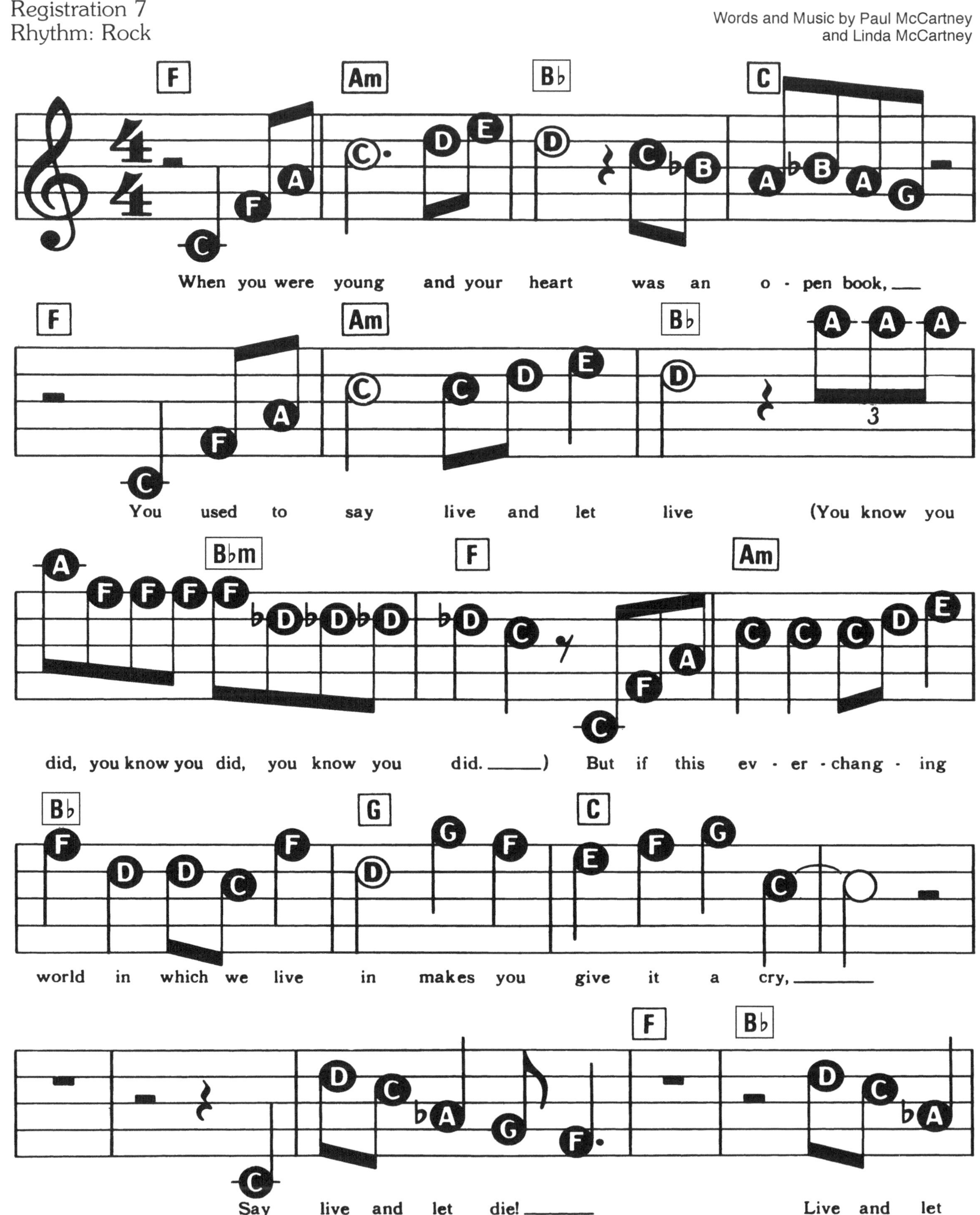

© 1973 (Renewed) PAUL and LINDA McCARTNEY and EMI UNART CATALOG INC.
All Rights for the U.S. and Canada Controlled by EMI UNART CATALOG INC.
All Rights Reserved Used by Permission

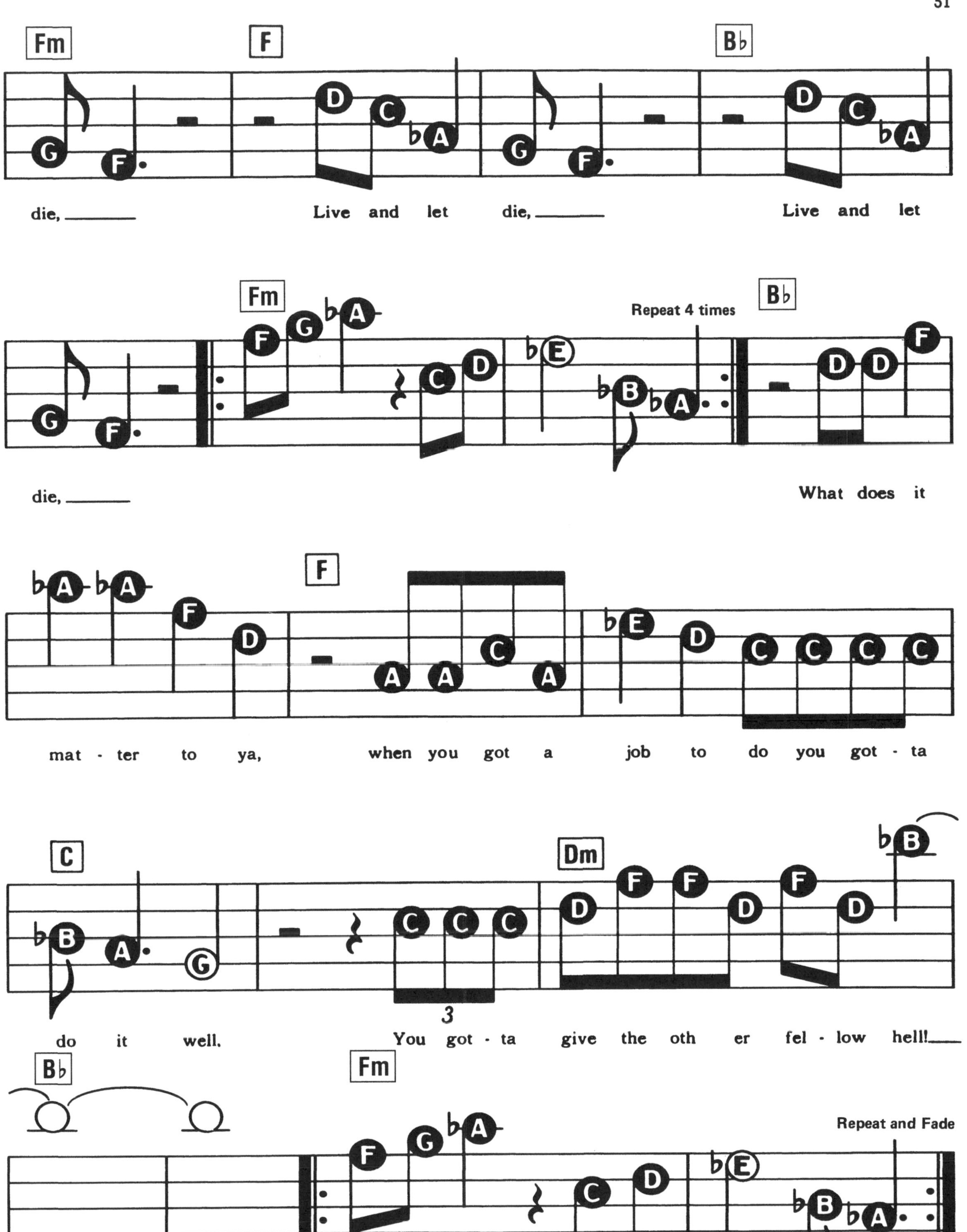
Fm
F
B♭
die, Live and let die, Live and let
Fm
Repeat 4 times
B♭
die, What does it
F
mat - ter to ya, when you got a job to do you got - ta
C
Dm
3
do it well. You got - ta give the oth er fel - low hell!
B♭
Fm
Repeat and Fade

Maybe I'm Amazed

Registration 1
Rhythm: Rock, Pops or Ballad

Words and Music by
Paul McCartney

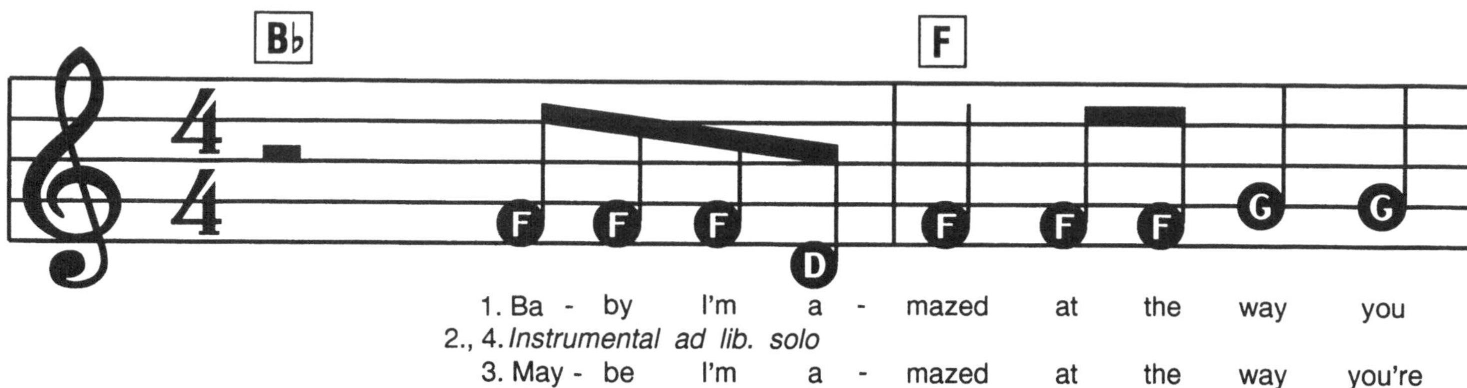

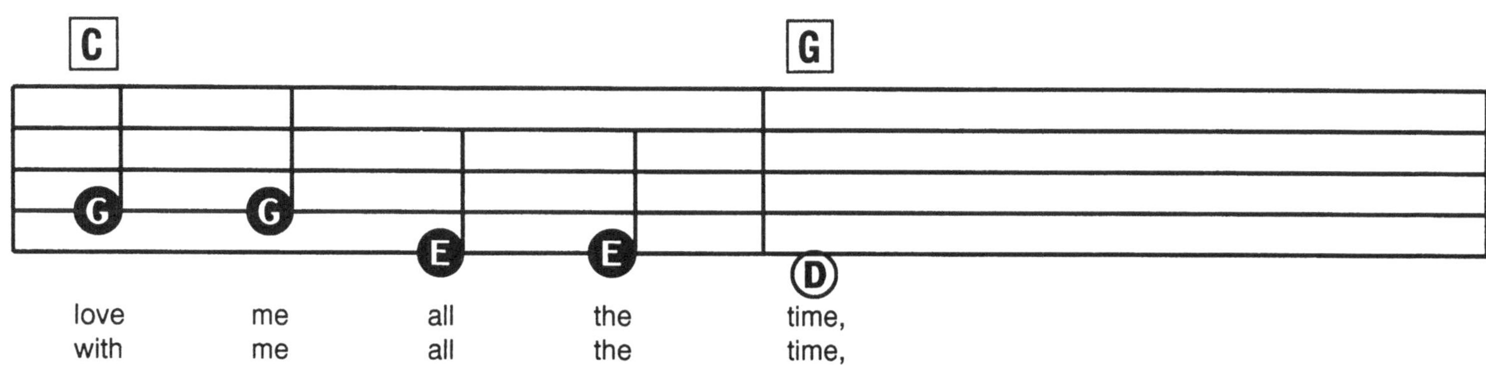

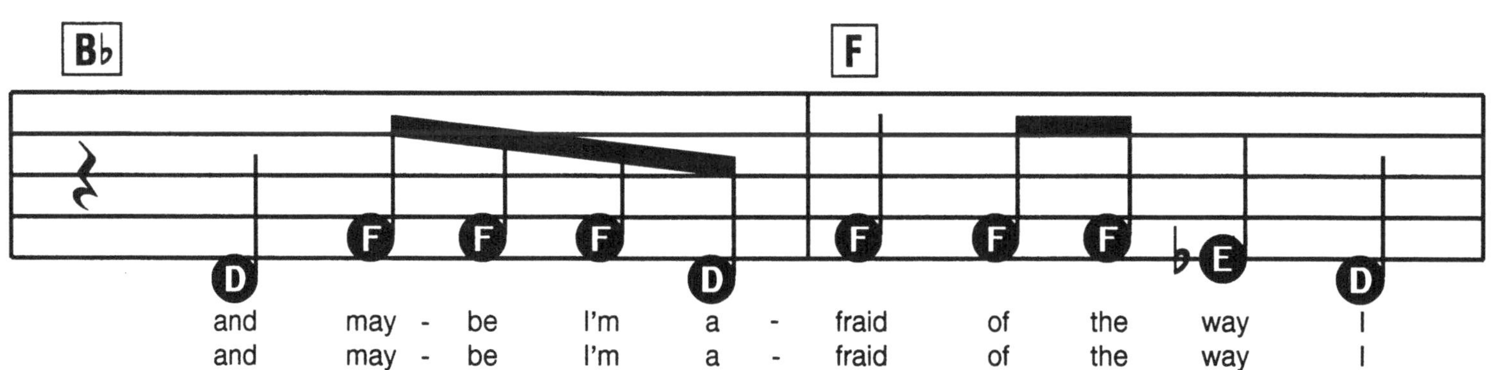

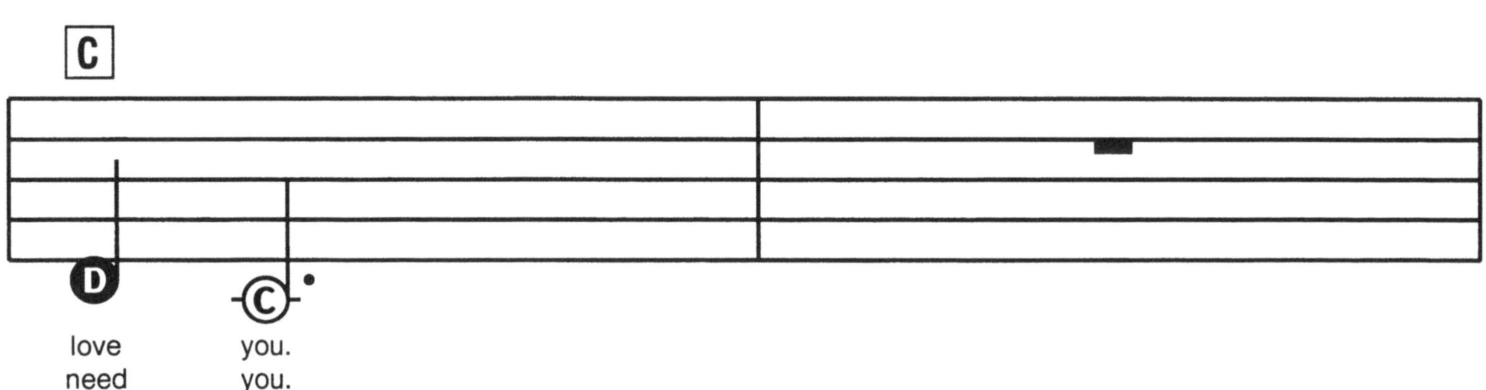

Copyright © 1970 Sony/ATV Music Publishing LLC
Copyright Renewed
All Rights Administered by Sony/ATV Music Publishing LLC, 8 Music Square West, Nashville, TN 37203
International Copyright Secured All Rights Reserved

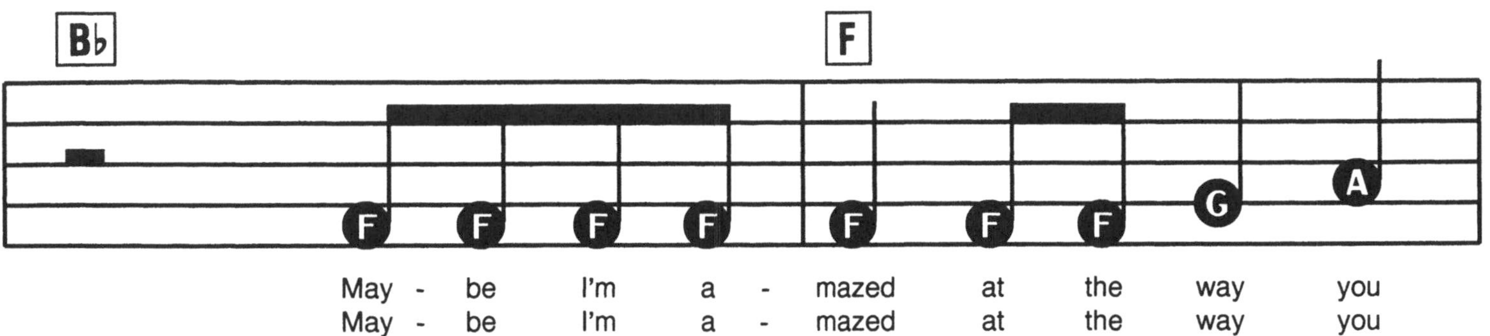

B♭
F
May - be I'm a - mazed at the way you
May - be I'm a - mazed at the way you

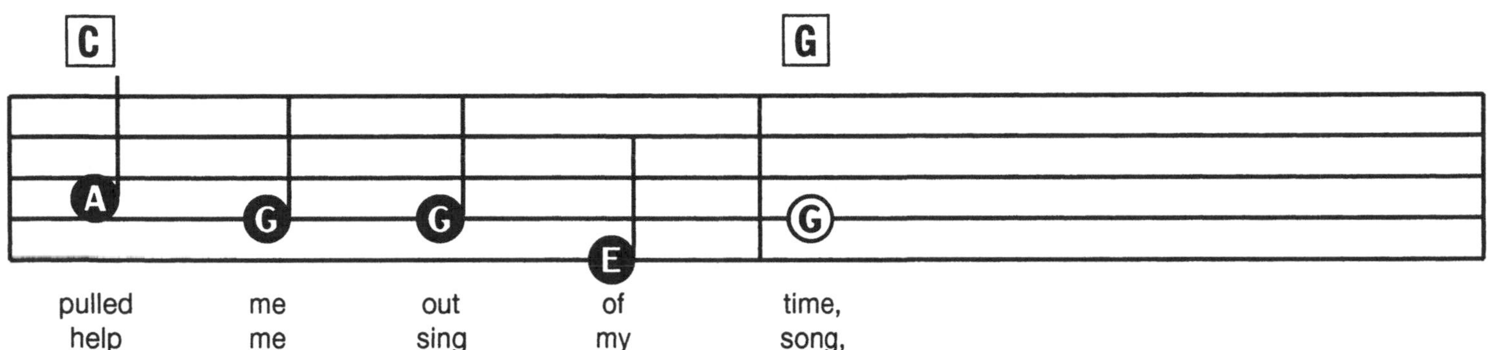

C
G
pulled me out of time,
help me sing my song,

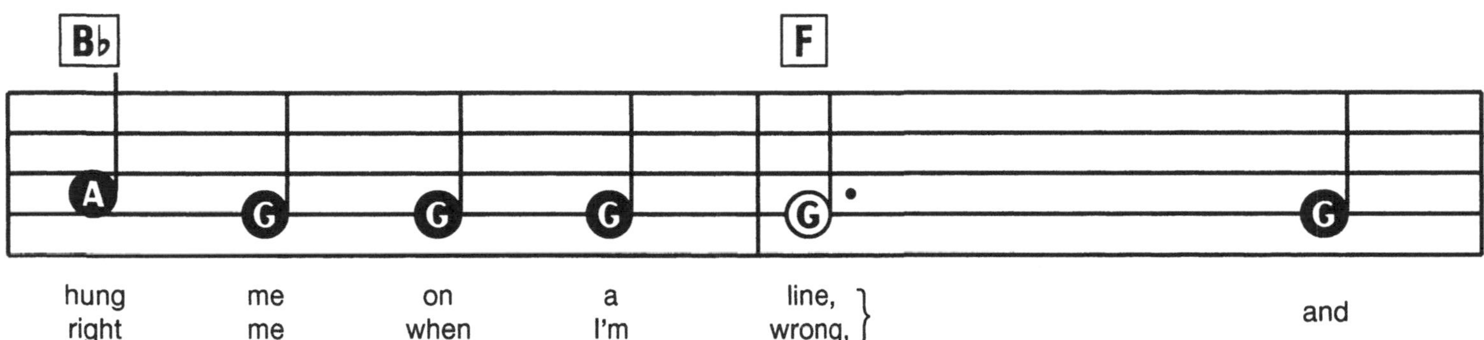

B♭
F
hung me on a line,
right me when I'm wrong,
and

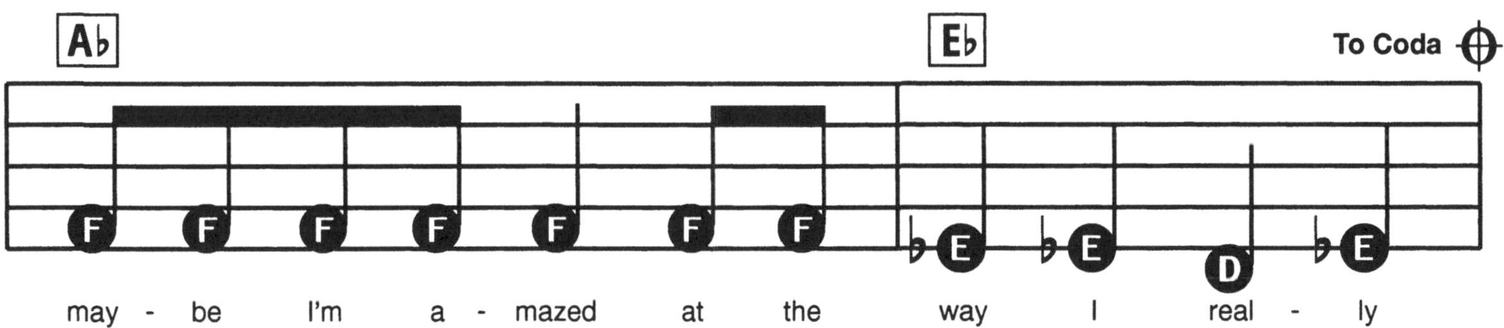

A♭
E♭
To Coda
may - be I'm a - mazed at the way I real - ly

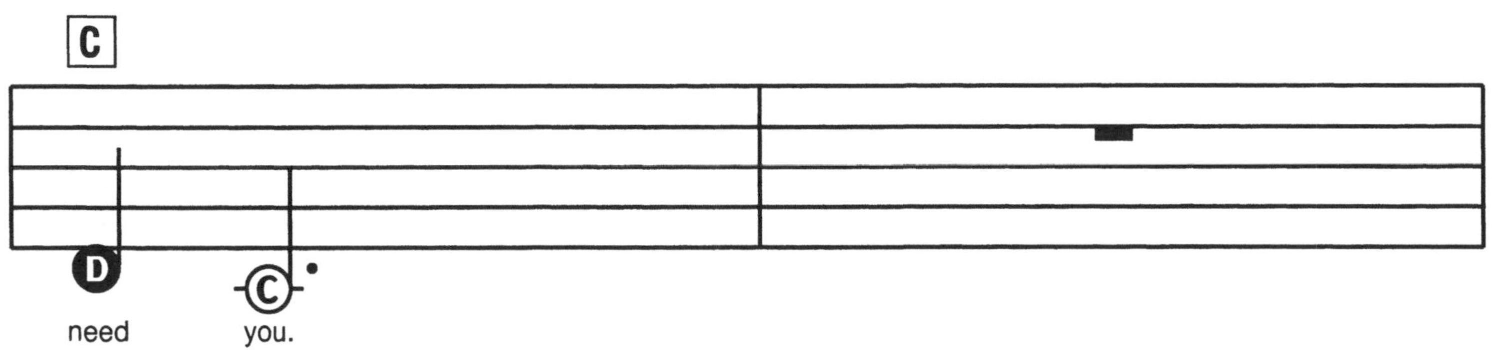

C
need you.

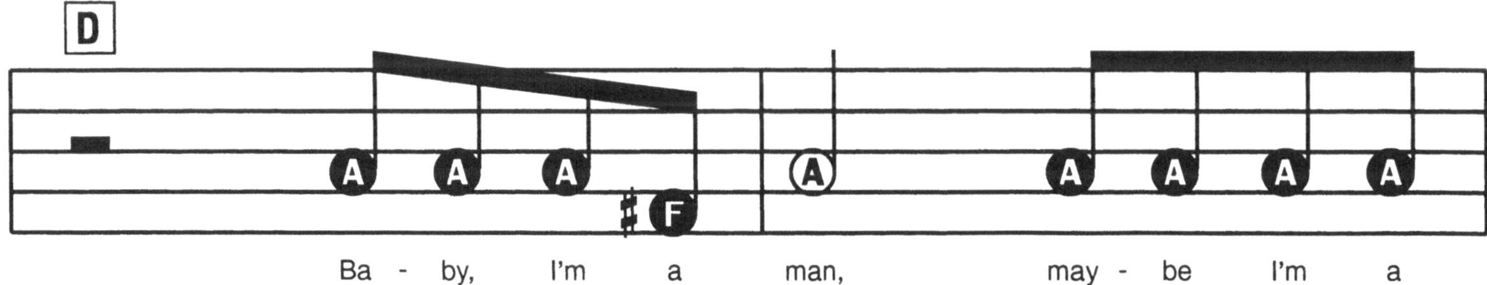
D
A
A
A
F
A
A
A
A
A
Ba - by, I'm a man, may - be I'm a

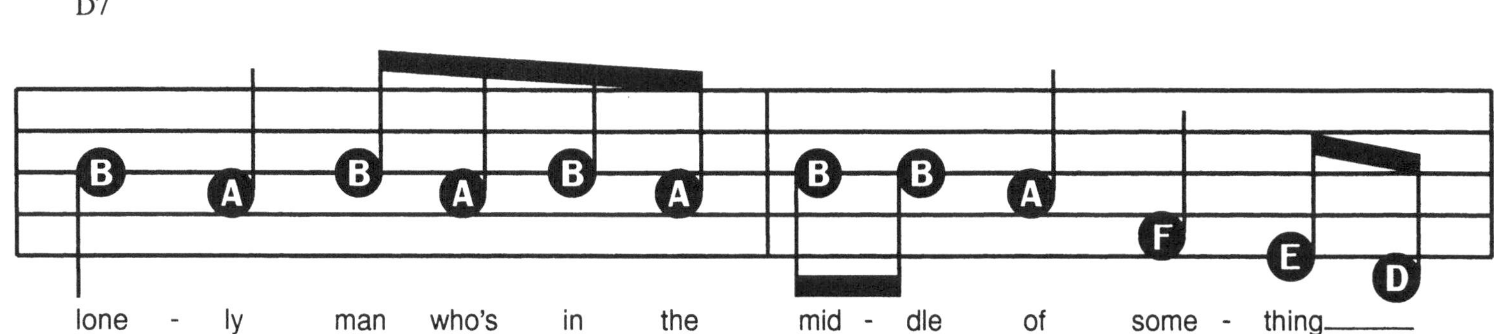
D7
B
A
B
A
B
A
B
B
A
F
E
D
lone - ly man who's in the mid - dle of some - thing

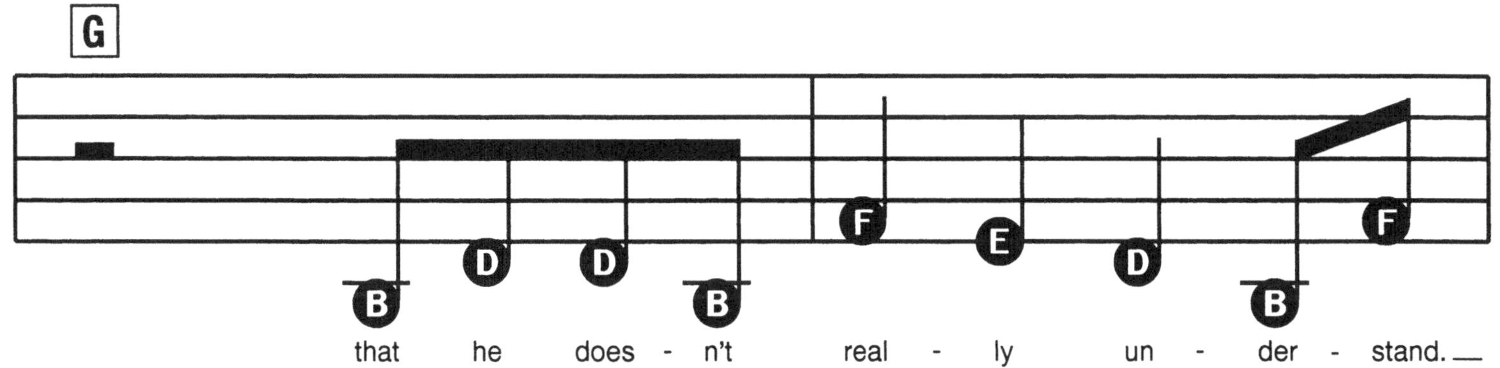
G
B
D
D
B
F
E
D
B
F
that he does - n't real - ly un - der - stand.

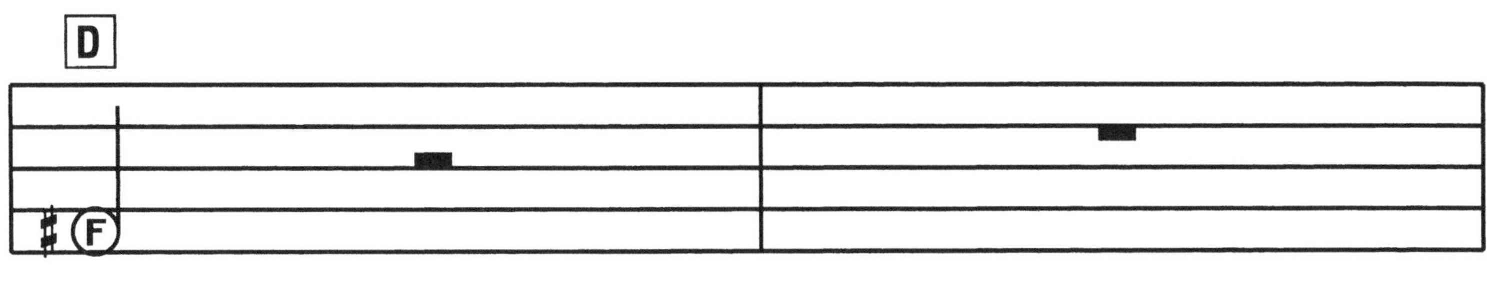
D
F

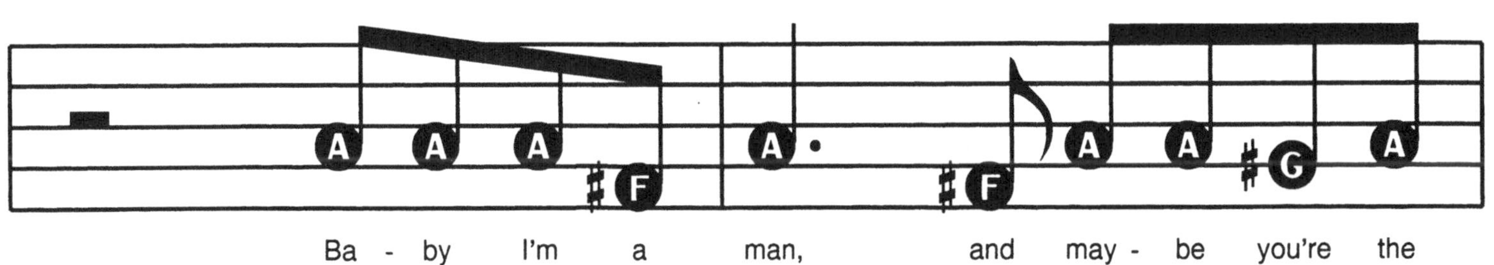
A
A
A
F
A
F
A
A
G
A
Ba - by I'm a man, and may - be you're the

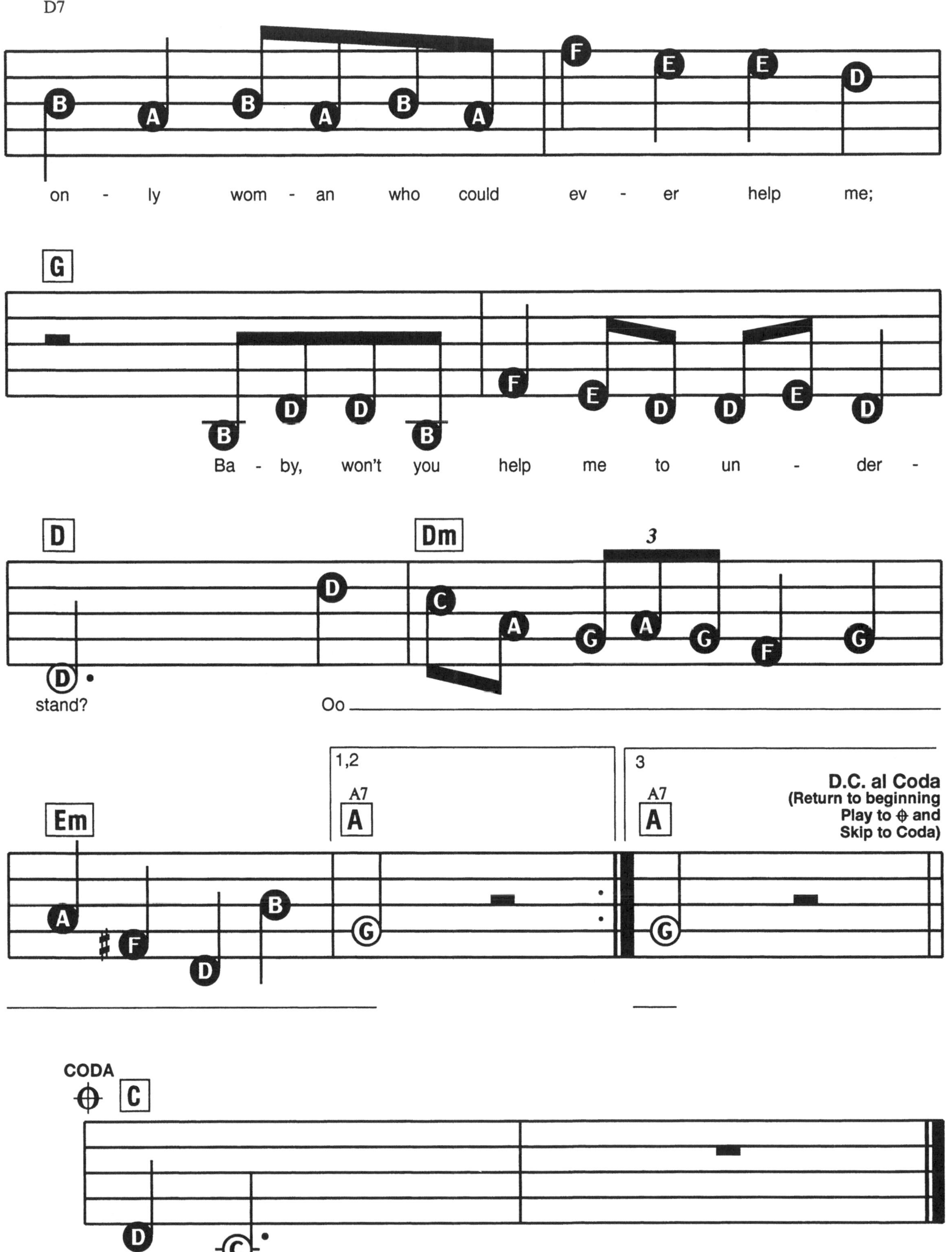
D7
on - ly wom - an who could ev - er help me;
G
Ba - by, won't you help me to un - der -
D
Dm
3
stand? Oo
Em
1,2
A7
A
3
A7
A
D.C. al Coda
(Return to beginning
Play to ⊕ and
Skip to Coda)
CODA
C
need you.

Mull of Kintyre

Registration 8
Rhythm: Waltz

Words and Music by Paul McCartney
and Denny Laine

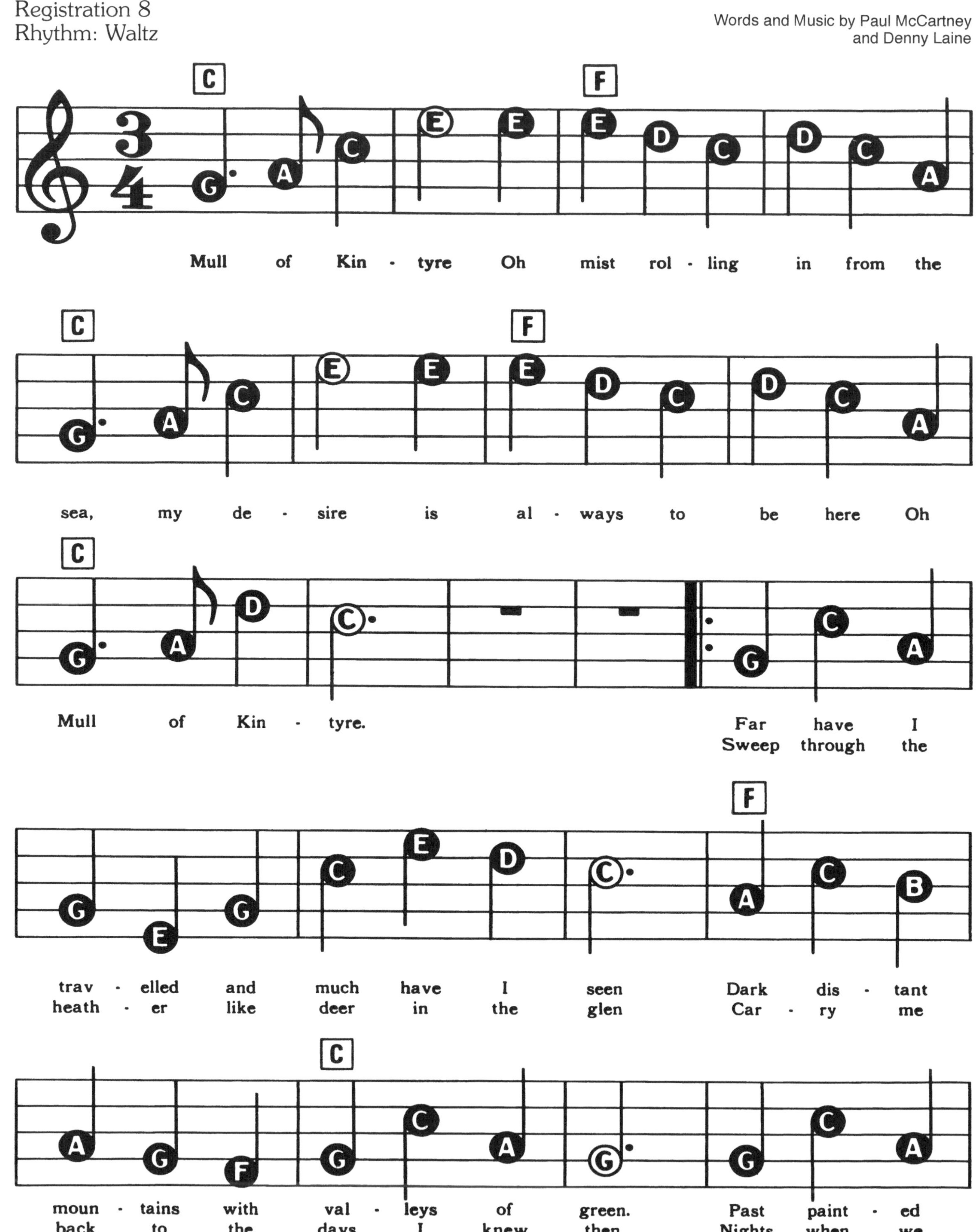

© 1977 (Renewed) MPL COMMUNICATIONS LTD.
Administered by MPL COMMUNICATIONS, INC.
All Rights Reserved

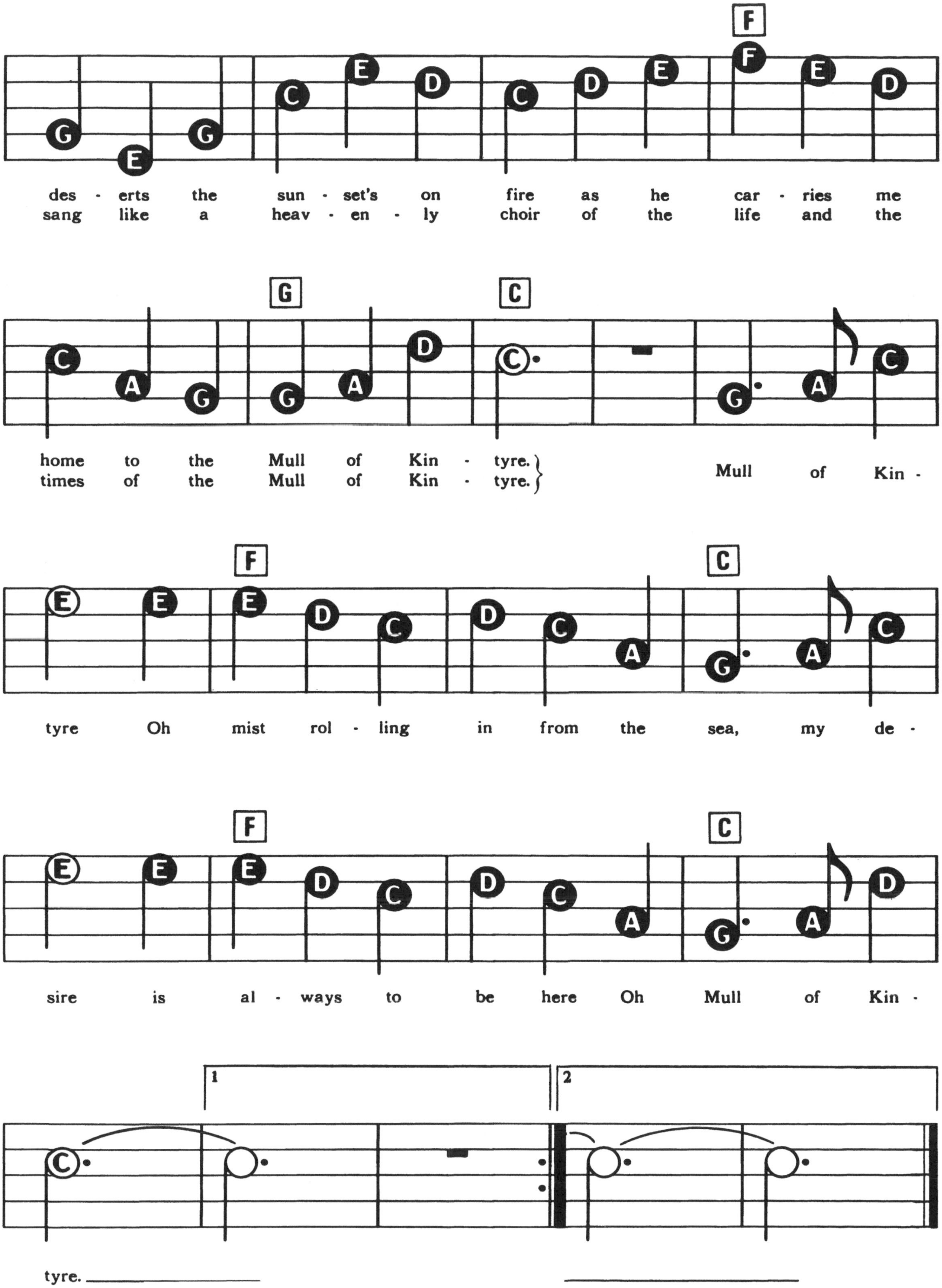

F

des - erts the sun - set's on fire as he car - ries me
sang like a heav - en - ly choir of the life and the

G C

home to the Mull of Kin - tyre.
times of the Mull of Kin - tyre.
Mull of Kin -

F C

tyre Oh mist rol - ling in from the sea, my de -

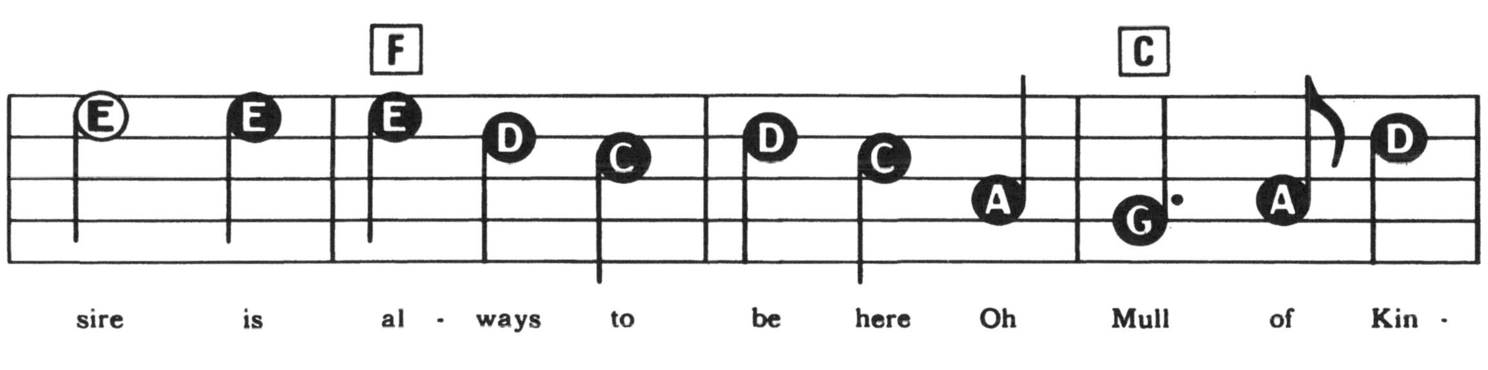

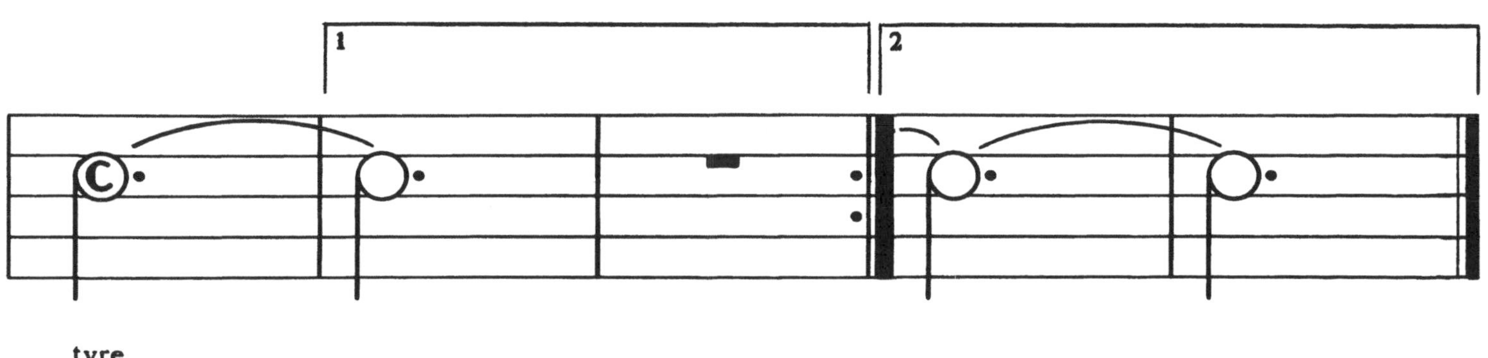

My Love

Registration 10
Rhythm: Ballad

Words and Music by Paul McCartney
and Linda McCartney

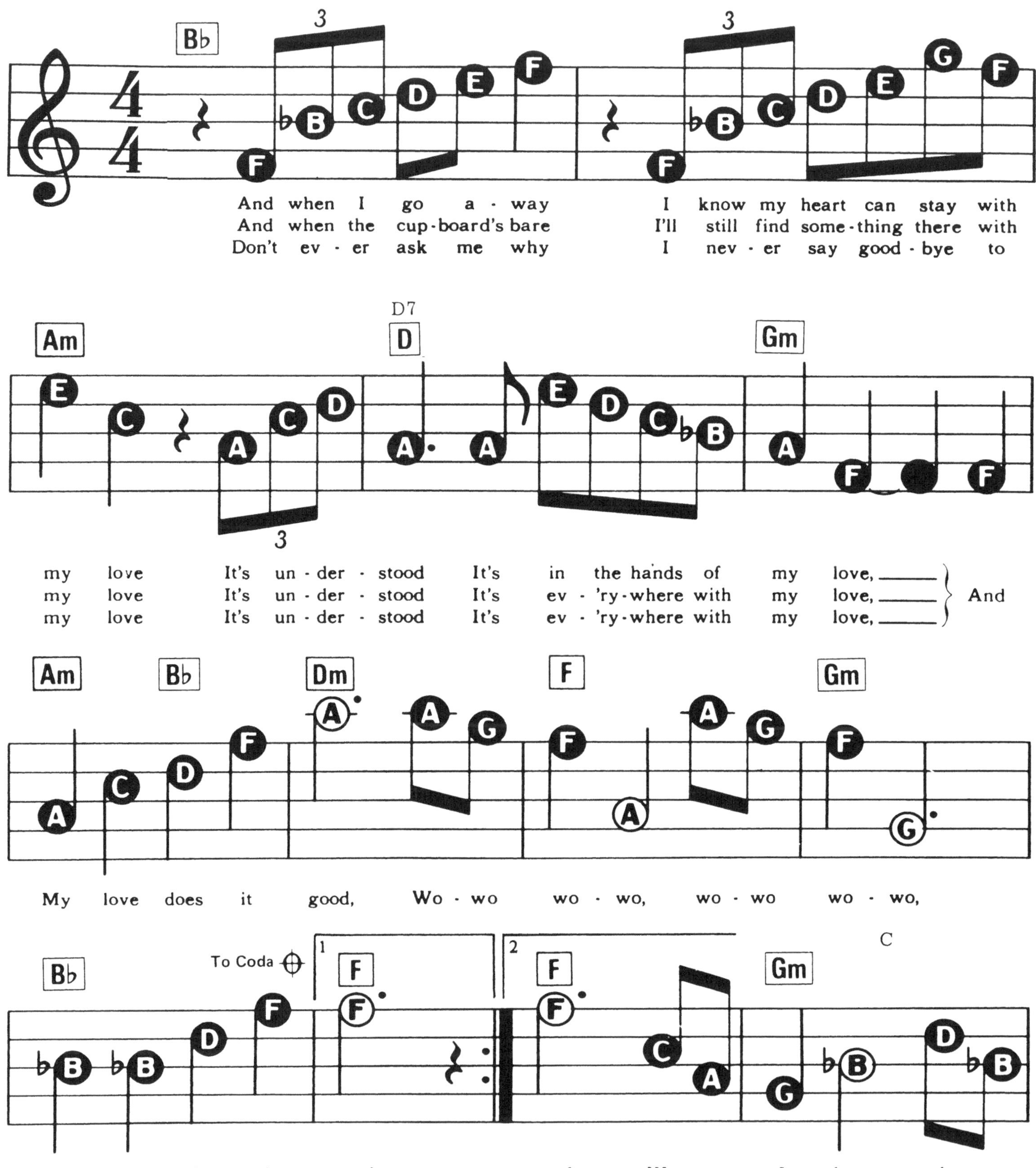

© 1973 (Renewed) PAUL and LINDA McCARTNEY
Administered by MPL COMMUNICATIONS, INC.
All Rights Reserved

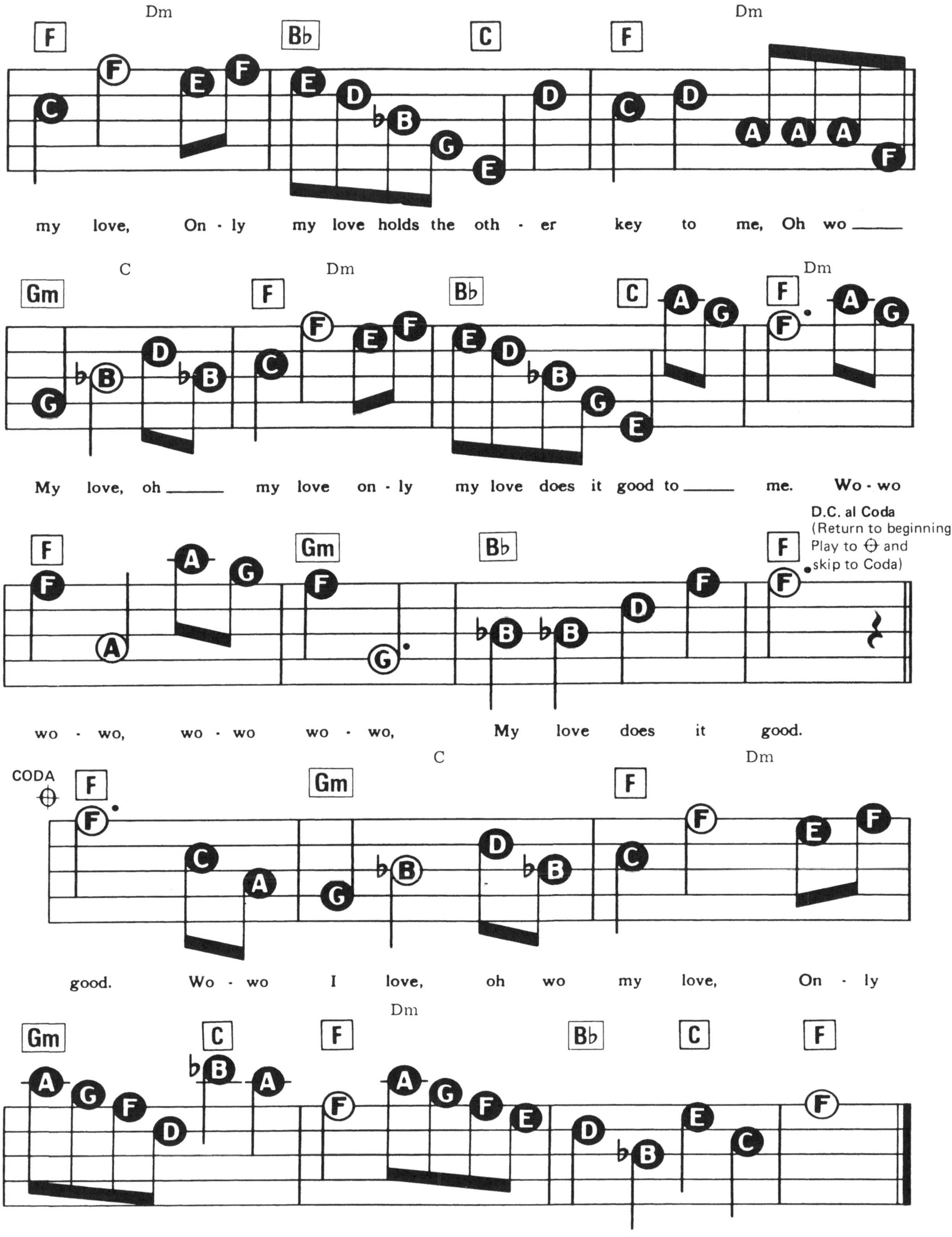
Dm
F
Bb
C
F
Dm
my love, On - ly my love holds the oth - er key to me, Oh wo
C
Gm
F
Dm
Bb
C
F
Dm
My love, oh my love on - ly my love does it good to me. Wo - wo
F
Gm
Bb
F
D.C. al Coda
(Return to beginning
Play to ⊕ and
skip to Coda)
wo - wo, wo - wo wo - wo, My love does it good.
CODA
F
Gm
C
F
Dm
good. Wo - wo I love, oh wo my love, On - ly
Gm
C
F
Dm
Bb
C
F
My love does it good to me. Wo wo wo wo wo wo wo.

No More Lonely Nights

from the Motion Picture GIVE MY REGARDS TO BROAD STREET

Registration 4
Rhythm: 8-Beat or Rock

Words and Music by
Paul McCartney

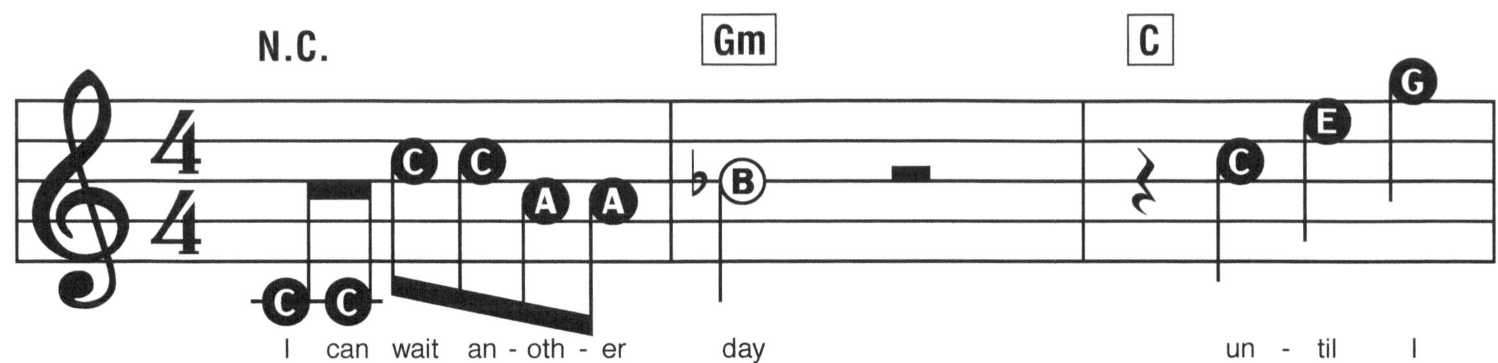

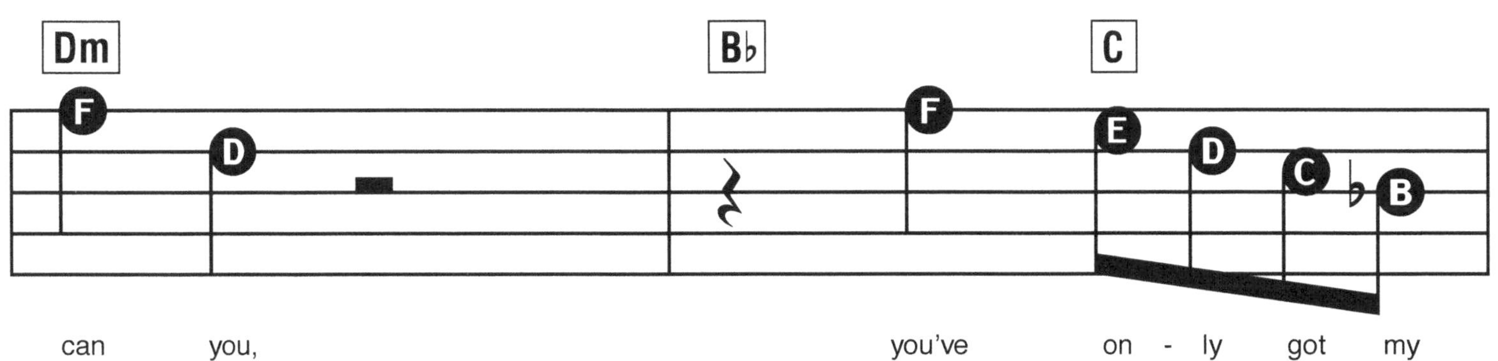

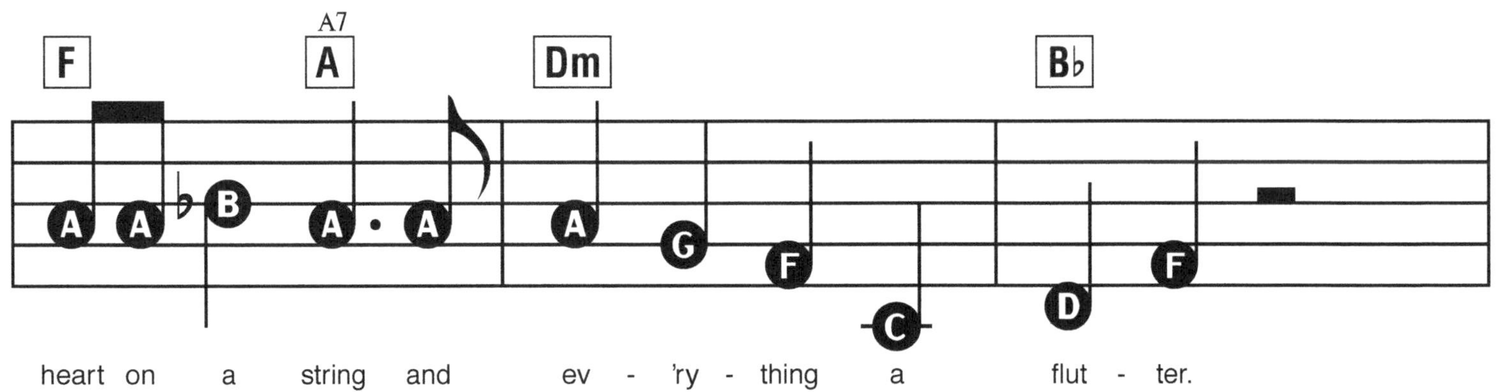

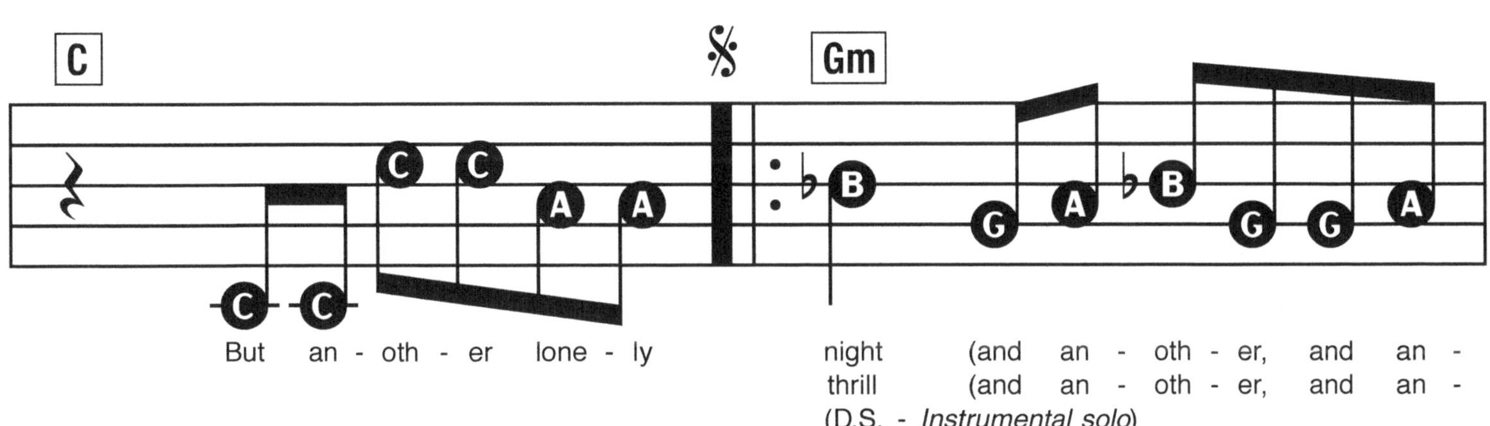

© 1984 MPL COMMUNICATIONS, INC.
All Rights Reserved

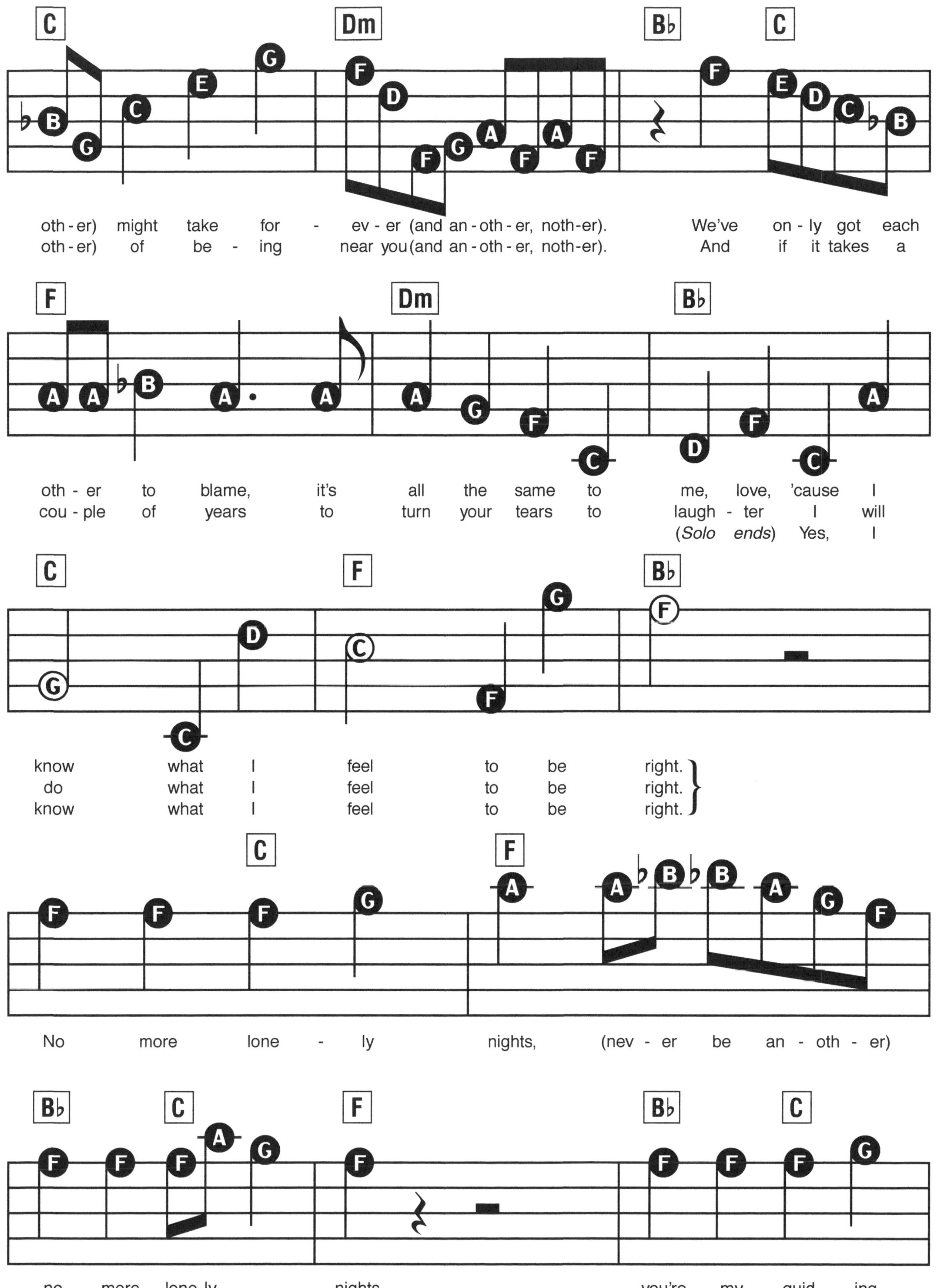
C
Dm
B♭
C
oth - er) might take for - ev - er (and an - oth - er, noth-er). We've on - ly got each
oth - er) of be - ing near you (and an - oth - er, noth-er). And if it takes a
F
Dm
B♭
oth - er to blame, it's all the same to me, love, 'cause I
cou - ple of years to turn your tears to laugh - ter I will
(Solo ends) Yes, I
C
F
B♭
know what I feel to be right.
do what I feel to be right.
know what I feel to be right.
C
F
No more lone - ly nights, (nev - er be an - oth - er)
B♭
C
F
B♭
C
no more lone-ly nights, you're my guid - ing

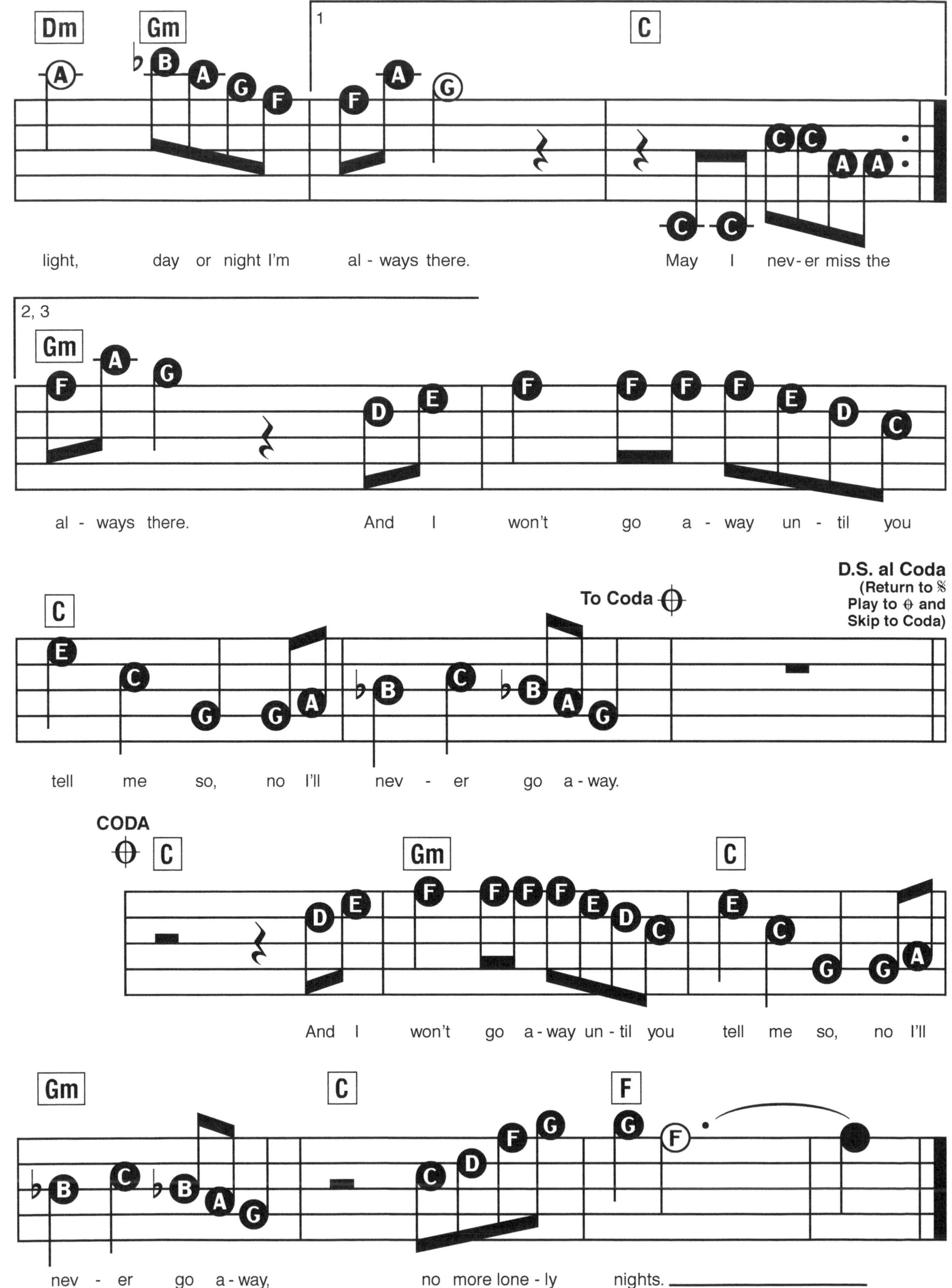
Dm
Gm
1
C
light, day or night I'm al - ways there. May I nev-er miss the
2, 3
Gm
al - ways there. And I won't go a - way un - til you
C
To Coda
D.S. al Coda
(Return to 𝄋
Play to ⊕ and
Skip to Coda)
tell me so, no I'll nev - er go a - way.
CODA
C
Gm
C
And I won't go a - way un - til you tell me so, no I'll
Gm
C
F
nev - er go a - way, no more lone - ly nights.

Say Say Say

Registration 4
Rhythm: Rock

Words and Music by Paul McCartney
and Michael Jackson

Am D

Say, say, say ___ what you want but
go, go, go ___ where you want but
You, you, you can nev - er say that

Dm Am

don't play ___ games with my af - fec - tion. Take, take, take ___
don't leave ___ me here for - ev - er. You, you, you ___
I'm not the one who real - ly loves ___ you. I pray, pray, pray ___

D Dm

___ what you need but don't leave ___ me ___
___ stay a - way, so long, girl ___ I ___
___ ev - 'ry day that you'll see ___ things ___

Am Dm

with no di - rec - tion. All a - lone I sit home
see you nev - er. What can I do girl, to get
girl, like I ___ do. What can I do girl, to get

© 1982, 1983 MPL COMMUNICATIONS, INC., WARNER-TAMERLANE PUBLISHING CORP. and MIJAC MUSIC
All Rights Reserved

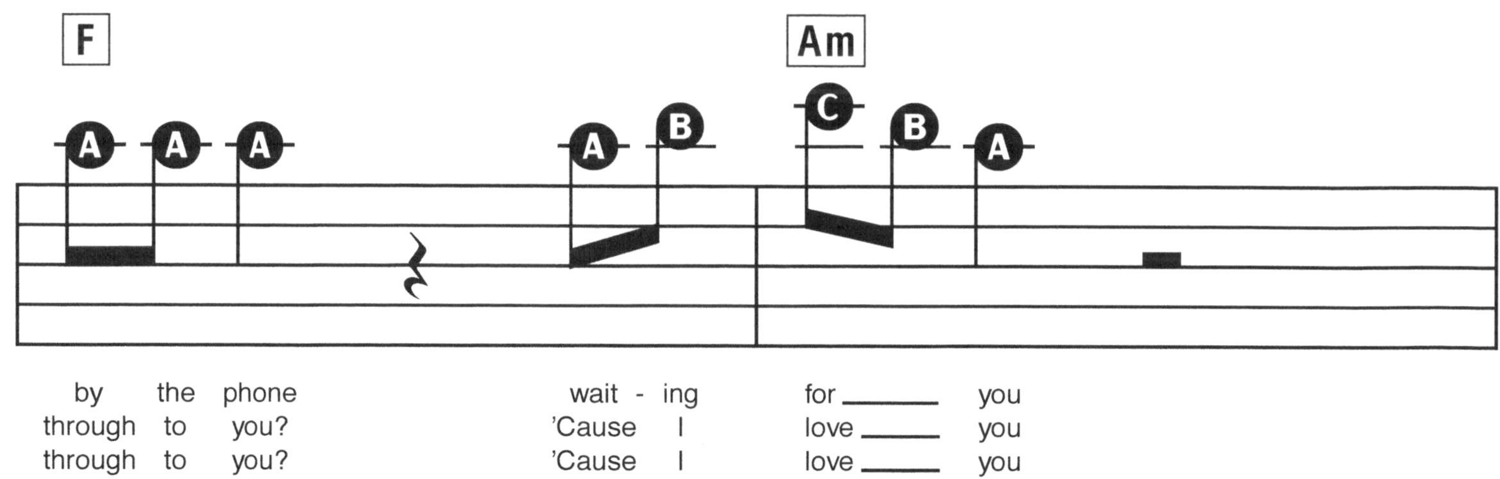
F
A A A A B
Am
C B A
by the phone wait - ing for ___ you
through to you? 'Cause I love ___ you
through to you? 'Cause I love ___ you

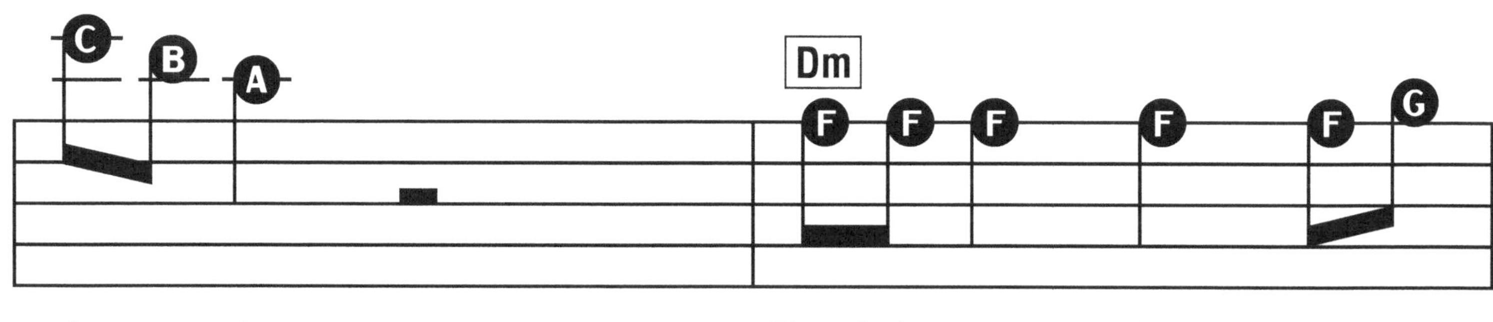
C B A
Dm
F F F F F G
ba - by. Through the years how can you
ba - by. Stand - ing here bap - tized in
ba - by. Stand - ing here bap - tized in

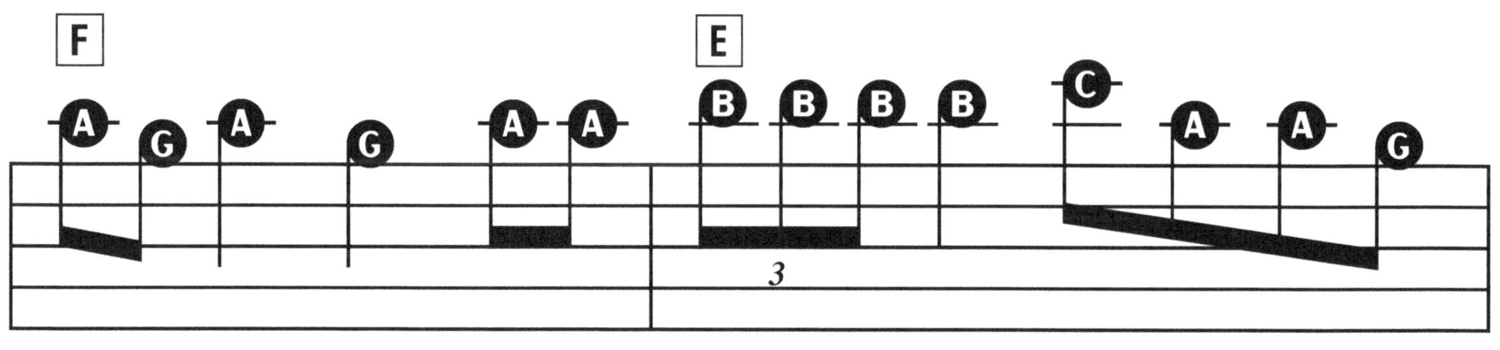
F
A G A G A A
E
B B B B C A A G
3
stand to hear my plead - ing for you dear? You know I'm cry - ing,
all my tears, ba - by through the years, you know I'm cry - ing,
all my tears, ba - by through the years, you know I'm cry - ing,

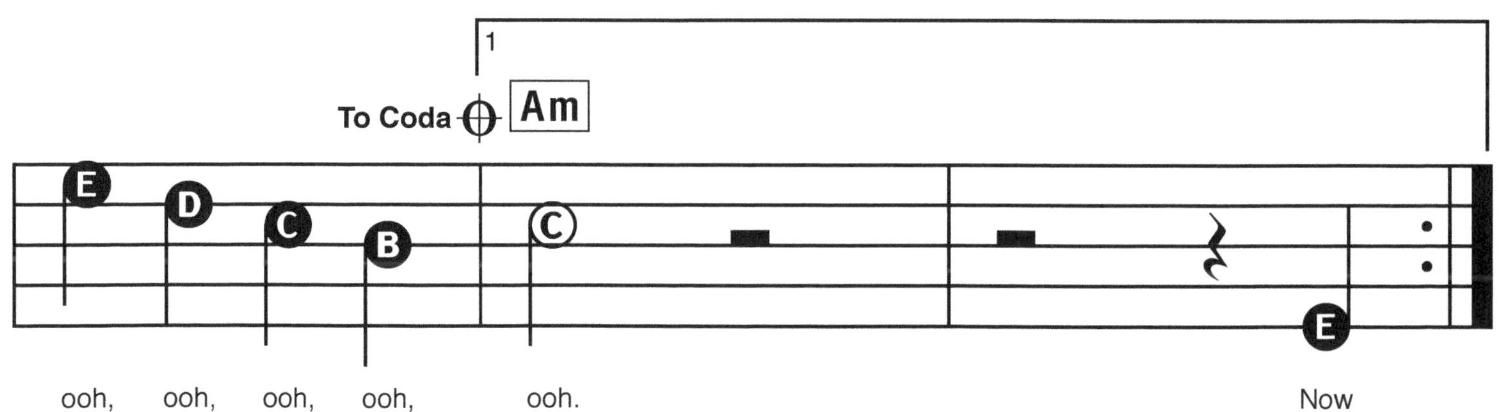
1
To Coda
Am
E D C B C E
ooh, ooh, ooh, ooh, ooh. Now

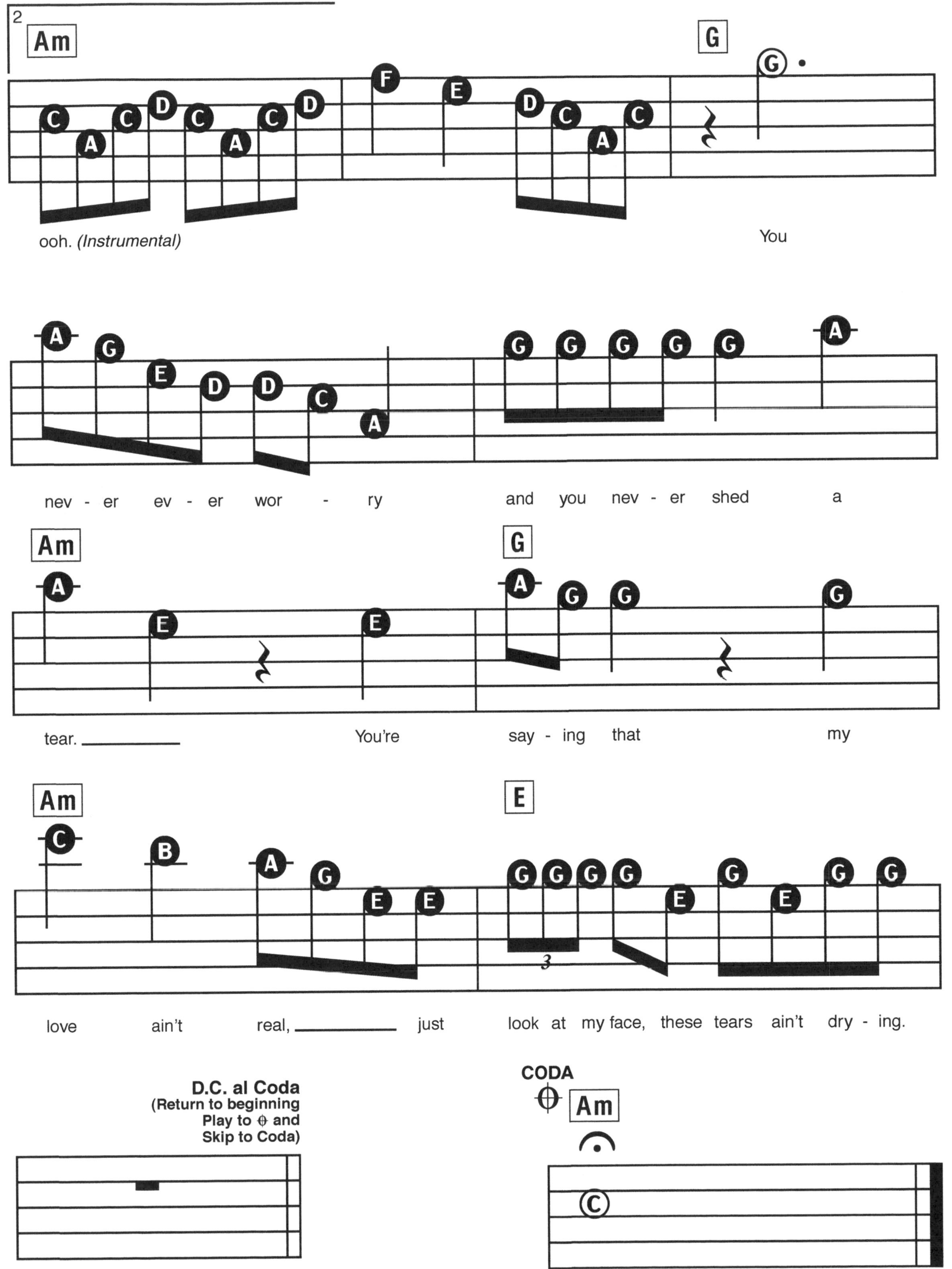
2
Am
G
ooh. (Instrumental)
You
nev - er ev - er wor - ry
and you nev - er shed a
Am
G
tear.
You're
say - ing that my
Am
E
love ain't real, just
look at my face, these tears ain't dry - ing.
D.C. al Coda
(Return to beginning
Play to ⊕ and
Skip to Coda)
CODA
Am
ooh.

Silly Love Songs

Registration 4
Rhythm: Rock or Pops

Words and Music by Paul McCartney
and Linda McCartney

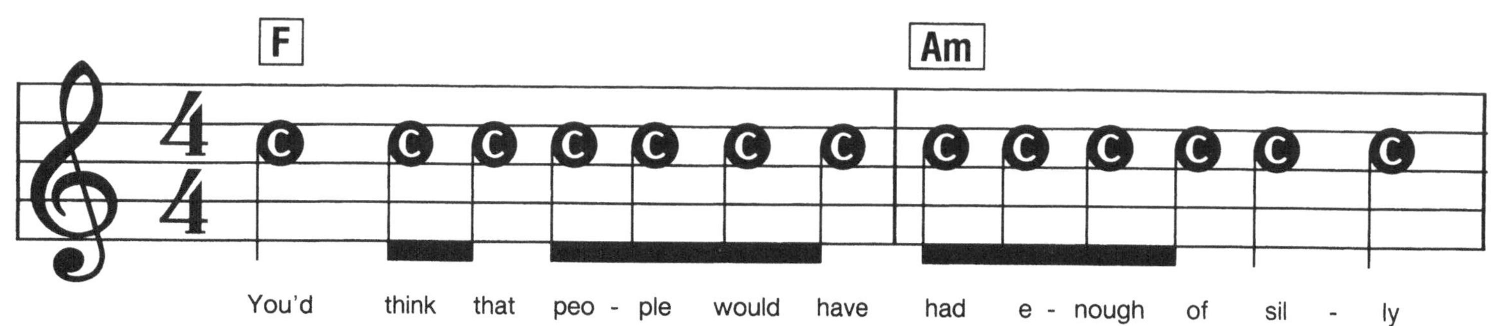

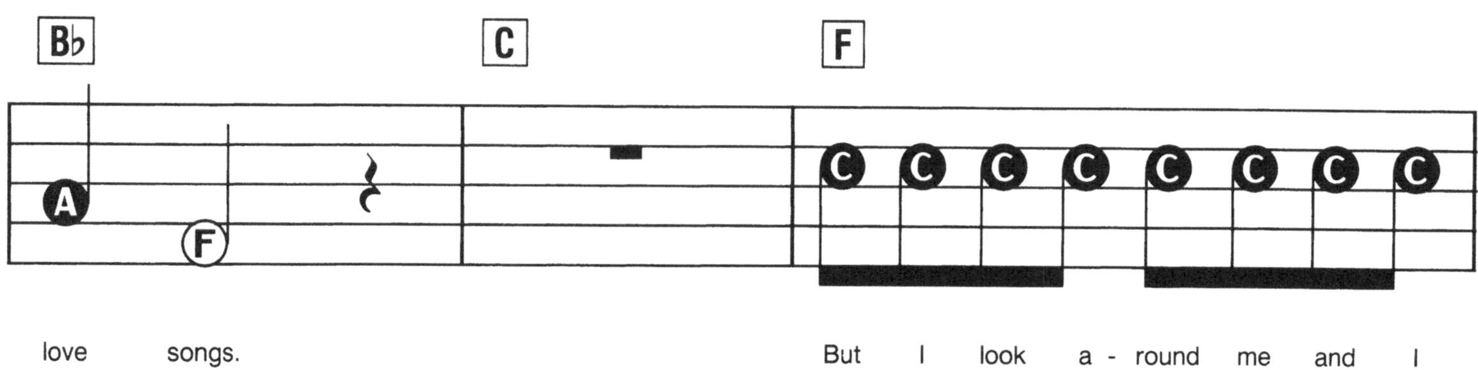

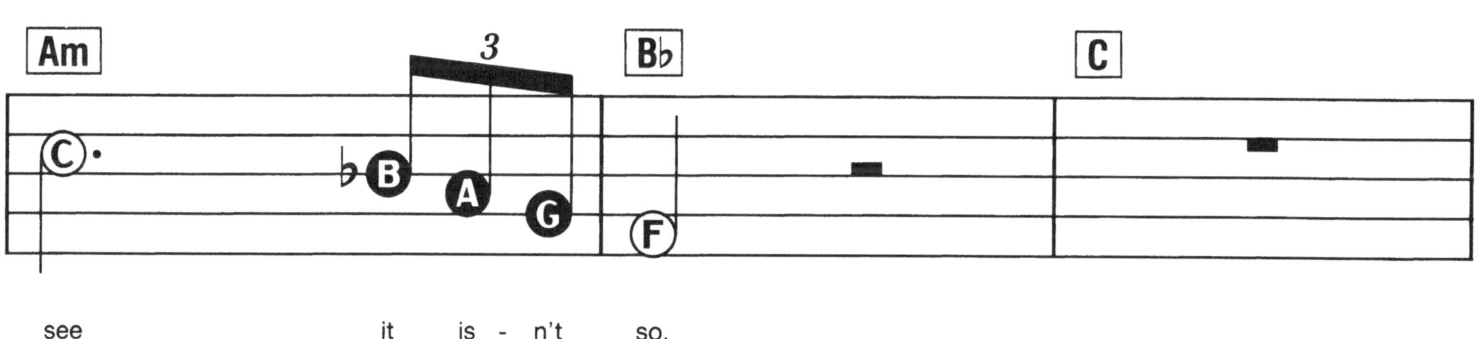

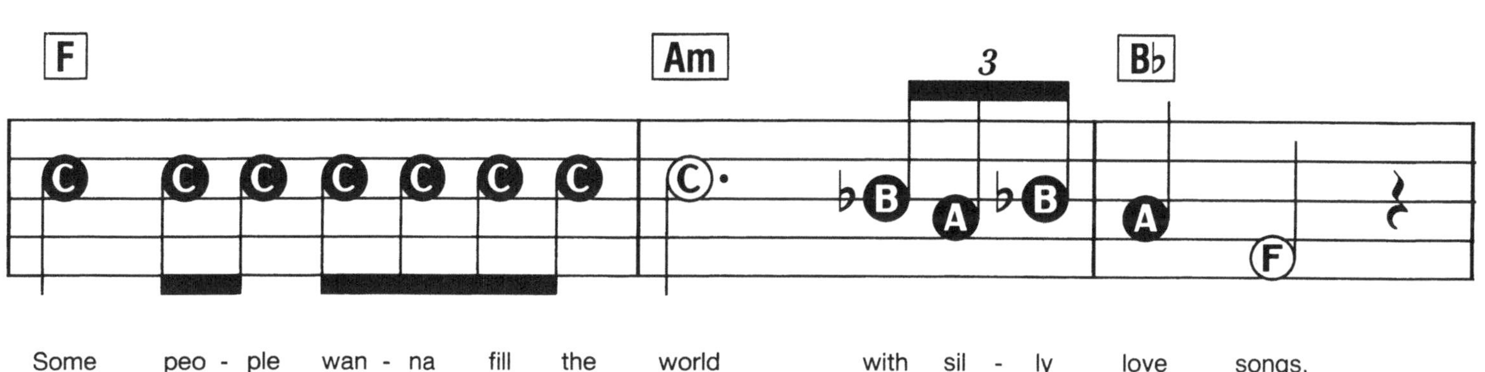

© 1976 (Renewed) MPL COMMUNICATIONS LTD.
Administered by MPL COMMUNICATIONS, INC.
All Rights Reserved

Am
To Coda
B♭
D
F
G
A
G
C
F
G
F
And what's wrong with that?
I'd like to know,

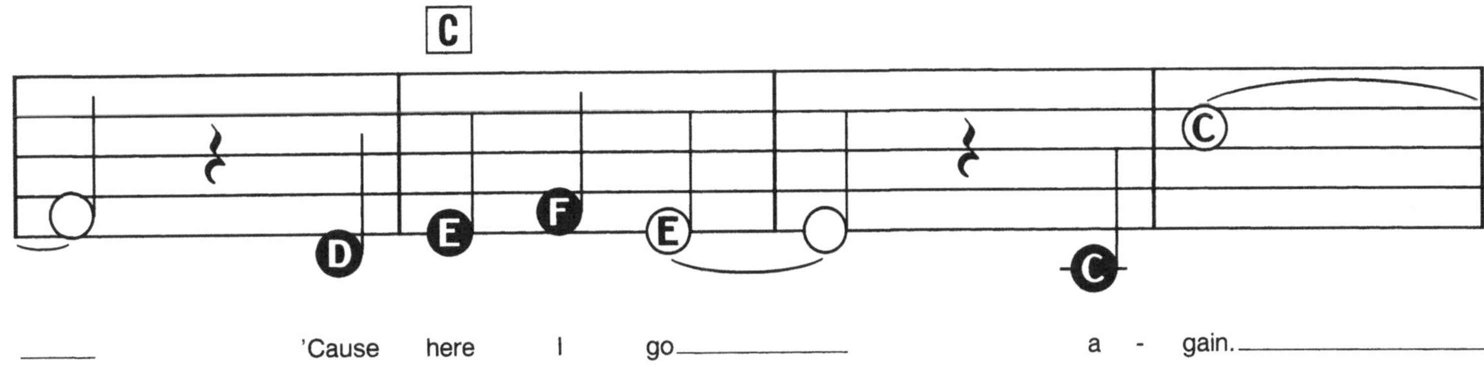
C
D
E
F
E
C
C
'Cause here I go
a - gain.

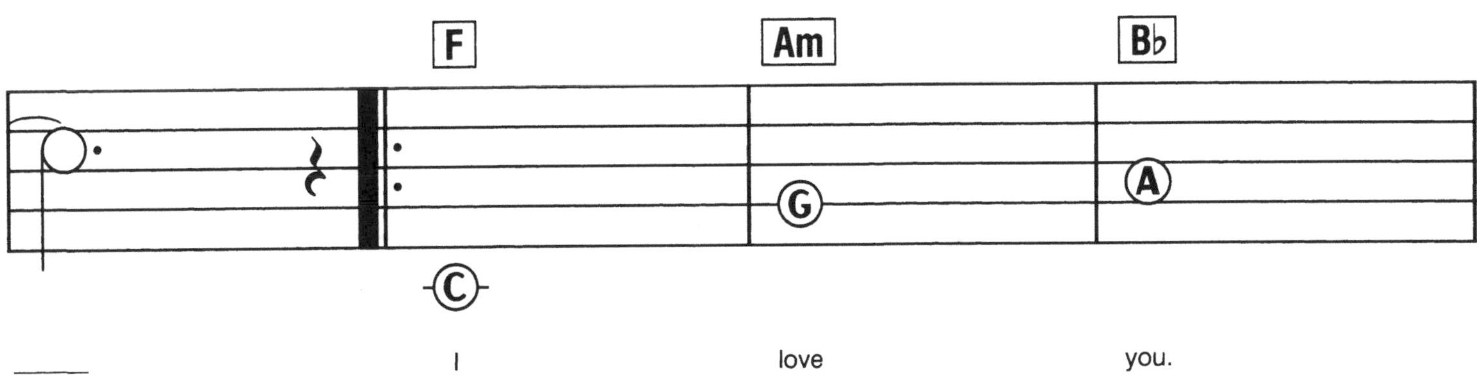
F
Am
B♭
C
G
A
I love you.

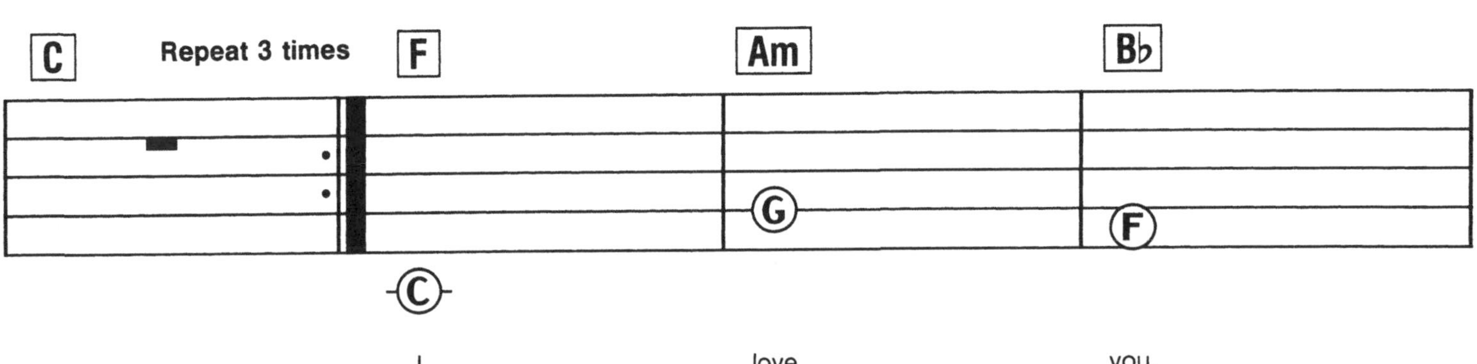
C
Repeat 3 times
F
Am
B♭
C
G
F
I love you.

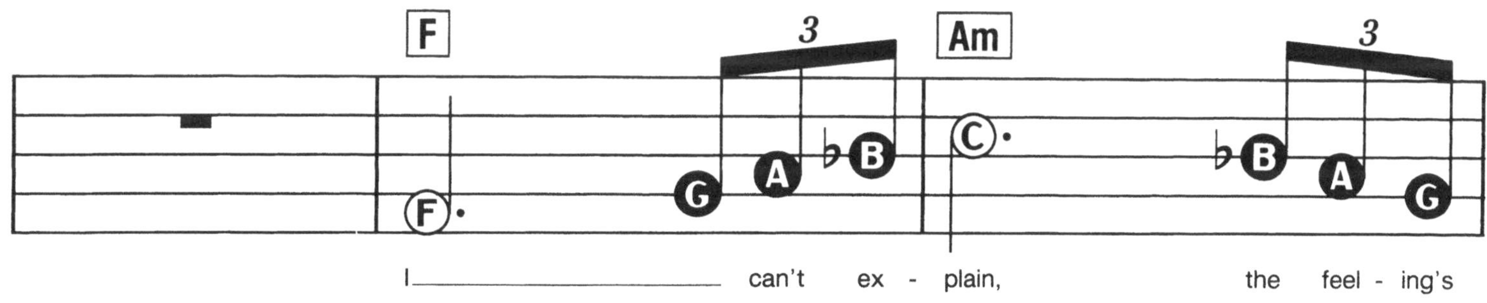
F
Am
3
F
G
A
♭B
C
♭B
A
G
I can't ex - plain, the feel - ing's

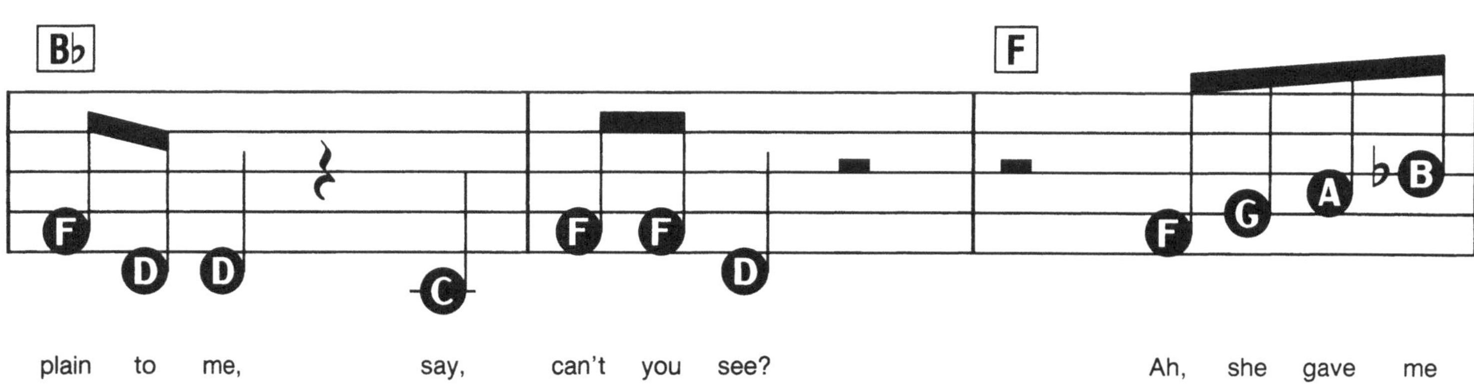
B♭
F
F
D
D
C
F
F
D
F
G
A
♭B
plain to me, say, can't you see? Ah, she gave me

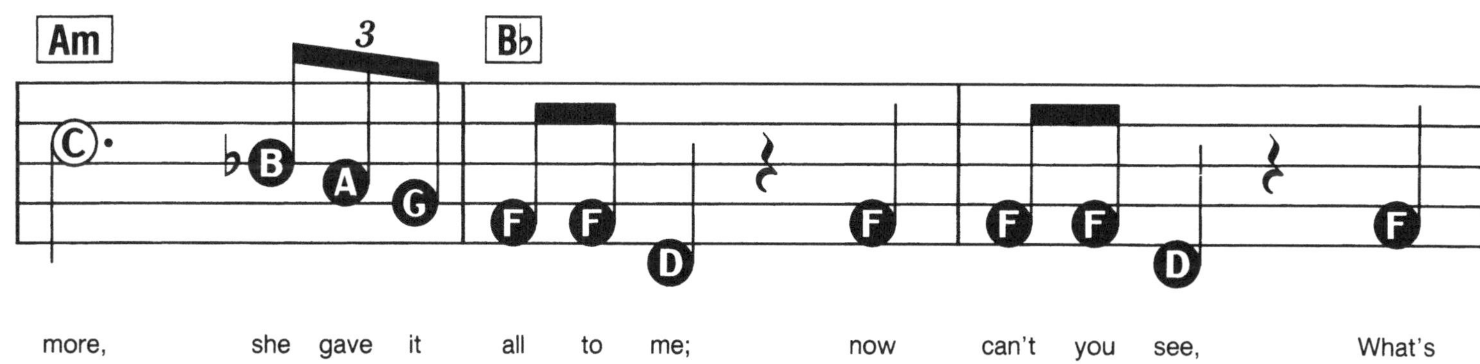
Am
3
B♭
C
♭B
A
G
F
F
D
F
F
F
D
F
more, she gave it all to me; now can't you see, What's

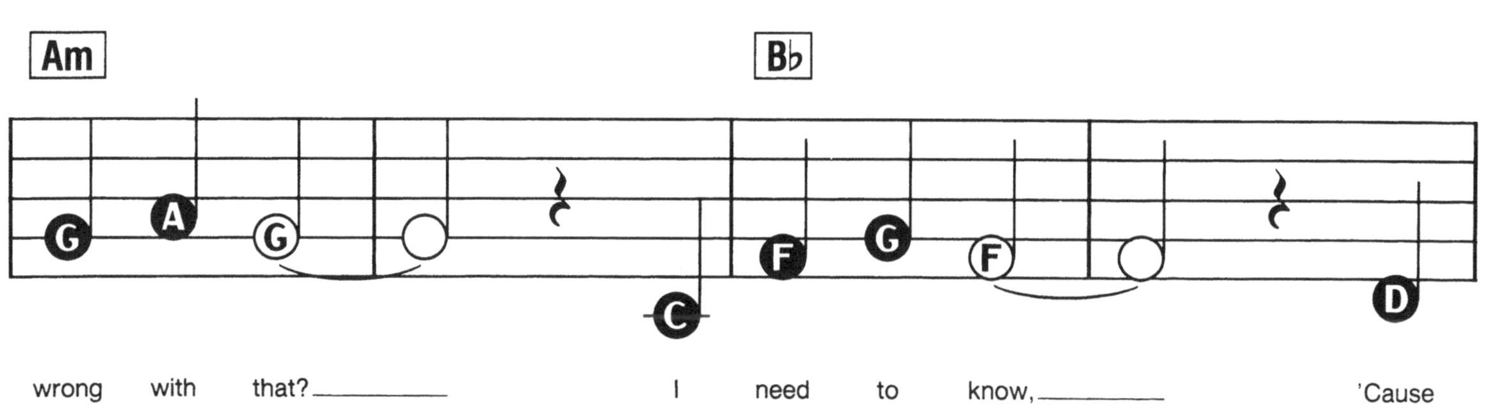
Am
B♭
G
A
G
C
F
G
F
D
wrong with that? I need to know, 'Cause

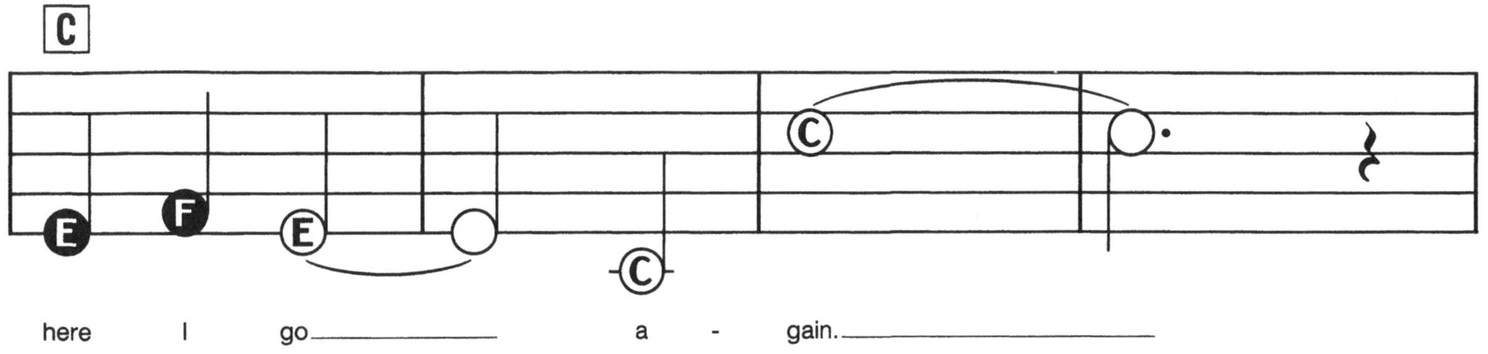
C
E
F
E
C
C
here I go a - gain.

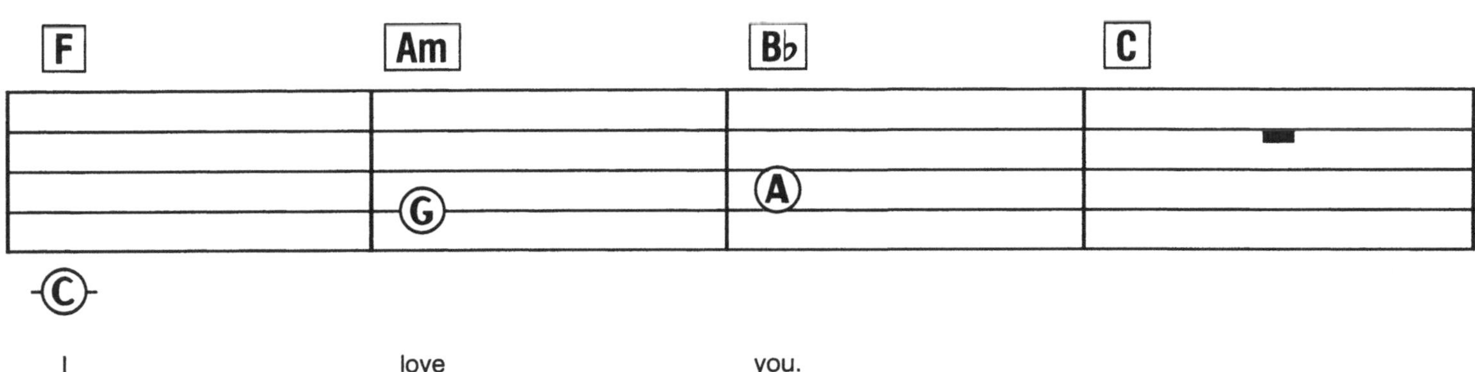
F
Am
B♭
C
C
G
A
I love you.

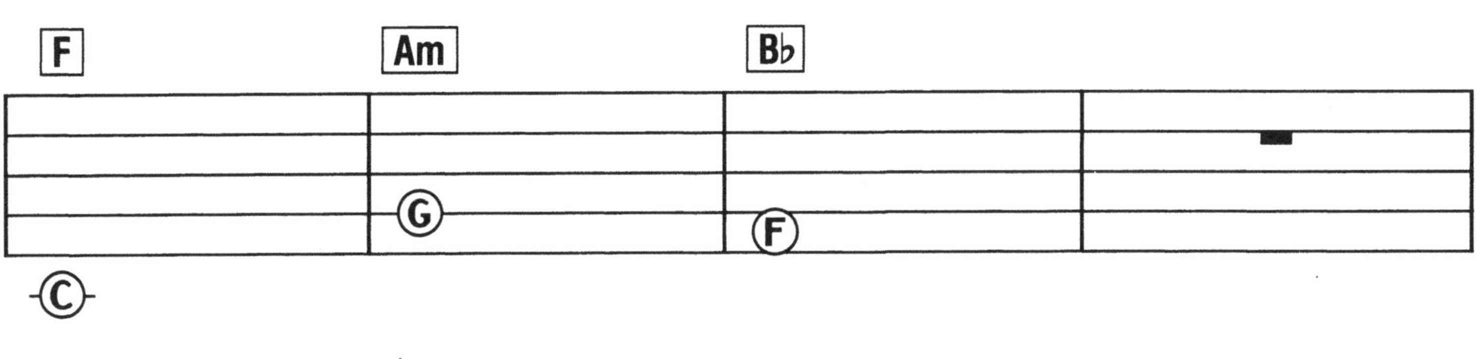
F
Am
B♭
C
G
F
I love you.

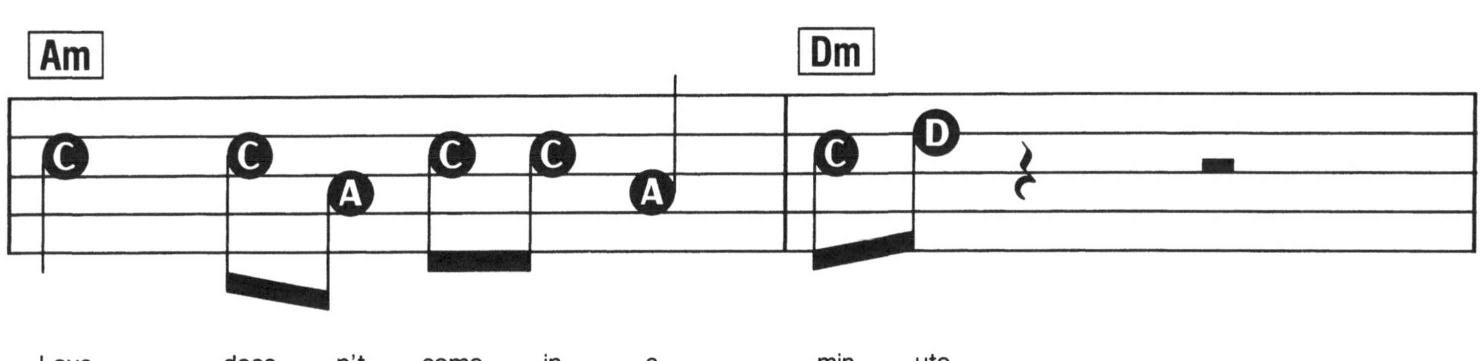
Am
Dm
C
C
A
C
C
A
C
D
Love does - n't come in a min - ute,

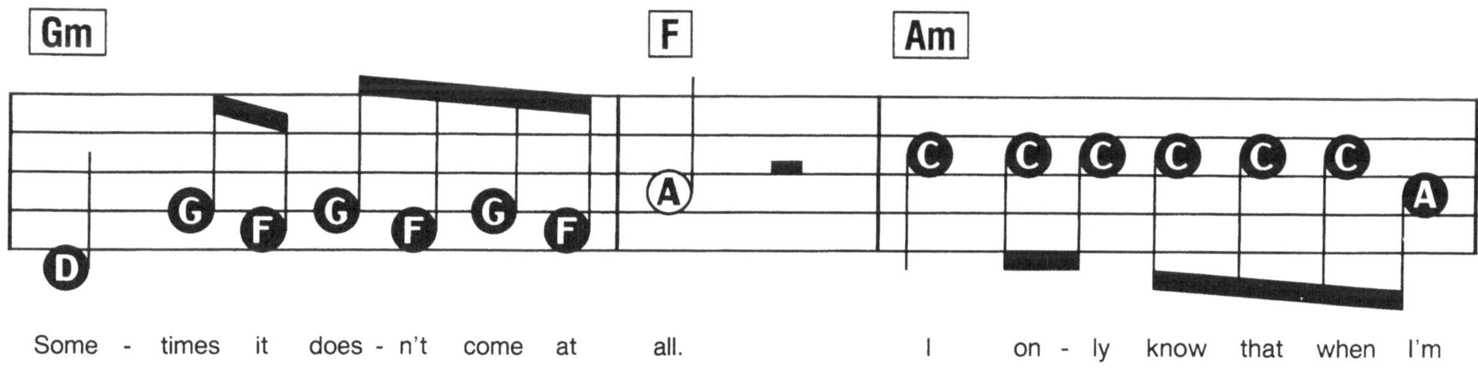
Gm
F
Am
D
G
F
G
F
G
F
A
C
C
C
C
C
C
A
Some - times it does - n't come at all. I on - ly know that when I'm

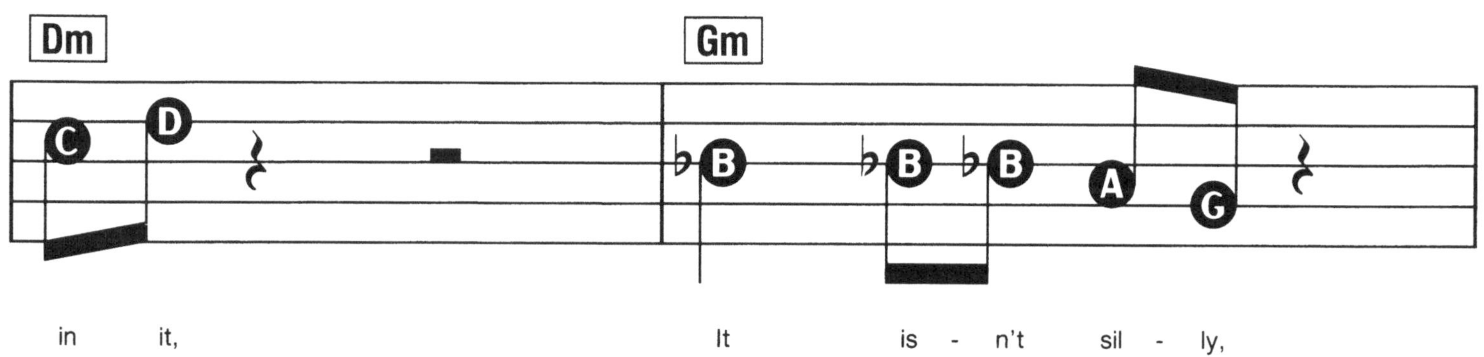
Dm
Gm
C
D
B
B
B
A
G
in it, It is - n't sil - ly,

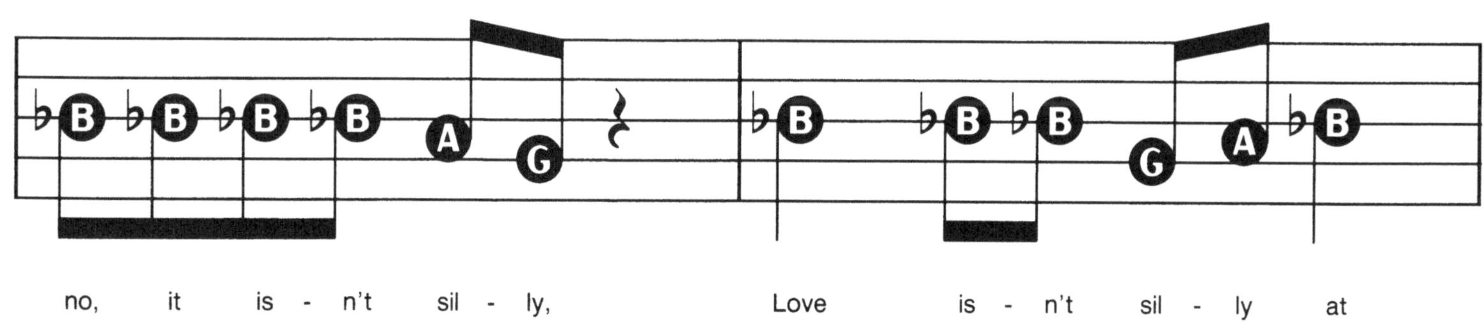
B
B
B
B
A
G
B
B
B
G
A
B
no, it is - n't sil - ly, Love is - n't sil - ly at

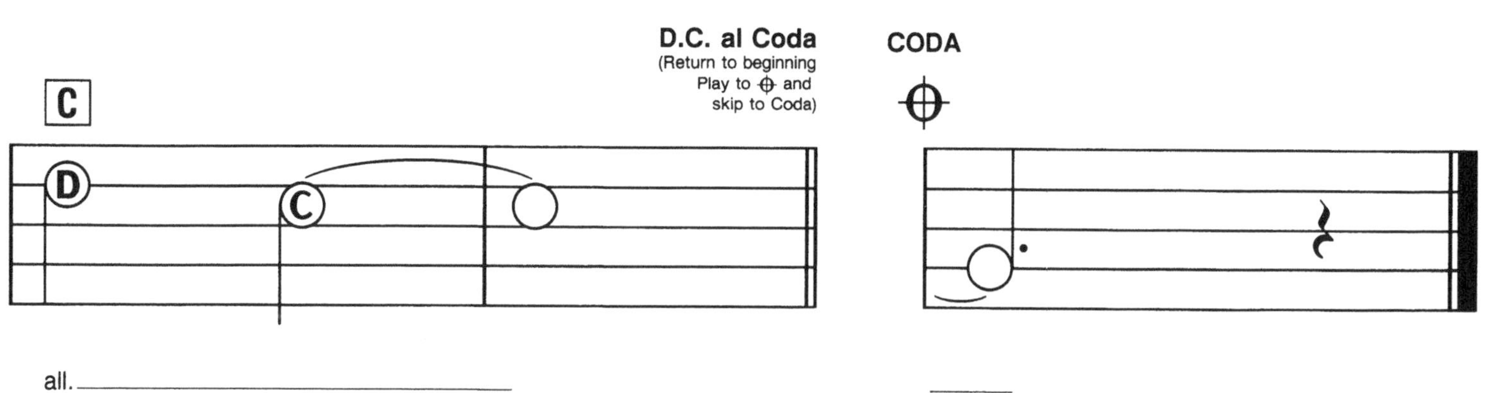
D.C. al Coda
(Return to beginning
Play to ⊕ and
skip to Coda)
CODA
C
D
C
all.

Take It Away

Registration 4
Rhythm: 8-Beat or Rock

Words and Music by
Paul McCartney

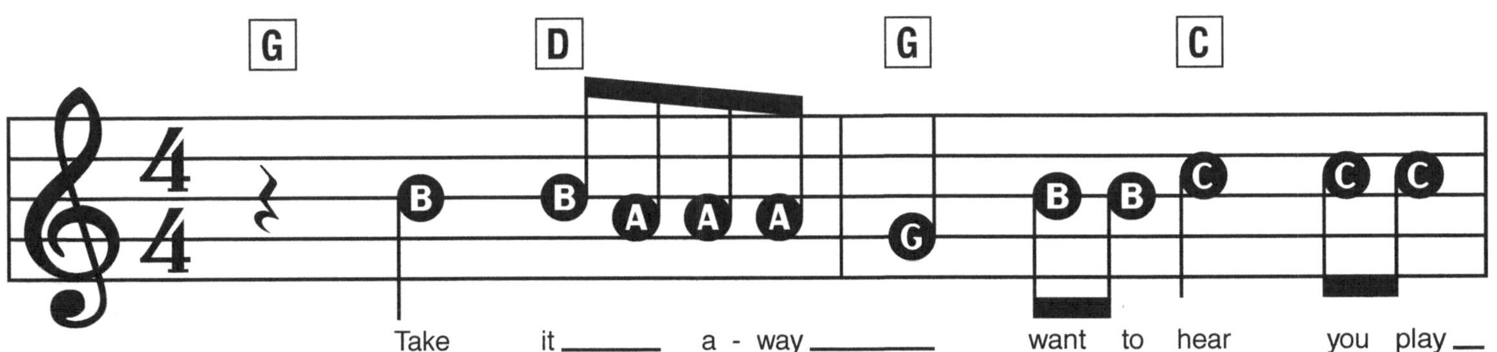

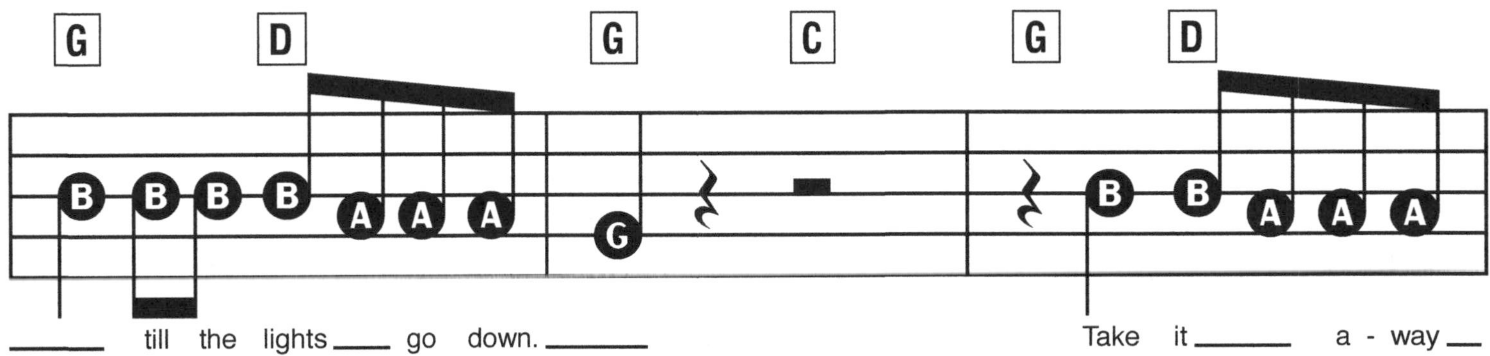

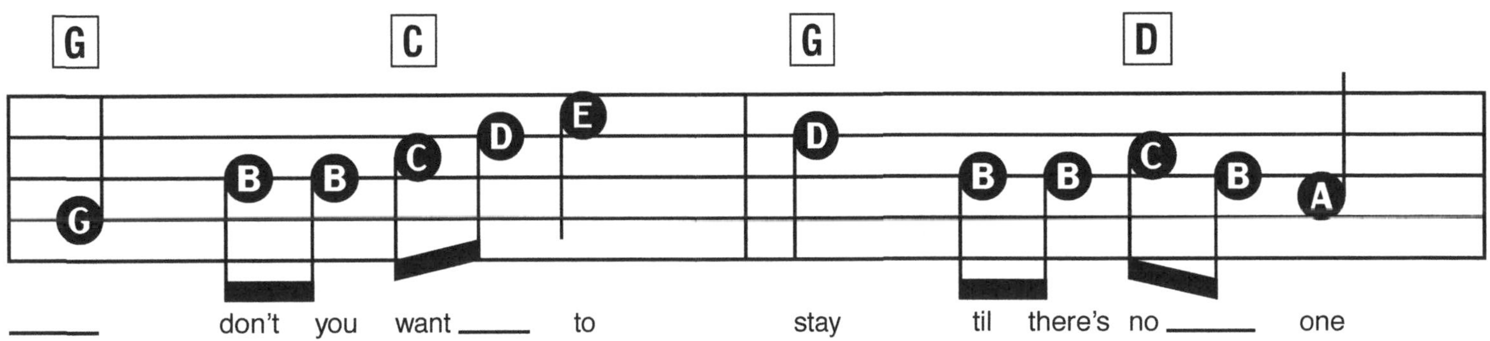

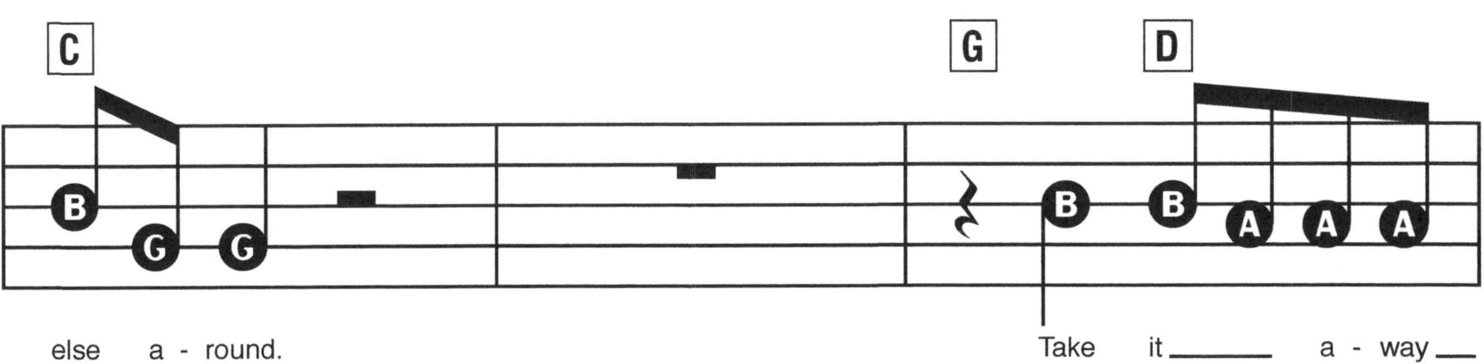

© 1982 MPL COMMUNICATIONS, INC.
All Rights Reserved

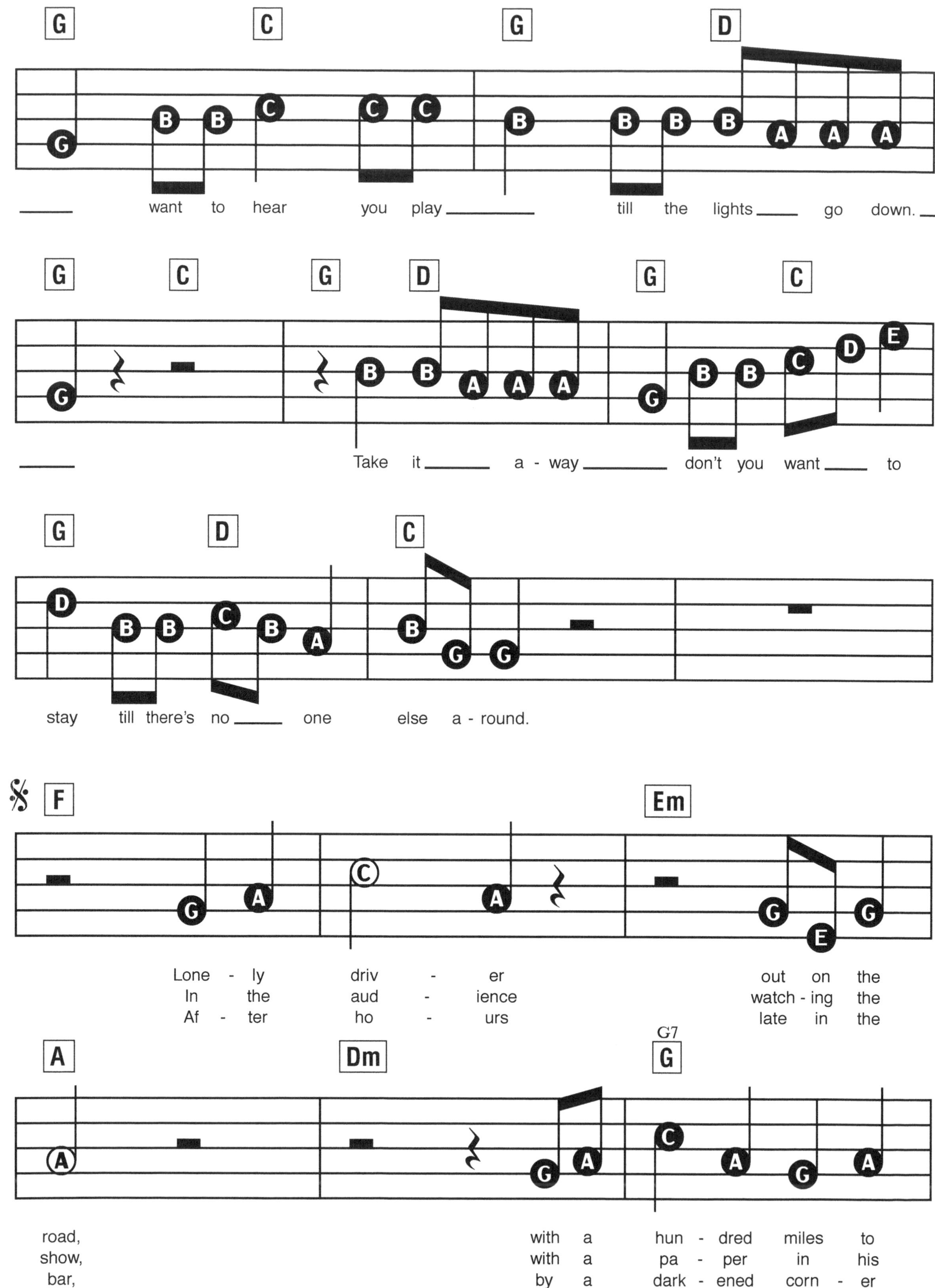
G C G D
want to hear you play till the lights go down.
G C G D G C
Take it a - way don't you want to
G D C
stay till there's no one else a - round.
F Em
Lone - ly driv - er out on the
In the aud - ience watch - ing the
Af - ter ho - urs late in the
A Dm G7 G
road, with a hun - dred miles to
show, with a pa - per in his
bar, by a dark - ened corn - er

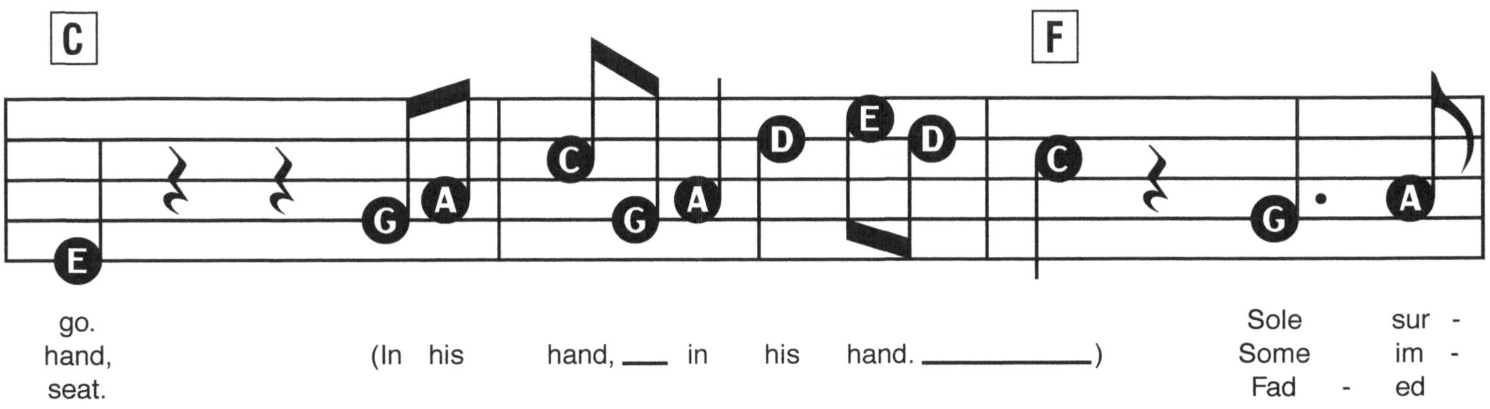
C
F
E
G
A
C
G
A
D
E
D
C
G
A
go.
hand, (In his hand, in his hand.)
seat.
Sole sur -
Some im -
Fad - ed

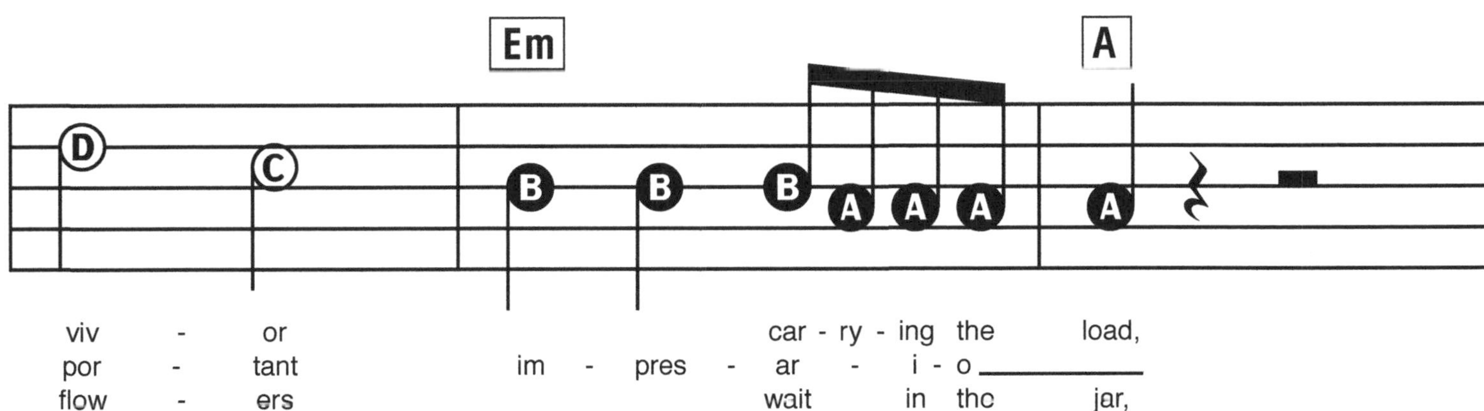
Em
A
D
C
B
B
B
A
A
A
A
viv - or car - ry - ing the load,
por - tant im - pres - ar - i - o
flow - ers wait in the jar,

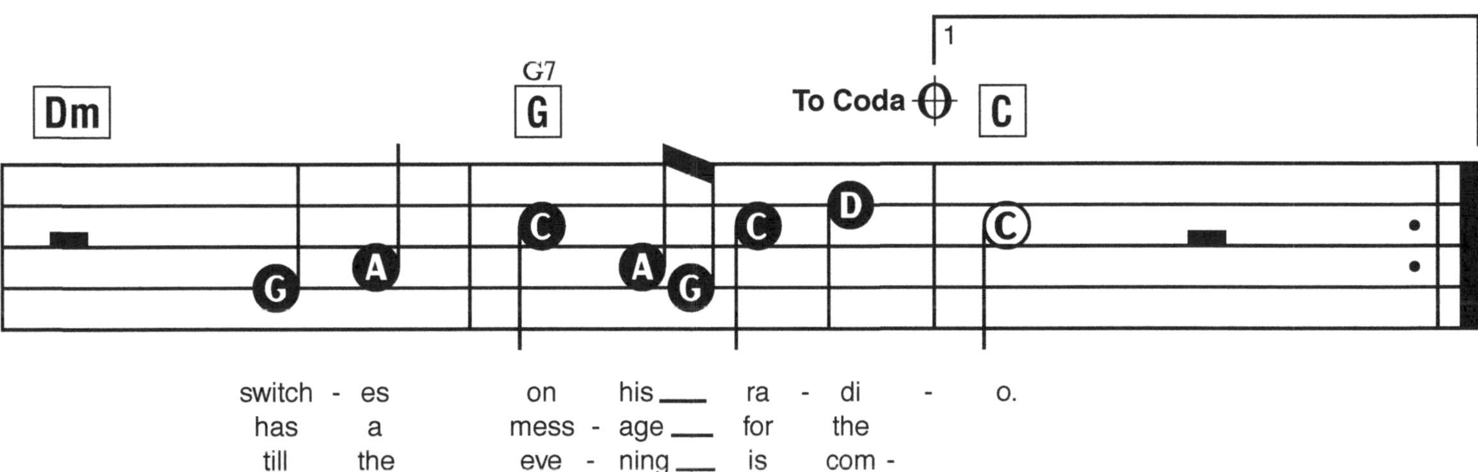
1
Dm
G7
G
To Coda
C
G
A
C
A
G
C
D
C
switch - es on his ra - di - o.
has a mess - age for the
till the eve - ning is com -

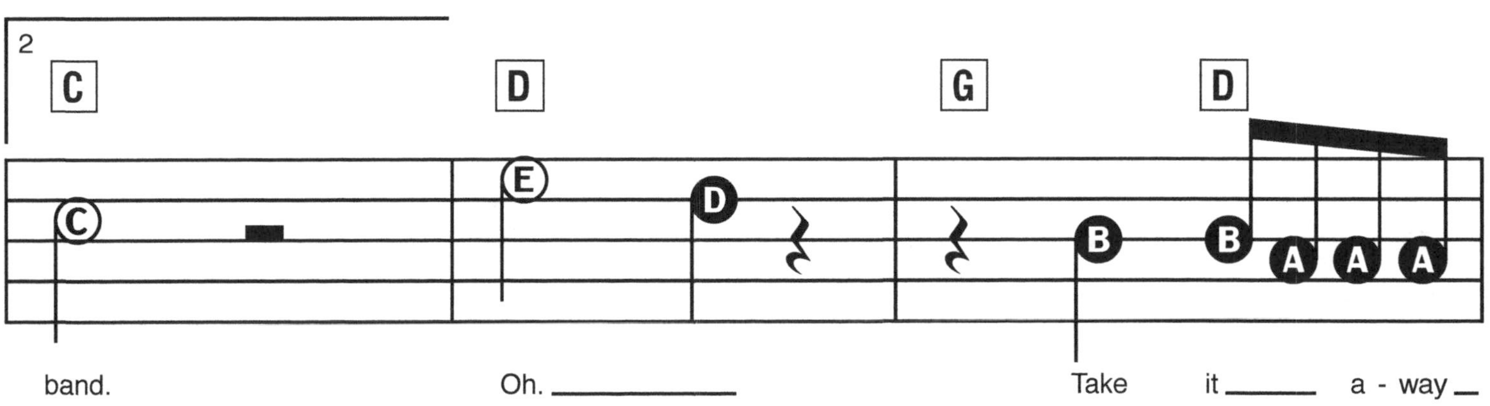
2
C
D
G
D
C
E
D
B
B
A
A
A
band.
Oh.
Take it a - way

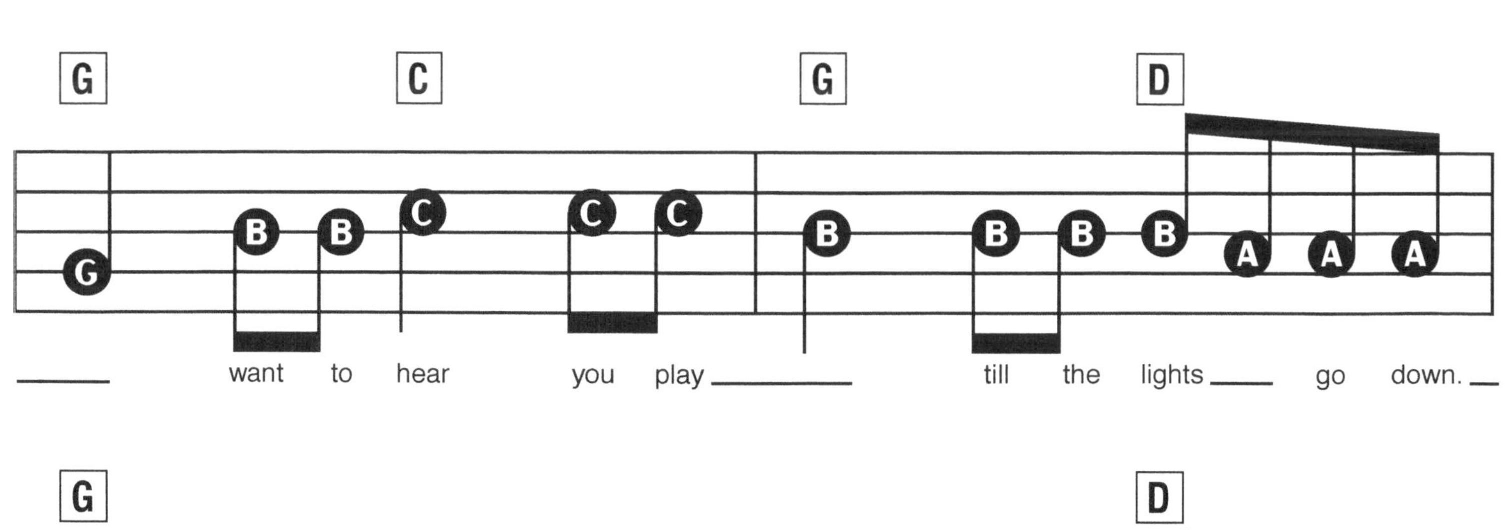
G
C
G
D
G B B C C C B B B B A A A
want to hear you play till the lights go down.

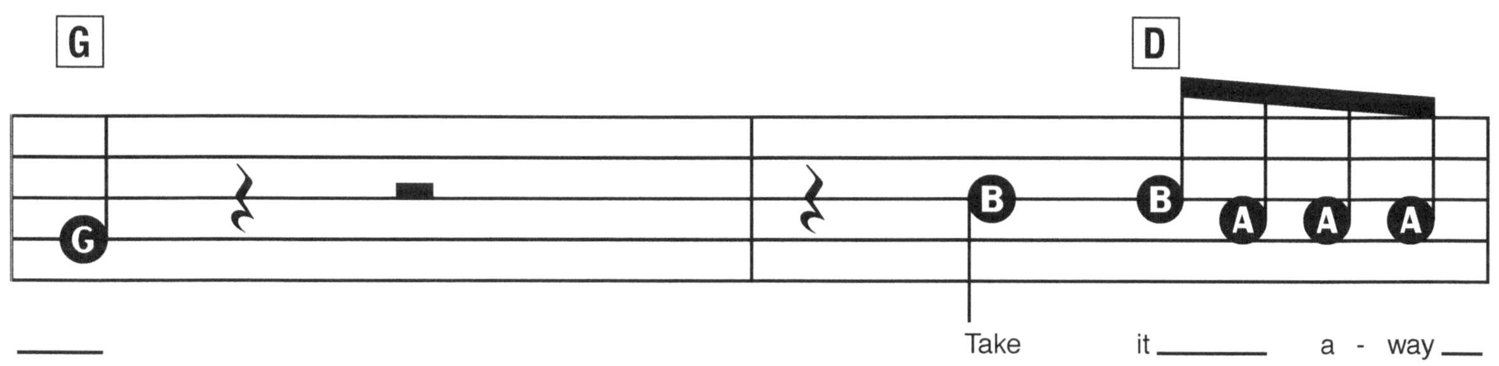
G
D
G B B A A A
Take it a - way

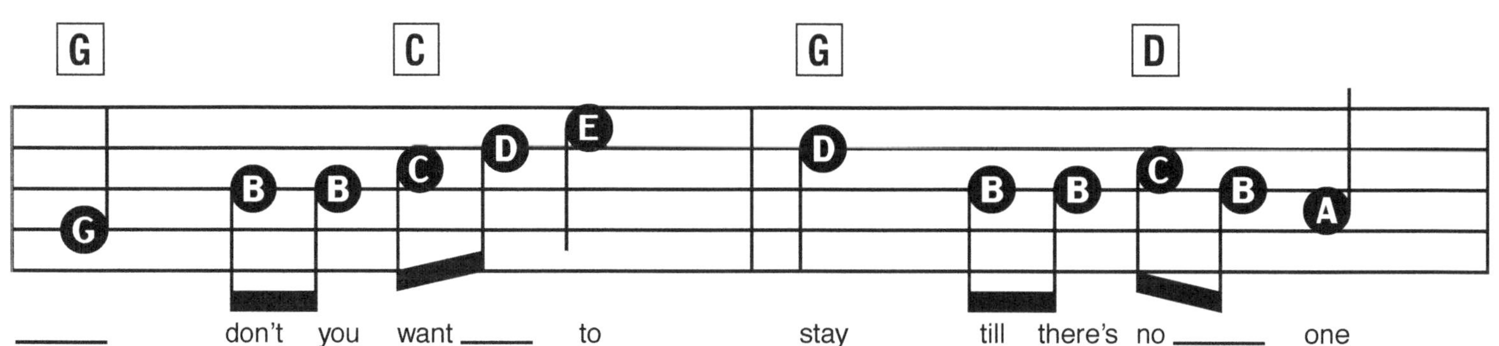
G
C
G
D
G B B C D E D B B C B A
don't you want to stay till there's no one

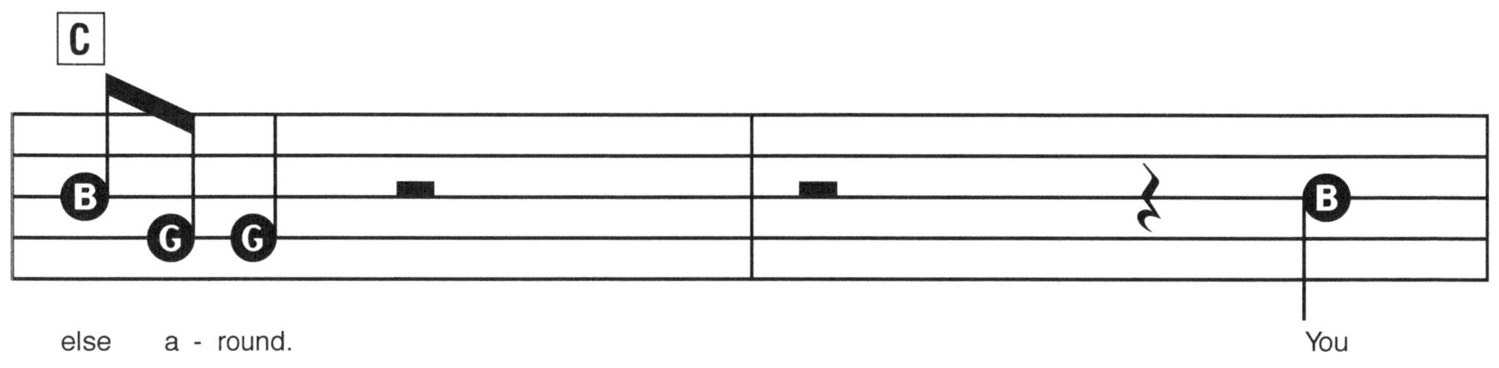
C
B G G B
else a - round. You

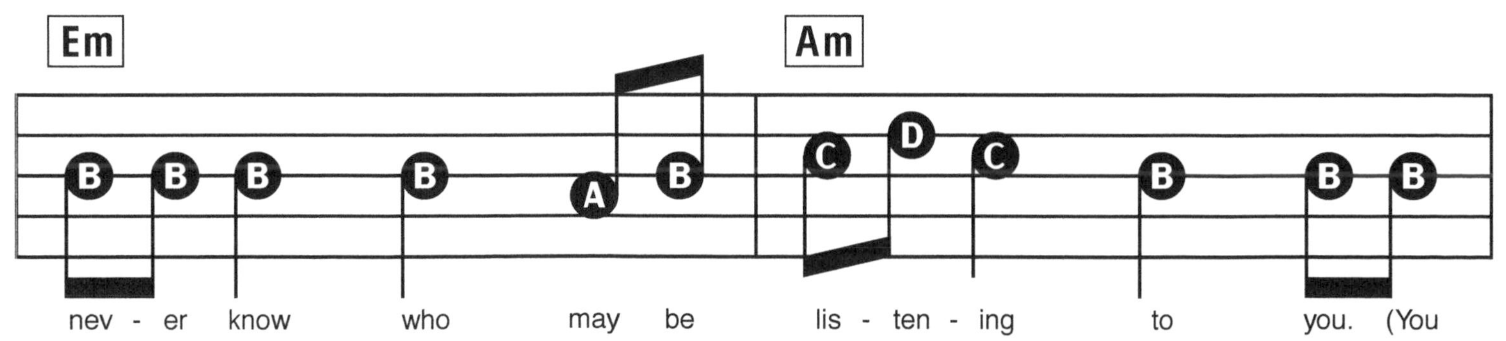
Em
Am
B B B B A B C D C B B B
nev - er know who may be lis - ten - ing to you. (You

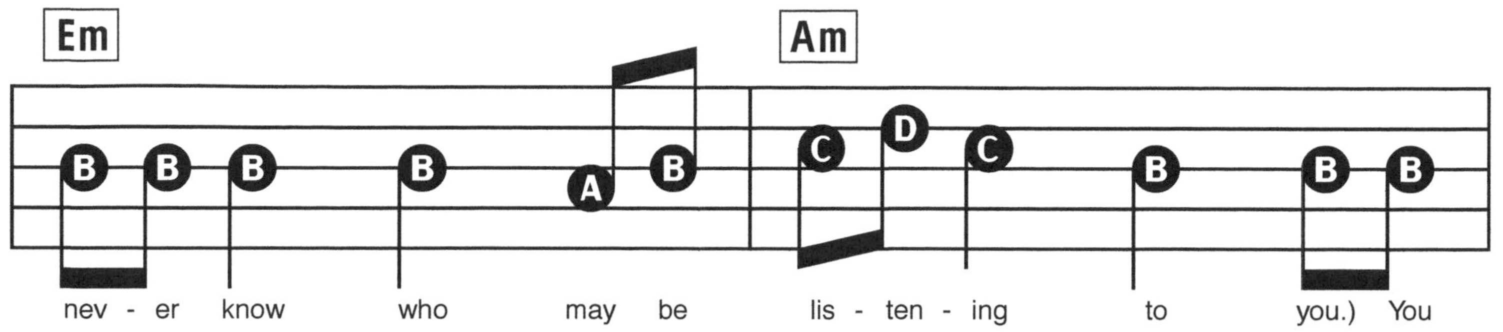
Em
Am
never know who may be listening to you.) You

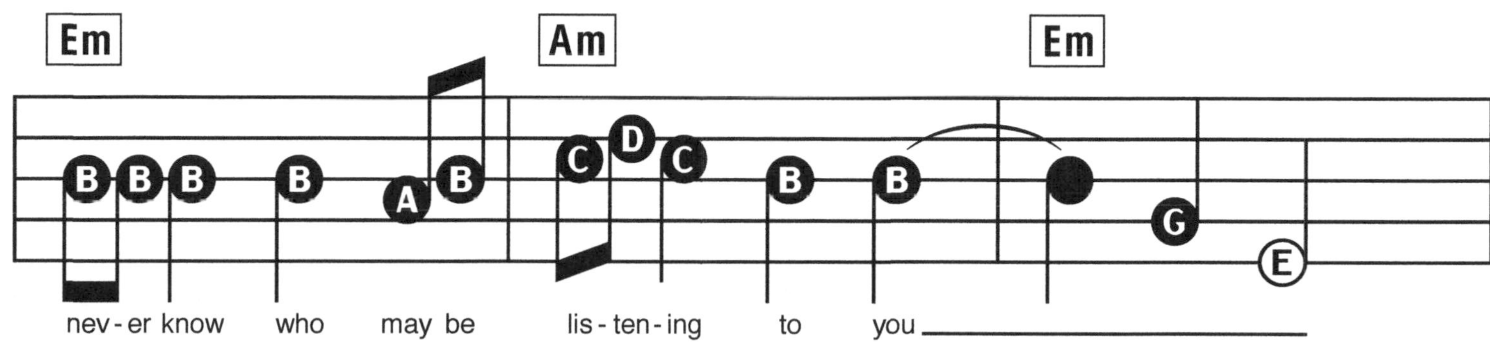
Em
Am
Em
never know who may be listening to you

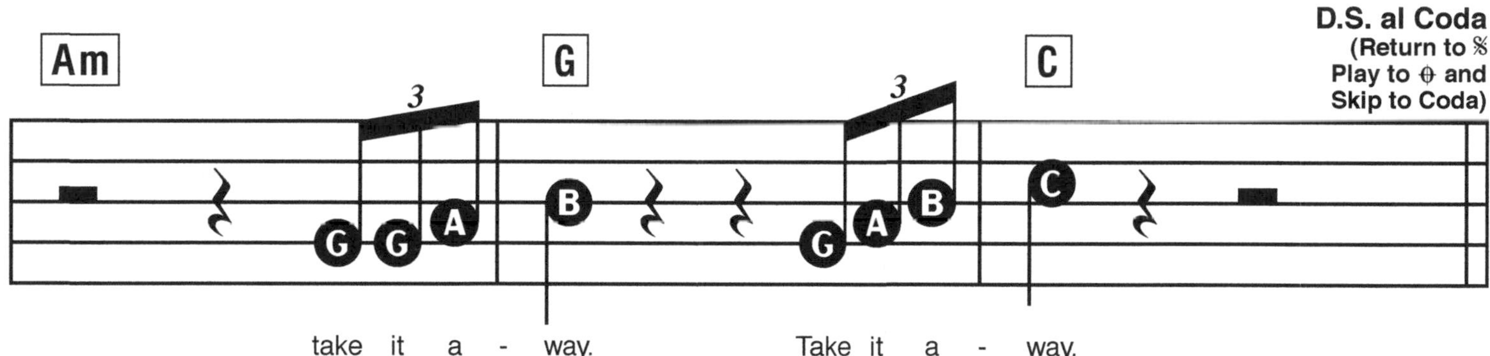
D.S. al Coda
(Return to 𝄋
Play to ⊕ and
Skip to Coda)
Am
G
C
3
3
take it a - way.
Take it a - way.

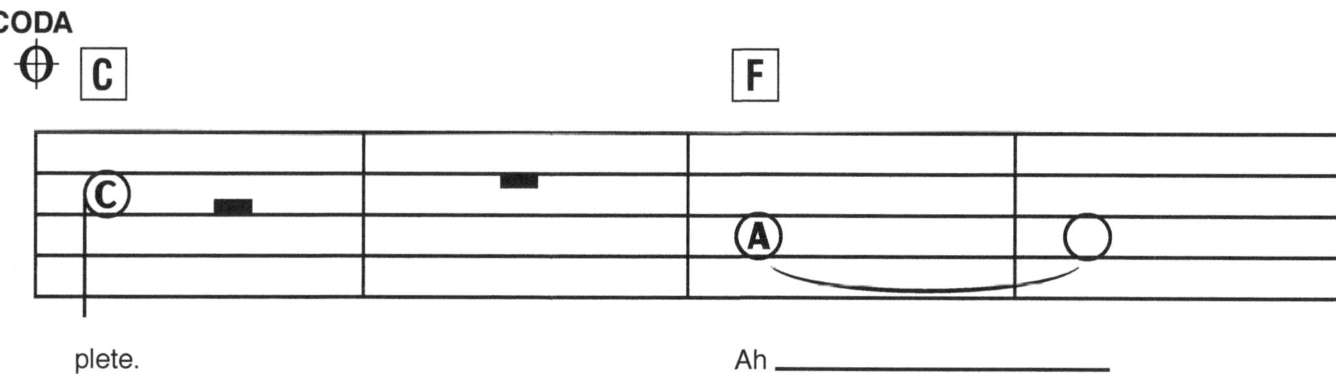
CODA
C
F
plete.
Ah

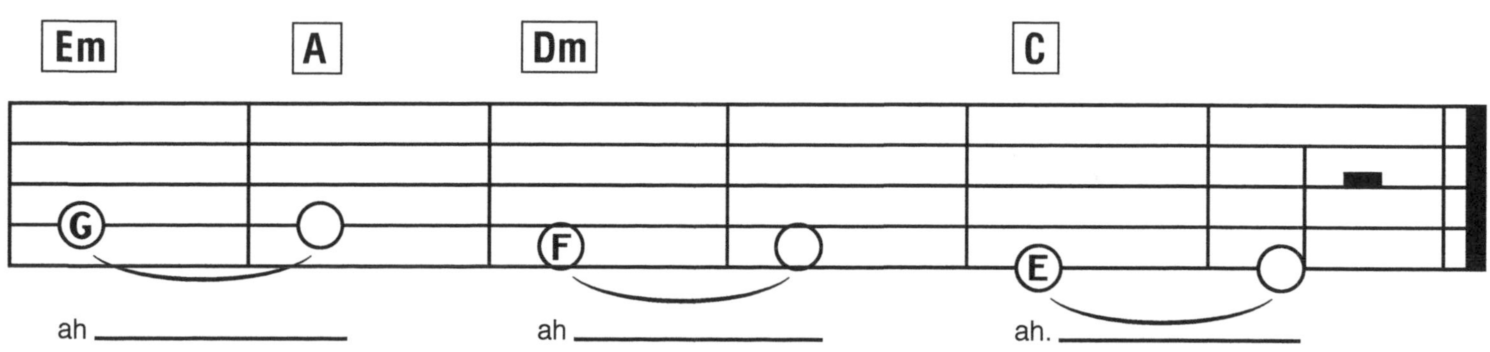
Em
A
Dm
C
ah
ah
ah.

Uncle Albert/Admiral Halsey

Registration 2
Rhythm: Rock or Pops

Words and Music by Paul McCartney
and Linda McCartney

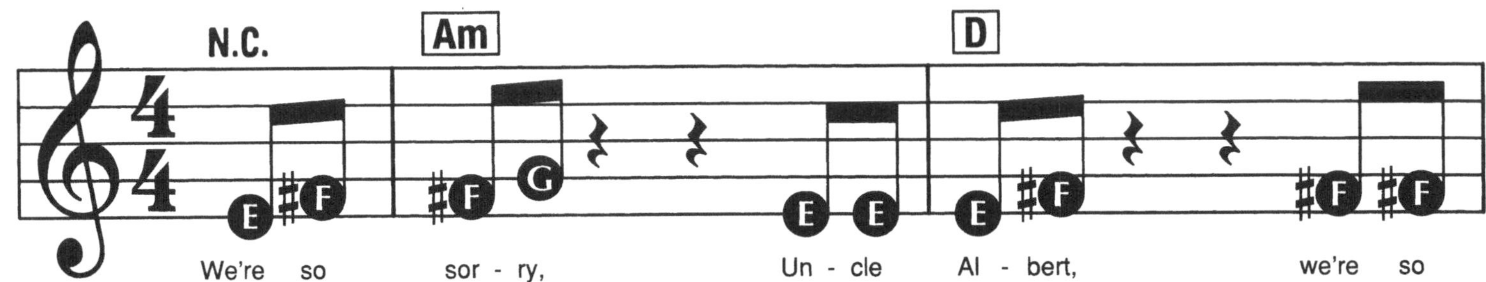

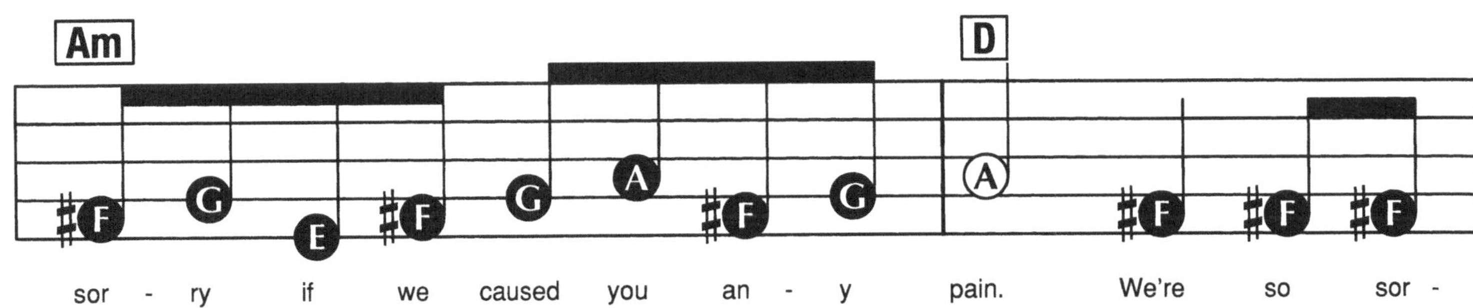

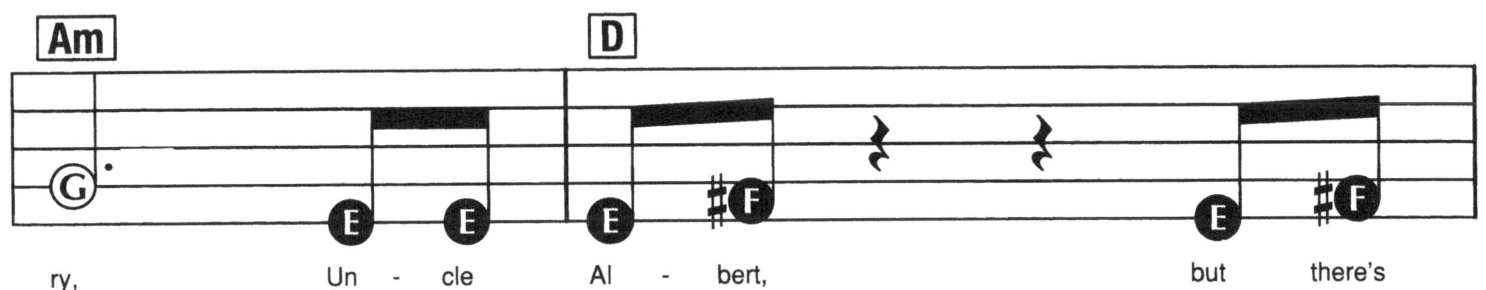

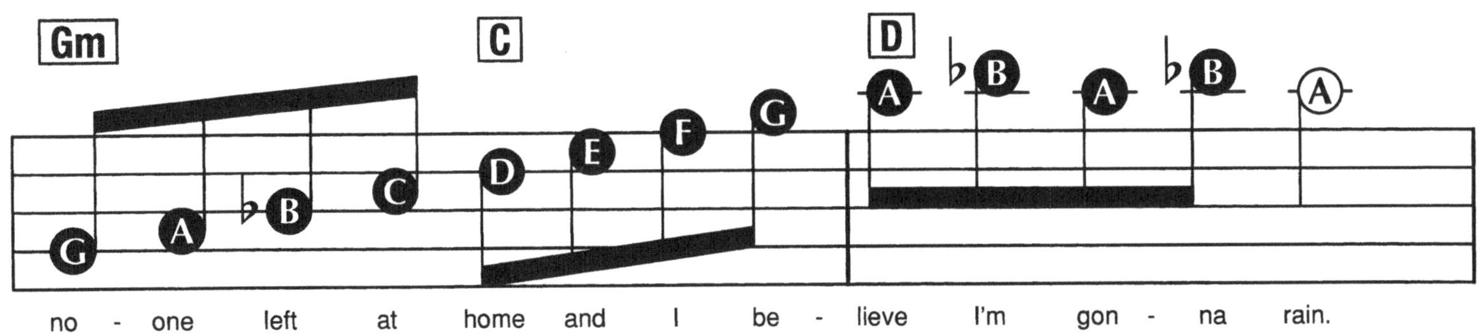

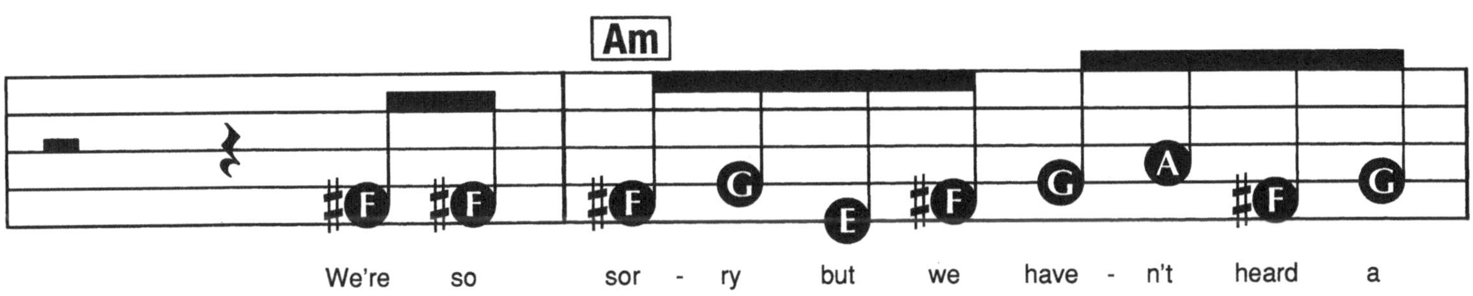

© 1971 (Renewed) PAUL and LINDA McCARTNEY
Administered by MPL COMMUNICATIONS, INC.
All Rights Reserved

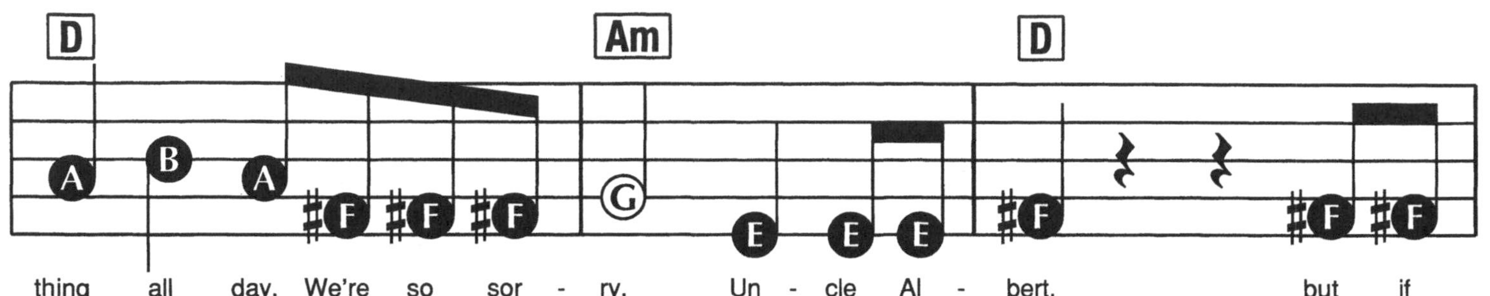
D
Am
D
A
B
A
♯F
♯F
♯F
G
E
E
E
♯F
♯F
♯F
thing all day. We're so sor - ry, Un - cle Al - bert, but if

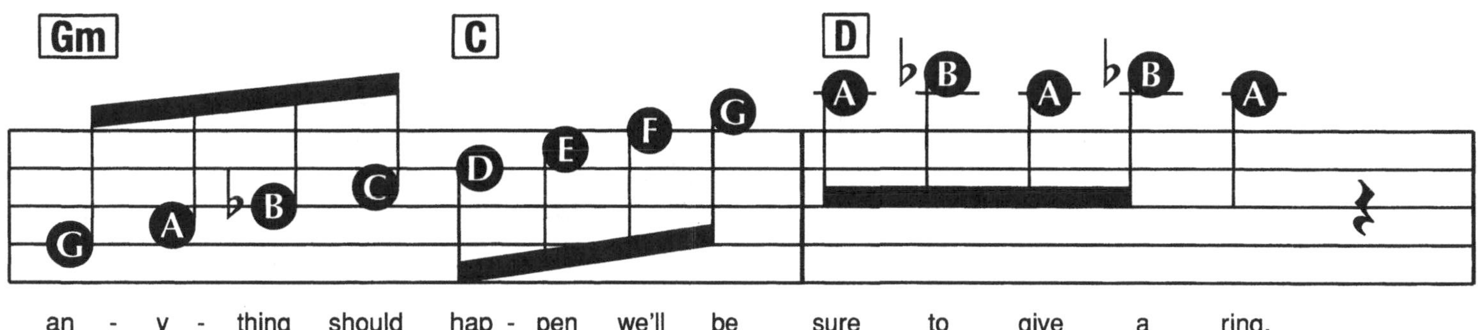
Gm
C
D
G
A
♭B
C
D
E
F
G
A
♭B
A
♭B
A
an - y - thing should hap - pen we'll be sure to give a ring.

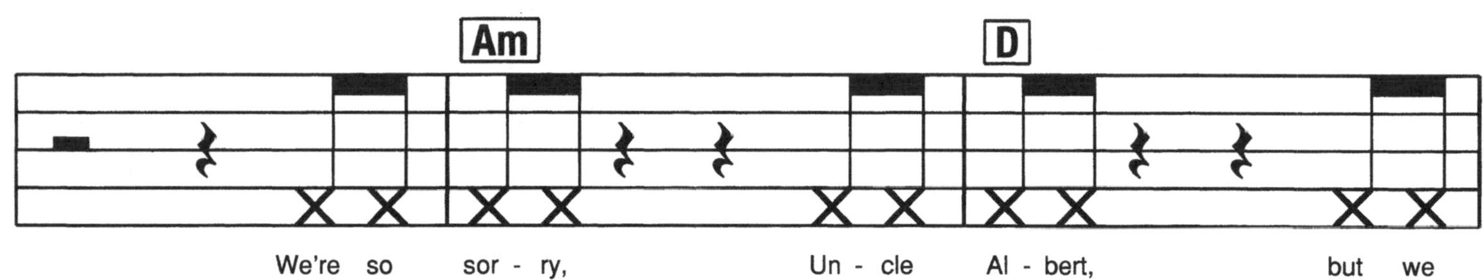
Am
D
We're so sor - ry, Un - cle Al - bert, but we

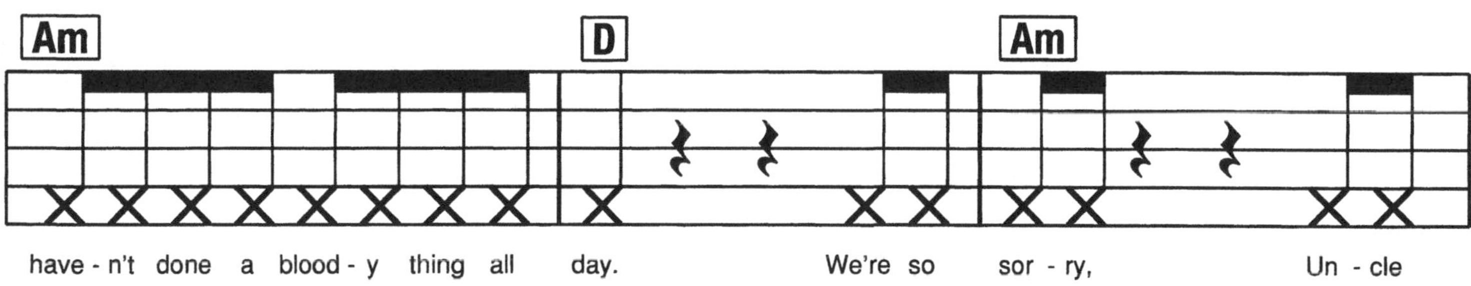
Am
D
Am
have - n't done a blood - y thing all day. We're so sor - ry, Un - cle

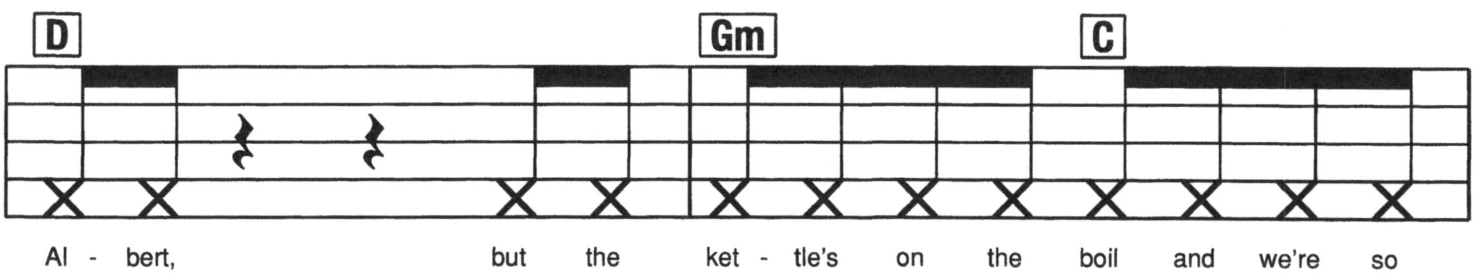
D
Gm
C
Al - bert, but the ket - tle's on the boil and we're so

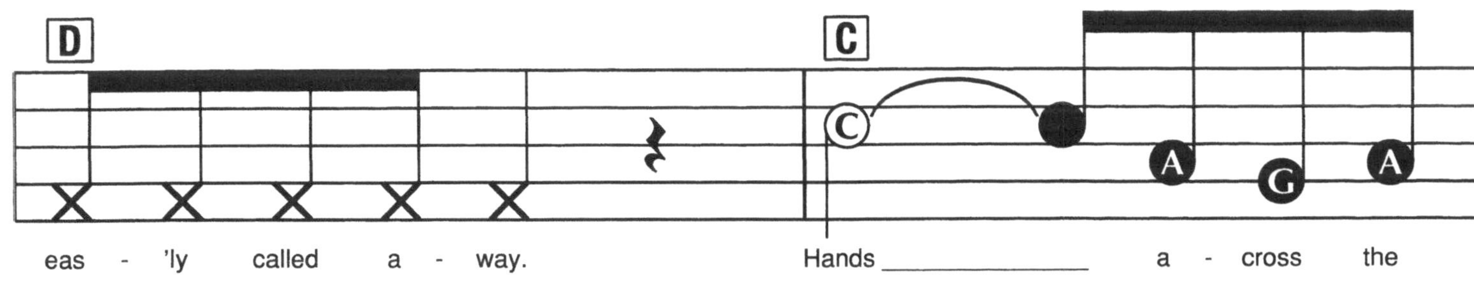
D
C
C A G A
eas - 'ly called a - way. Hands a - cross the

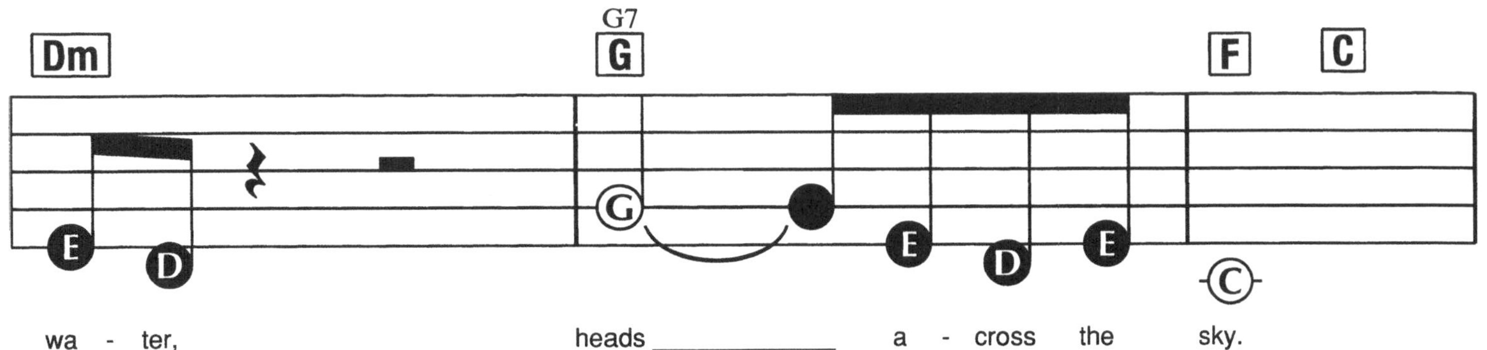
Dm
G7
G
F
C
E D
G E D E
C
wa - ter, heads a - cross the sky.

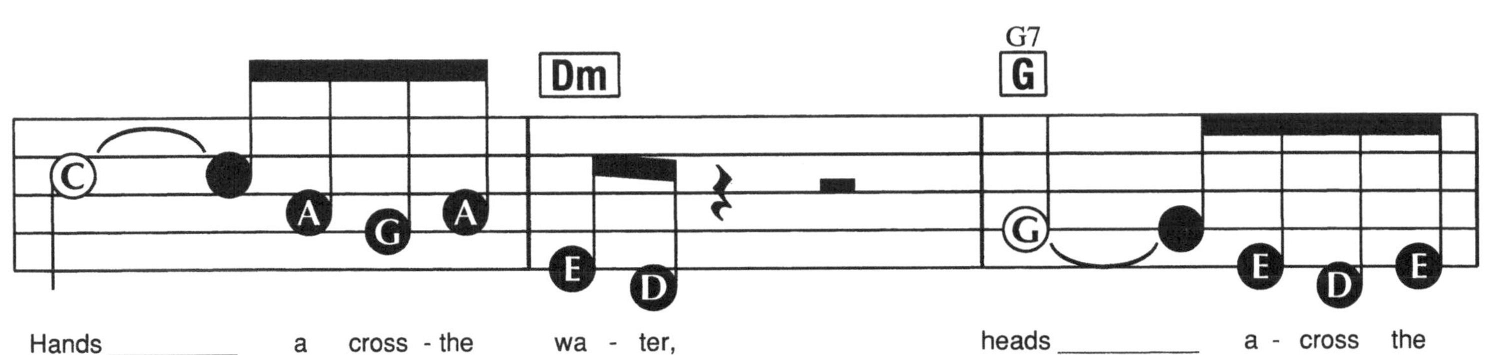
Dm
G7
G
C A G A
E D
G E D E
Hands a cross - the wa - ter, heads a - cross the

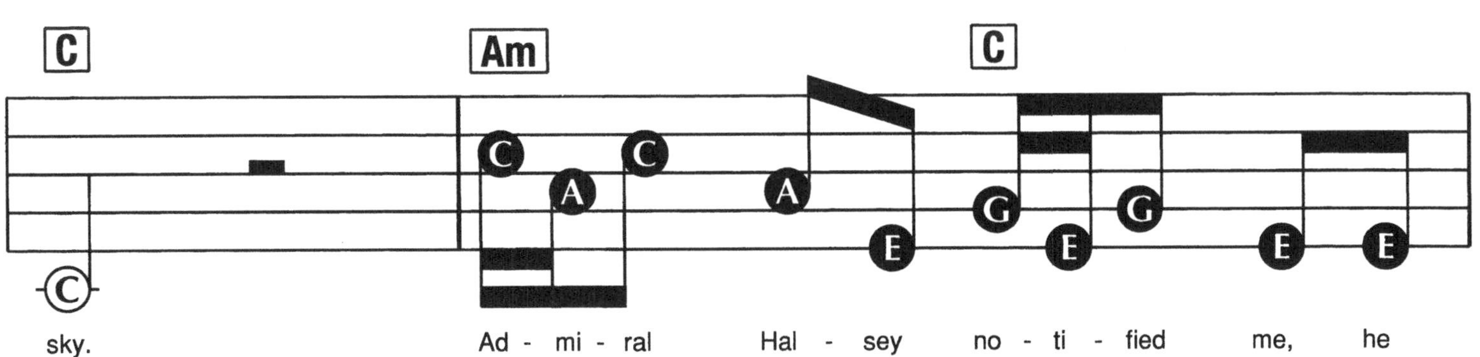
C
Am
C
C
C A C A E
G E G E E
sky. Ad - mi - ral Hal - sey no - ti - fied me, he

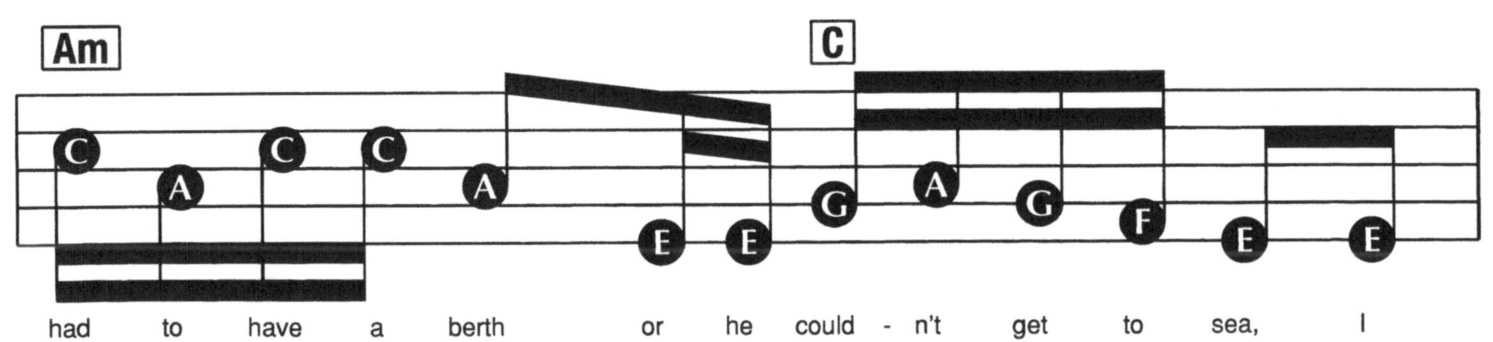
Am
C
C A C C A E E
G A G F E E
had to have a berth or he could - n't get to sea, I

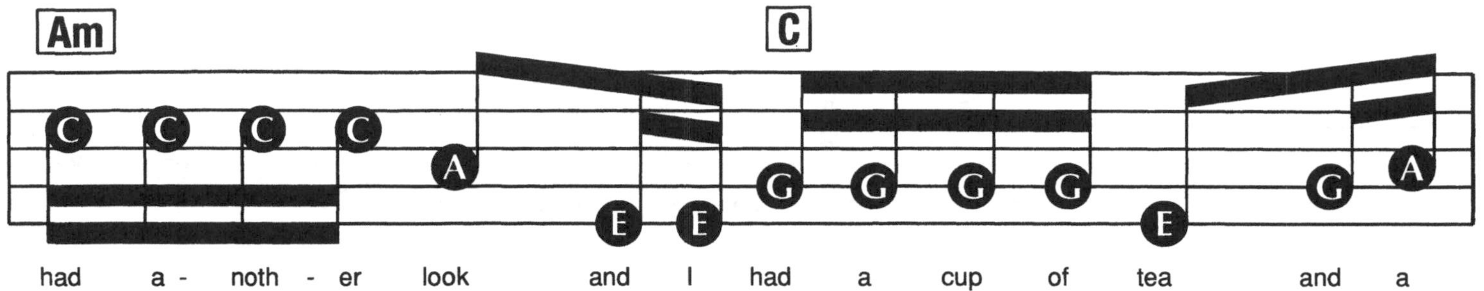
Am
C
had a - noth - er look and I had a cup of tea and a

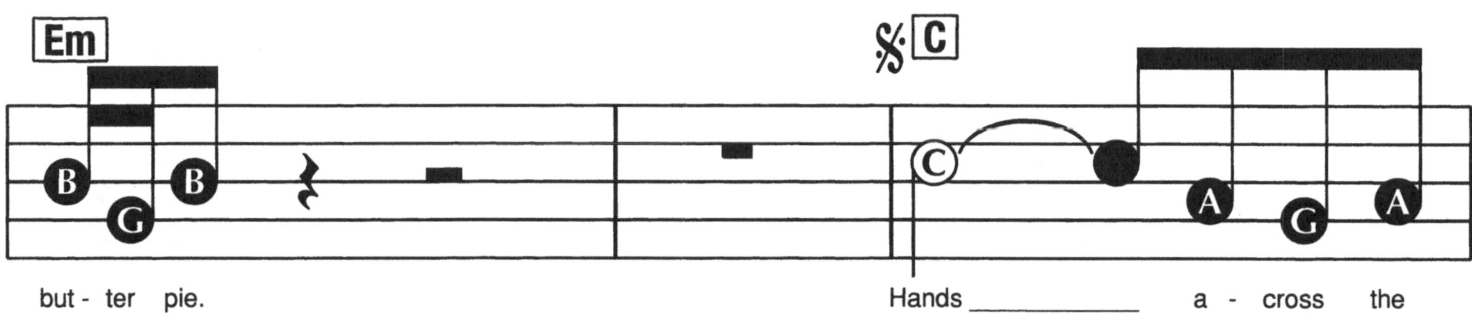
Em
C
but - ter pie.
Hands a - cross the

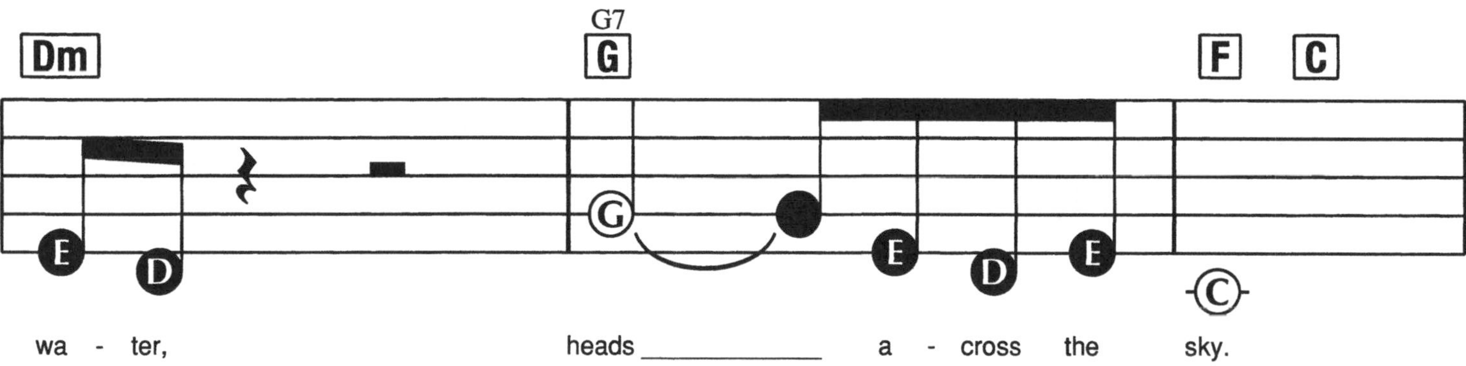
Dm
G7
G
F
C
wa - ter,
heads a - cross the
sky.

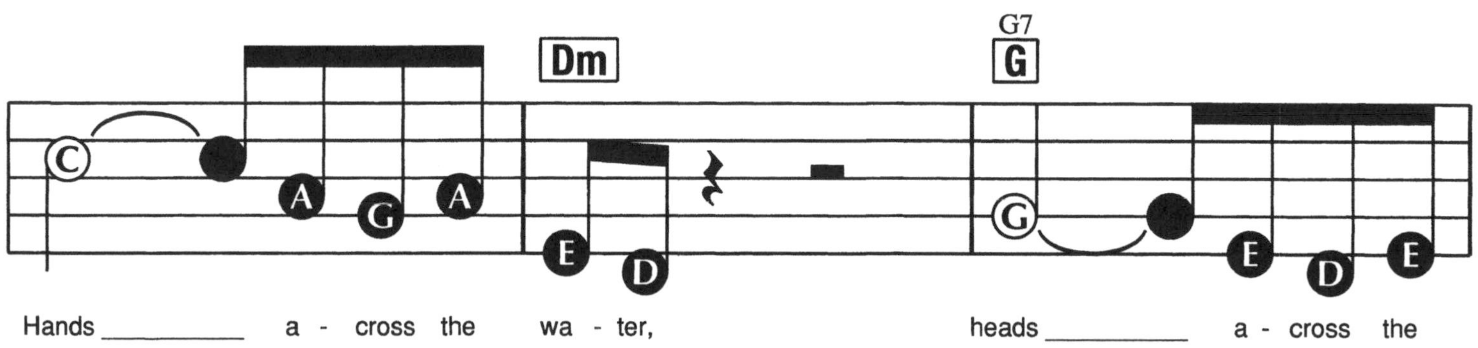
Dm
G7
G
Hands a - cross the wa - ter,
heads a - cross the

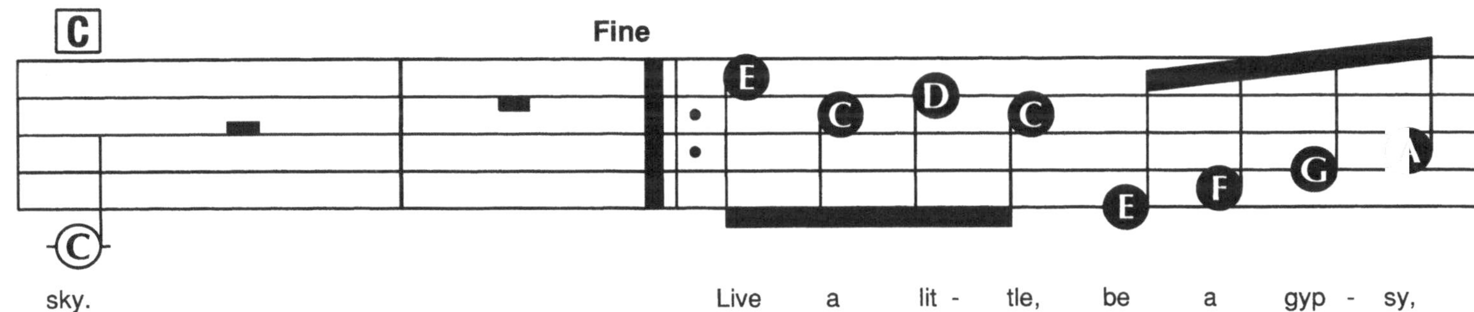
C
Fine
sky.
Live a lit - tle, be a gyp - sy,

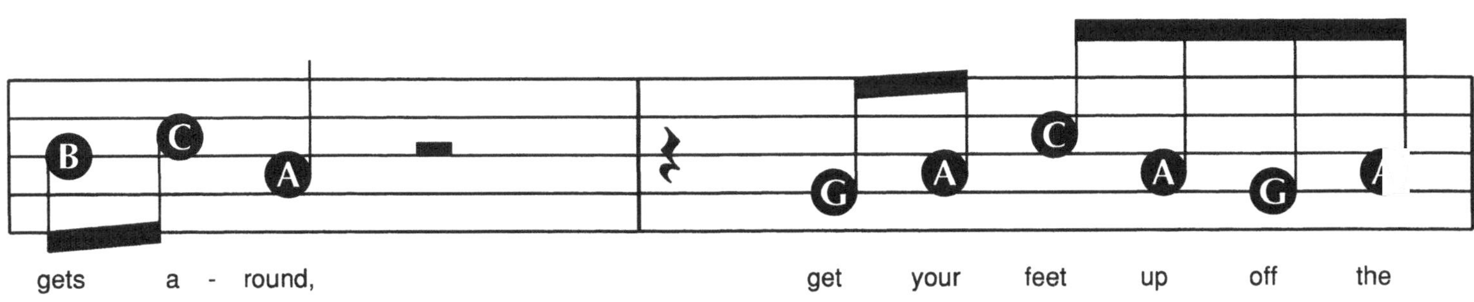
gets a - round,
get your feet up off the

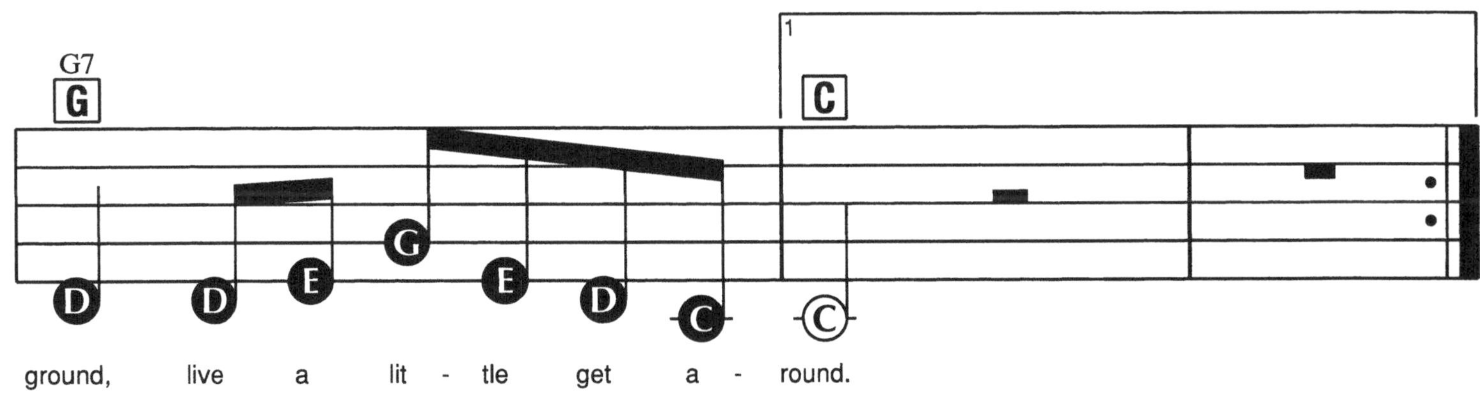
G7
G
1
C
ground, live a lit - tle get a - round.

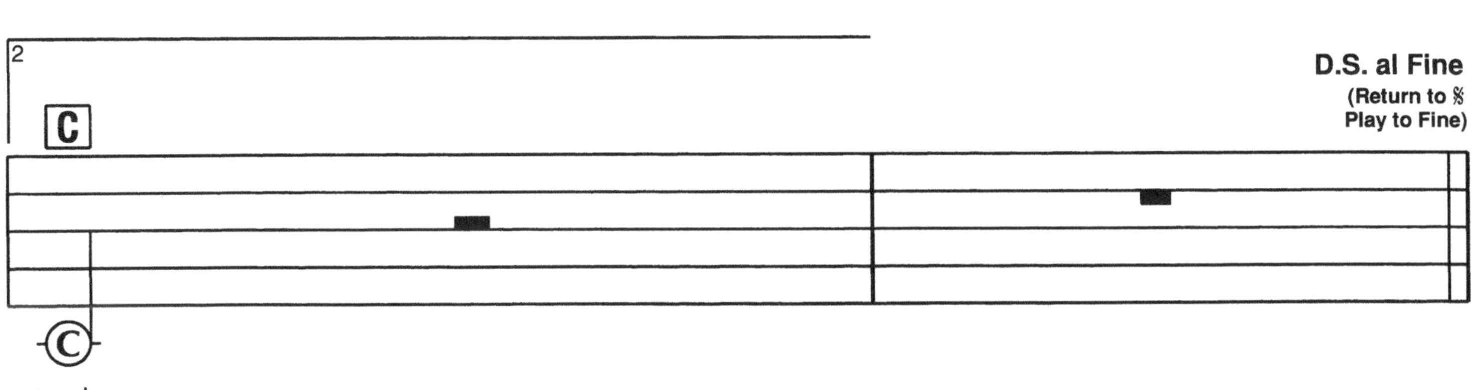
2
C
D.S. al Fine
(Return to 𝄋
Play to Fine)
round.

With a Little Luck

Registration 1
Rhythm: 8-Beat or Rock

Words and Music by
Paul McCartney

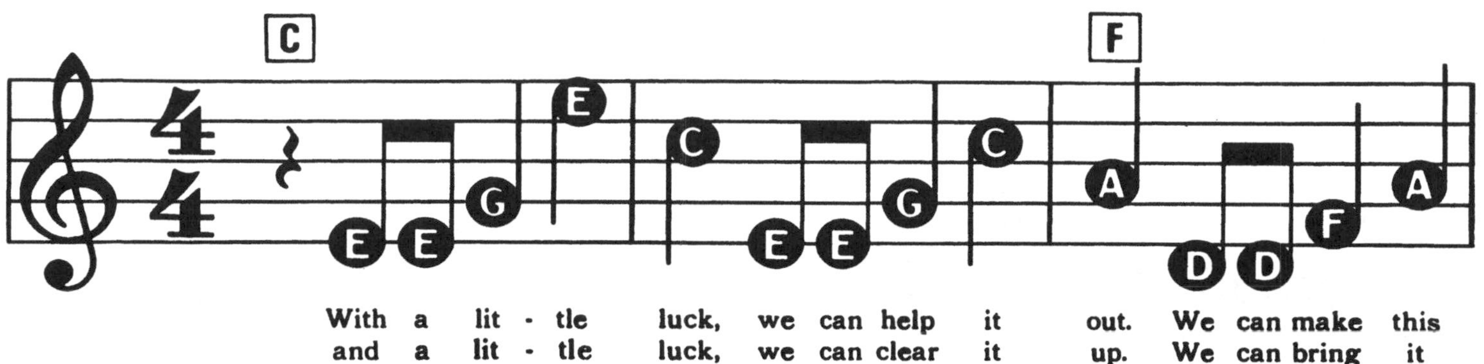

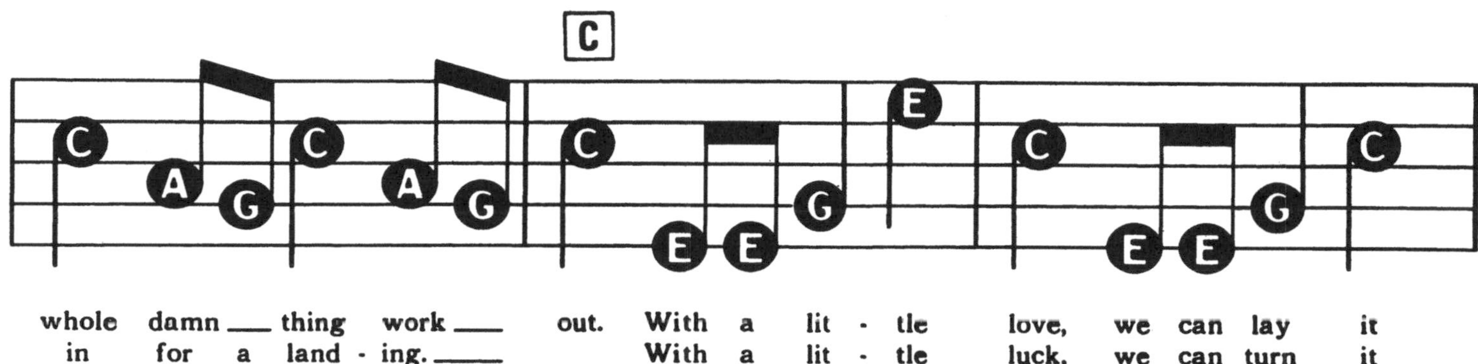

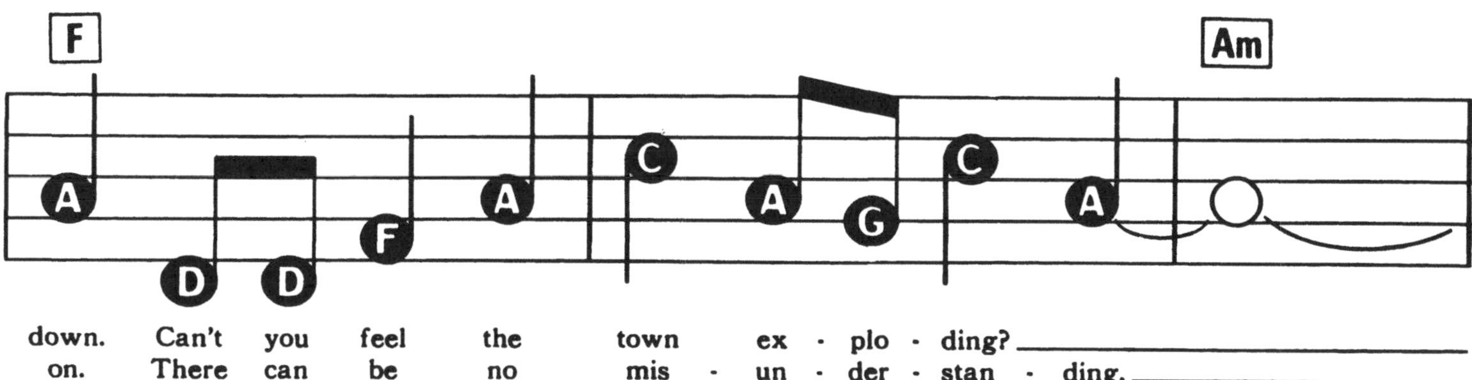

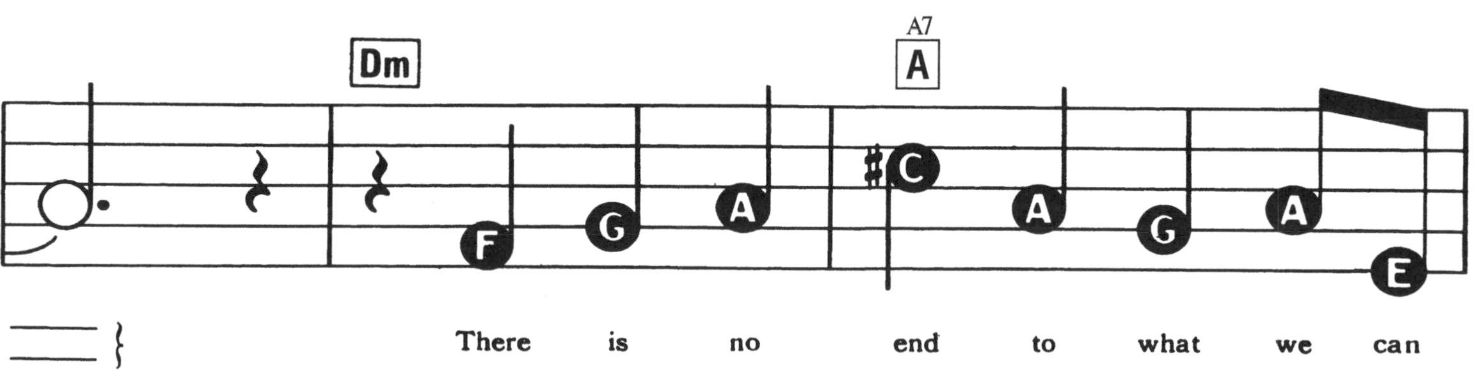

© 1978 MPL COMMUNICATIONS, INC.
All Rights Reserved

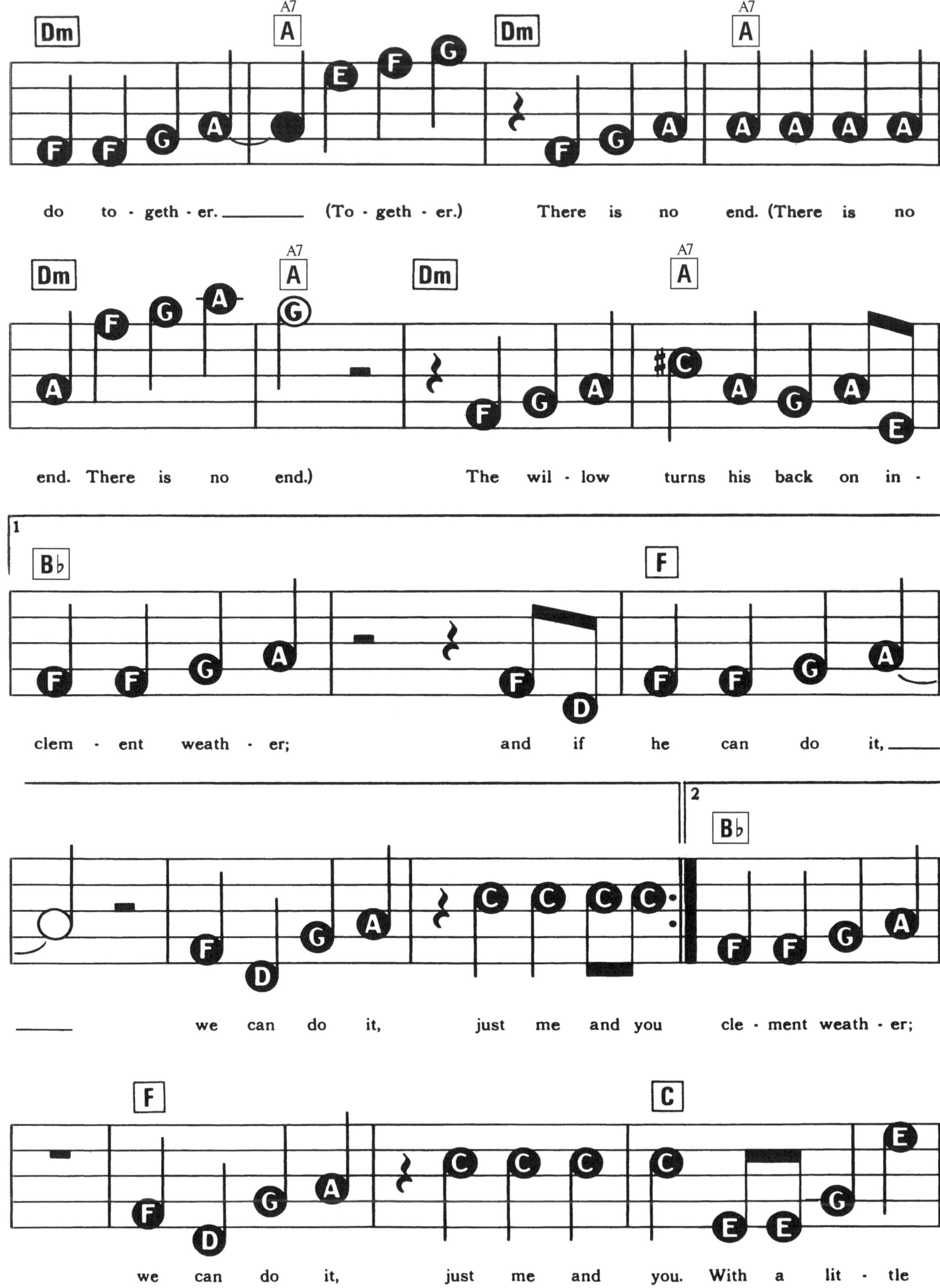
Dm A7 A Dm A7 A
do to - geth - er. (To - geth - er.) There is no end. (There is no
Dm A7 A Dm A7 A
end. There is no end.) The wil - low turns his back on in -
1
B♭ F
clem - ent weath - er; and if he can do it,
2
B♭
we can do it, just me and you cle - ment weath - er;
F C
we can do it, just me and you. With a lit - tle

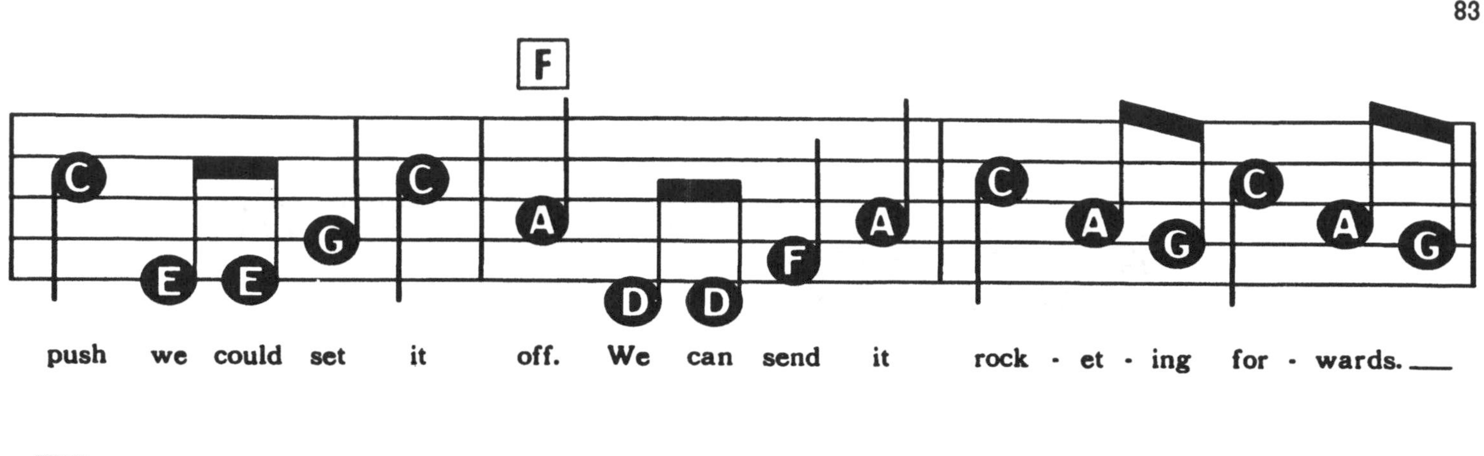
F
push we could set it off. We can send it rock - et - ing for - wards.

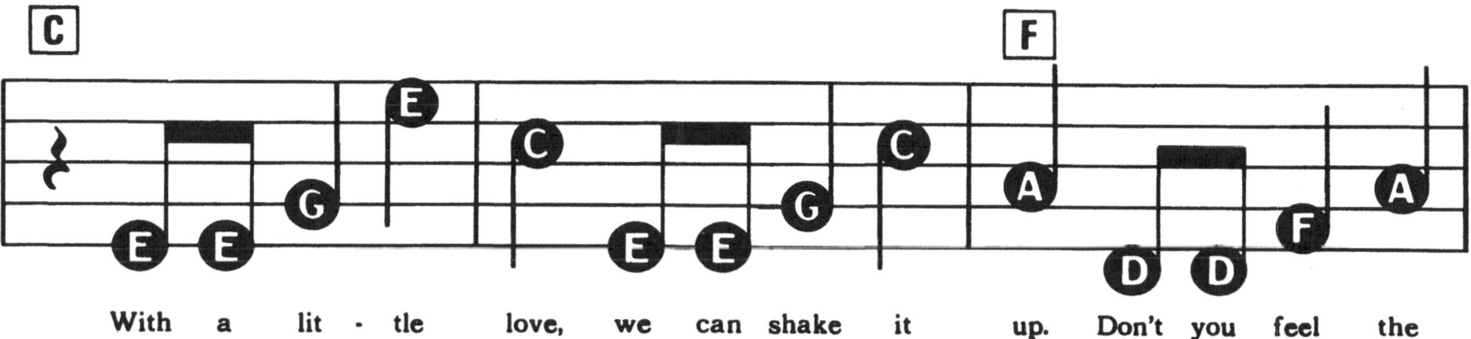
C
F
With a lit - tle love, we can shake it up. Don't you feel the

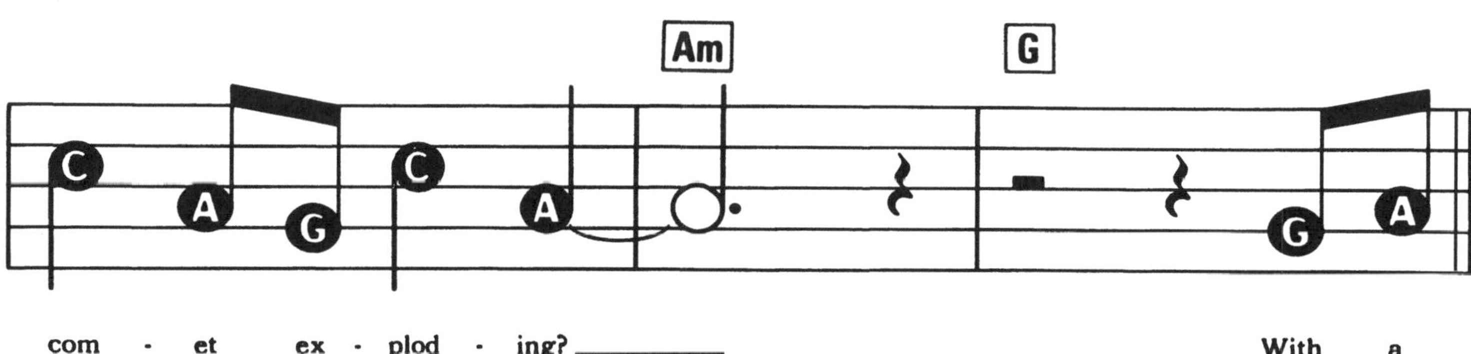
Am
G
com - et ex - plod - ing?
With a

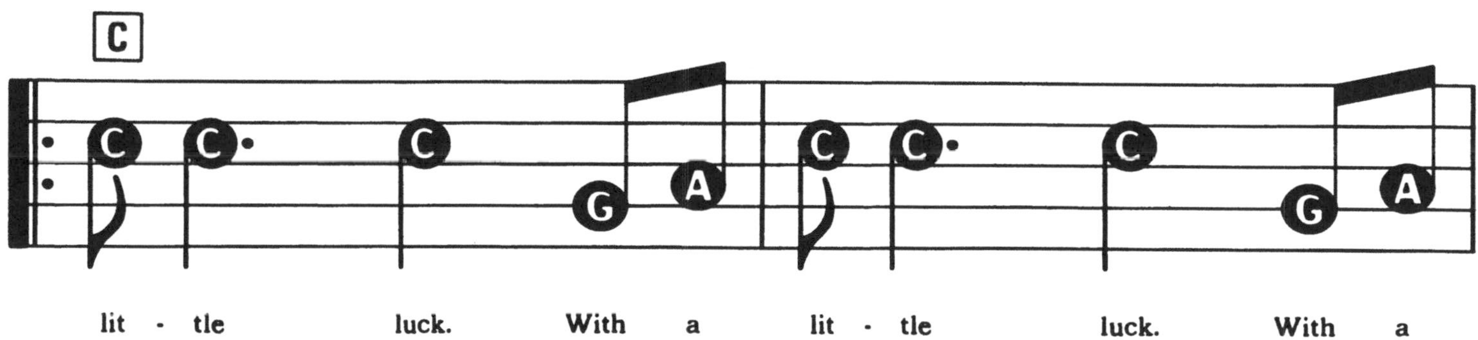
C
lit - tle luck. With a lit - tle luck. With a

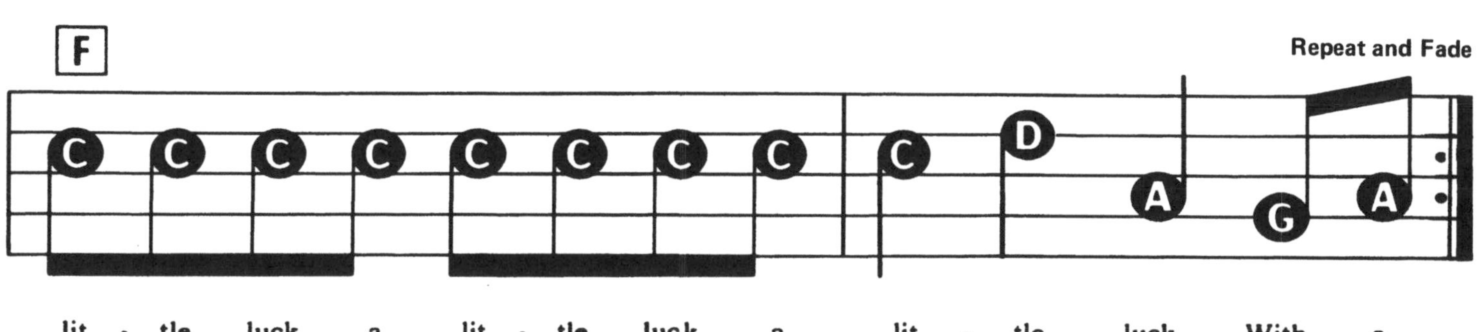
F
Repeat and Fade
lit - tle luck, a lit - tle luck, a lit - tle luck. With a

Registration Guide

- Match the Registration number on the song to the corresponding numbered category below. Select and activate an instrumental sound available on your instrument.
- Choose an automatic rhythm appropriate to the mood and style of the song. (Consult your Owner's Guide for proper operation of automatic rhythm features.)
- Adjust the tempo and volume controls to comfortable settings.

Registration

1	Mellow	Flutes, Clarinet, Oboe, Flugel Horn, Trombone, French Horn, Organ Flutes
2	Ensemble	Brass Section, Sax Section, Wind Ensemble, Full Organ, Theater Organ
3	Strings	Violin, Viola, Cello, Fiddle, String Ensemble, Pizzicato, Organ Strings
4	Guitars	Acoustic/Electric Guitars, Banjo, Mandolin, Dulcimer, Ukulele, Hawaiian Guitar
5	Mallets	Vibraphone, Marimba, Xylophone, Steel Drums, Bells, Celesta, Chimes
6	Liturgical	Pipe Organ, Hand Bells, Vocal Ensemble, Choir, Organ Flutes
7	Bright	Saxophones, Trumpet, Mute Trumpet, Synth Leads, Jazz/Gospel Organs
8	Piano	Piano, Electric Piano, Honky Tonk Piano, Harpsichord, Clavi
9	Novelty	Melodic Percussion, Wah Trumpet, Synth, Whistle, Kazoo, Perc. Organ
10	Bellows	Accordion, French Accordion, Mussette, Harmonica, Pump Organ, Bagpipes

R ORGANS, PIANOS & ELECTRONIC KEYBOARDS

E-Z PLAY® TODAY PUBLICATIONS

*The E-Z Play® Today songbook series is the shortest distance between beginning music and playing fun! Check out this list of highlights and visit **halleonard.com** for a complete listing of all volumes and songlists.*

2278 1. Favorite Songs with 3 Chords $9.99
374 2. Country Sound $12.99
4446 3. Contemporary Disney $16.99
382 4. Dance Band Greats $7.95
305 5. All-Time Standards $10.99
2553 6. Songs of the Beatles $14.99
442 7. Hits from Musicals $8.99
490 8. Patriotic Songs $8.99
5235 9. Christmas Time $9.99
3012 10. Songs of Hawaii $12.99
7580 11. 75 Light Classical Songs $19.99
284 12. Star Wars $10.99
248 13. 3-Chord Country Songs $14.99
248 14. All-Time Requests $8.99
1118 15. Simple Songs $14.99
5435 16. Broadway's Best $12.99
415 17. Fireside Singalong $14.99
113 18. 30 Classical Masterworks $8.99
7780 19. Top Country Songs $12.99
2277 20. Hymns $9.99
7200 21. Good Ol' Gospel $12.99
570 22. Sacred Sounds $8.99
4685 23. First 50 Songs You Should Play on Keyboard $16.99
9679 24. Songs with 3 Chords $14.99
724 25. Happy Birthday to You & Other Great Songs $10.99
1364 26. Bob Dylan $12.99
1236 27. 60 of the Easiest to Play Songs with 3 Chords $9.99
598 28. 50 Classical Themes $9.99
0135 29. Love Songs $9.99
0030 30. Country Connection $12.99
0010 31. Big Band Favorites $9.99
9578 32. Songs with 4 Chords $14.99
0720 33. Ragtime Classics $9.99
0122 36. Good Ol' Songs $12.99
0410 37. Favorite Latin Songs $8.99
5394 38. Best of Adele $10.99
9567 39. Best Children's Songs Ever $17.99
9955 40. Coldplay $10.99
7762 41. Bohemian Rhapsody $14.99
0123 42. Baby Boomers Songbook $10.99
2135 44. Best of Willie Nelson $14.99
0460 45. Love Ballads $8.99
6236 46. 15 Chart Hits $12.99
0007 47. Duke Ellington $8.95
0343 48. Gospel Songs of Johnny Cash $9.99
6314 49. Beauty and the Beast $12.99
2114 50. Best of Patsy Cline $9.99
0208 51. Essential Songs: 1950s $17.99
0209 52. Essential Songs: 1960s $19.99
8318 53. 100 Most Beautiful Christmas Songs $22.99
9268 54. Acoustic Songs $12.99
0342 55. Johnny Cash $12.99
7703 56. Jersey Boys $12.99
0118 57. More of the Best Songs Ever $19.99
0285 58. Four-Chord Songs $10.99
0353 59. Christmas Songs $10.99
0304 60. Songs for All Occasions $16.99
0409 62. Favorite Hymns $7.99
8397 63. Classical Music $7.99
0223 64. Wicked $12.99
0217 65. Hymns with 3 Chords $8.99
2258 66. La La Land $12.99
0268 68. Pirates of the Caribbean $12.99
0449 69. It's Gospel $9.99
0432 70. Gospel Greats $8.99
6744 71. 21 Top Hits $12.99
0117 72. Canciones Románticas $10.99
7558 73. Michael Jackson $12.99
7049 74. Over the Rainbow & 40 More Great Songs $12.99
0568 75. Sacred Moments $6.95
0572 76. The Sound of Music $10.99

00238941 77. Andrew Lloyd Webber $12.99
00100530 78. Oklahoma! $6.95
00248709 79. Roadhouse Country $12.99
00100200 80. Essential Paul Anka $8.95
00100262 82. Big Book of Folk Pop Rock $14.99
00100584 83. Swingtime $7.95
00265416 84. Ed Sheeran $14.99
00100221 85. Cowboy Songs $7.95
00265488 86. Leonard Cohen $12.99
00100286 87. 50 Worship Standards $14.99
00100287 88. Glee $9.99
00100577 89. Songs for Children $9.99
00290104 90. Elton John Anthology $16.99
00100034 91. 30 Songs for a Better World $10.99
00100288 92. Michael Bublé Crazy Love $10.99
00100036 93. Country Hits $12.99
00100219 95. Phantom of the Opera $12.99
00100263 96. Mamma Mia $10.99
00102317 97. Elvis Presley $14.99
00109768 98. Flower Power $16.99
00275360 99. The Greatest Showman $12.99
00282486 100. The New Standards $19.99
00100000 101. Annie $10.99
00286388 102. Dear Evan Hansen $12.99
00119237 103. Two-Chord Songs $9.99
00147057 104. Hallelujah & 40 More Great Songs $14.99
00287417 105. River Flows in You & Other Beautiful Songs $12.99
00139940 106. 20 Top Hits $14.99
00100256 107. The Best Praise & Worship Songs Ever $16.99
00100363 108. Classical Themes $7.99
00102232 109. Motown's Greatest Hits $12.95
00101566 110. Neil Diamond Collection $15.99
00100119 111. Season's Greetings $15.99
00101498 112. Best of the Beatles $21.99
00100134 113. Country Gospel USA $14.99
00100264 114. Pride and Prejudice $9.99
00101612 115. The Greatest Waltzes $9.99
00287931 116. A Star Is Born, La La Land, Greatest Showman & More $14.99
00289026 117. Tony Bennett $14.99
00100136 118. 100 Kids' Songs $14.99
00139985 119. Blues $12.99
00100433 120. Bill & Gloria Gaither $14.95
00100333 121. Boogies, Blues & Rags $9.99
00100146 122. Songs for Praise & Worship $9.99
00100266 123. Pop Piano Hits $14.99
00101440 124. The Best of Alabama $7.95
00100001 125. The Great Big Book of Children's Songs $14.99
00101563 127. John Denver $12.99
00116947 128. John Williams $12.99
00140764 129. Campfire Songs $12.99
00116956 130. Taylor Swift Hits $10.99
00102318 131. Doo-Wop Songbook $12.99
00100258 132. Frank Sinatra: Christmas Collection $10.99
00100306 133. Carole King $12.99
00100226 134. AFI's Top 100 Movie Songs $24.95
00289978 135. Mary Poppins Returns $10.99
00291475 136. Disney Fun Songs $14.99
00100144 137. Children's Movie Hits $9.99
00100038 138. Nostalgia Collection $16.99
00100289 139. Crooners $19.99
00101956 140. Best of George Strait $16.99
00294969 141. A Sentimental Christmas $12.99
00300288 142. Aladdin $10.99
00101946 143. Songs of Paul McCartney $8.99
00140768 144. Halloween $10.99
00100291 145. Traditional Gospel $9.99
00319452 146. The Lion King (2019) $10.99
00147061 147. Great Instrumentals $9.99
00100222 148. Italian Songs $9.99
00329569 149. Frozen 2 $10.99
00100152 151. Beach Boys Greatest Hits $14.99

00101592 152. Fiddler on the Roof $9.99
00140981 153. 50 Great Songs $14.99
00100228 154. Walk the Line $8.95
00101549 155. Best of Billy Joel $12.99
00101769 158. Very Best of John Lennon $12.99
00326434 159. Cats $10.99
00100315 160. Grammy Awards Record of the Year 1958-2011 $19.99
00100293 161. Henry Mancini $10.99
00100049 162. Lounge Music $10.95
00100295 163. Very Best of the Rat Pack $12.99
00277916 164. Best Christmas Songbook $9.99
00101895 165. Rodgers & Hammerstein Songbook $10.99
00149300 166. The Best of Beethoven $8.99
00149736 167. The Best of Bach $8.99
00100148 169. Charlie Brown Christmas $10.99
00100900 170. Kenny Rogers $12.99
00101537 171. Best of Elton John $9.99
00101796 172. The Music Man $9.99
00100321 173. Adele: 21 $12.99
00100229 175. Party Songs $14.99
00100149 176. Charlie Brown Collection $9.99
00100019 177. I'll Be Seeing You $15.99
00102325 179. Love Songs of the Beatles $14.99
00149881 180. The Best of Mozart $8.99
00101610 181. Great American Country Songbook $16.99
00001246 182. Amazing Grace $12.99
00450133 183. West Side Story $9.99
00290252 184. Merle Haggard $14.99
00100151 185. Carpenters $12.99
00101606 186. 40 Pop & Rock Song Classics $14.99
00100155 187. Ultimate Christmas $18.99
00102276 189. Irish Favorites $9.99
00100053 191. Jazz Love Songs $9.99
00123123 193. Bruno Mars $11.99
00124609 195. Opera Favorites $8.99
00101609 196. Best of George Gershwin $14.99
00119857 199. Jumbo Songbook $24.99
00295070 200. Best Songs Ever $19.99
00101540 202. Best Country Songs Ever $17.99
00101541 203. Best Broadway Songs Ever $19.99
00101542 204. Best Easy Listening Songs Ever $17.99
00284127 205. Best Love Songs Ever $17.99
00101570 209. Disney Christmas Favorites $9.99
00100059 210. '60s Pop Rock Hits $14.99
14041777 211. Big Book of Nursery Rhymes & Children's Songs $15.99
00126895 212. Frozen $9.99
00101546 213. Disney Classics $15.99
00101533 215. Best Christmas Songs Ever $22.99
00131100 216. Frank Sinatra Centennial Songbook $19.99
00100040 217. Movie Ballads $9.99
00100156 219. Christmas Songs with Three Chords $9.99
00102190 221. Carly Simon Greatest Hits $8.95
00102080 225. Lawrence Welk Songbook $10.99
00283385 234. Disney Love Songs $12.99
00101581 235. Elvis Presley Anthology $16.99
00100165 236. God Bless America & Other Songs for a Better Nation $26.99
00290209 242. Les Misérables $10.95
00100158 243. Oldies! Oldies! Oldies! $12.99
00100041 245. Simon & Garfunkel $10.99
00100267 246. Andrew Lloyd Webber Favorites $10.99
00100296 248. Love Songs of Elton John $12.99
00102113 251. Phantom of the Opera $14.99
00100203 256. Very Best of Lionel Richie $10.99
00100302 258. Four-Chord Worship $9.99
00286504 260. Mister Rogers' Songbook $9.99
00100235 263. Grand Irish Songbook $19.95
00100063 266. Latin Hits $7.95
00100062 269. Love That Latin Beat $8.99
00101425 272. ABBA Gold Greatest Hits $9.99
00100024 274. 150 of the Most Beautiful Songs Ever $22.99

00102248 275. Classical Hits $8.99
00100186 277. Stevie Wonder $10.99
00100227 278. 150 More of the Most Beautiful Songs Ever $24.99
00100236 279. Alan Jackson $20.99
00100237 280. Dolly Parton $10.99
00100238 281. Neil Young $12.99
00100239 282. Great American Songbook $19.95
00100068 283. Best Jazz Standards Ever $15.95
00281046 284. Great American Songbook: The Singers $19.99
00100271 286. CMT's 100 Greatest Love Songs $24.99
00100244 287. Josh Groban $14.99
00102124 293. Movie Classics $10.99
00100303 295. Best of Michael Bublé $14.99
00100075 296. Best of Cole Porter $9.99
00102130 298. Beautiful Love Songs $9.99
00100077 299. The Vaudeville Songbook $7.99
00259570 301. Kids' Songfest $12.99
00110416 302. More Kids' Songfest $12.99
00100275 305. Rod Stewart $12.99
00102147 306. Irving Berlin Collection $16.99
00100276 307. Gospel Songs with 3 Chords $8.99
00100194 309. 3-Chord Rock 'n' Roll $9.99
02501515 312. Barbra Streisand $10.99
00100197 315. VH1's 100 Greatest Songs of Rock & Roll $19.95
00100234 316. E-Z Play® Today White Pages $27.99
00100277 325. Taylor Swift $10.99
00100249 328. French Songs $8.95
00100251 329. Antonio Carlos Jobim $7.99
00102275 330. The Nutcracker Suite $8.99
00100092 333. Great Gospel Favorites $8.99
00100273 336. Beautiful Ballads $19.99
00100278 338. The Best Hymns Ever $19.99
00100084 339. Grease Is Still the Word $12.99
00100235 346. The Big Book of Christmas Songs $16.99
00100089 349. The Giant Book of Christmas Songs $9.95
00100087 354. The Mighty Big Book of Christmas Songs $12.95
00100088 355. Smoky Mountain Gospel Favorites $9.99
00100093 358. Gospel Songs of Hank Williams $7.95
00100095 359. 100 Years of Song $19.99
00100096 360. More 100 Years of Song $19.95
00159568 362. Songs of the 1920s $19.99
00159569 363. Songs of the 1930s $19.99
00159570 364. Songs of the 1940s $19.99
00159571 365. Songs of the 1950s $19.99
00159572 366. Songs of the 1960s $19.99
00159573 367. Songs of the 1970s $19.99
00159574 368. Songs of the 1980s $19.99
00159575 369. Songs of the 1990s $19.99
00159576 370. Songs of the 2000s $19.99
00339094 370. Songs of the 2010s $19.99
00100103 375. Songs of Bacharach & David $9.99
00100107 392. Disney Favorites $19.99
00100108 393. Italian Favorites $9.99
00100111 394. Best Gospel Songs Ever $19.99
00100115 400. Classical Masterpieces $11.99

HAL•LEONARD®

Prices, contents and availability subject to change without notice

0421
330

CD PLAY-ALONG SERIES

Each book in this exciting new series comes with a CD of complete professional performances, and includes matching custom arrangements in our famous E-Z Play® Today format. With these books you can:

- **Listen to complete professional performances of each of the songs**
- **Play the arrangements along with the recorded performances**
- **Sing along with the full performances; and/or play the arrangements as solos, without the disk.**

SONG FAVORITES WITH 3 CHORDS • VOLUME 1

15 songs, including: Can Can Polka • For He's a Jolly Good Fellow • Kum Ba Yah • Oh! Susanna • On Top of Old Smoky • Ta-Ra-Ra-Boom-De-Ay • When the Saints Go Marching In • Yankee Doodle • and more. **00100180**

CHILDREN'S SONGS • VOLUME 2

16 songs, including: Alphabet Song • Chopsticks • Frere Jacques (Are You Sleeping?) • I've Been Working on the Railroad • Jack and Jill • Looby Loo • Mary Had a Little Lamb • The Mulberry Bush • This Old Man • Three Blind Mice • and more. **00100181**

HYMN FAVORITES • VOLUME 3

15 songs, including: Abide with Me • Blessed Assurance • The Church's One Foundation • Faith of Our Fathers • The Old Rugged Cross • Onward, Christian Soldiers • Rock of Ages • Sweet By and By • Were You There? • and more. **00100182**

COUNTRY • VOLUME 4

14 songs, including: Crazy • Gentle on My Mind • Green Green Grass of Home • I Walk the Line • Jambalaya (On the Bayou) • King of the Road • Make the World Go Away • Son-Of-A-Preacher Man • Your Cheatin' Heart • and more. **00100183**

LENNON & MCCARTNEY • VOLUME 7

10 songs, including: Eleanor Rigby • Hey Jude • In My Life • The Long and Winding Road • Love Me Do • Nowhere Man • Please Please Me • Sgt. Pepper's Lonely Hearts Club Band • Strawberry Fields Forever • Yesterday. **00100240**

THE SOUND OF MUSIC • VOLUME 8

10 songs, including: Climb Ev'ry Mountain • Do-Re-Mi • Edelweiss • The Lonely Goatherd • Maria • My Favorite Things • Sixteen Going on Seventeen • So Long, Farewell • Something Good • The Sound of Music. **00100241**

WICKED • VOLUME 9

10 songs, including: As Long as You're Mine • Dancing Through Life • Defying Gravity • For Good • I'm Not That Girl • No One Mourns the Wicked • Popular • What Is This Feeling? • The Wizard and I • Wonderful. **00100242**

LES MISÉRABLES • VOLUME 10

10 songs, including: Bring Him Home • Castle on a Cloud • Do You Hear the People Sing? • Drink with Me (To Days Gone By) • Empty Chairs at Empty Tables • A Heart Full of Love • I Dreamed a Dream • On My Own • Stars • Who Am I?. **00100243**

BOOK/CD PACKAGES ONLY $12.95 EACH!

7777 W. Bluemound Rd. P.O. Box 13819 Milwaukee, WI 53213

Visit Hal Leonard Online at **www.halleonard.com**

Prices, contents and availability subject to change without notice.